Rush Benjamin

An Account of the Bilious Remitting Yellow Fever as it Appeared in the City of Philadelphia

In the Year 1793

Rush Benjamin

An Account of the Bilious Remitting Yellow Fever as it Appeared in the City of Philadelphia
In the Year 1793

ISBN/EAN: 9783337149871

Printed in Europe, USA, Canada, Australia, Japan

Cover: Foto ©Andreas Hilbeck / pixelio.de

More available books at **www.hansebooks.com**

A N

ACCOUNT

OF THE

Bilious remitting Yellow Fever,

A S

IT APPEARED

IN THE

CITY OF PHILADELPHIA,

IN THE YEAR 1793.

By Benjamin Ruſh, M.D.

PROFESSOR OF THE INSTITUTES, AND OF CLINICAL MEDICINE,
IN THE UNIVERSITY OF PENNSYLVANIA.

PHILADELPHIA,
PRINTED BY THOMAS DOBSON,
AT THE STONE-HOUSE, N° 41, SOUTH SECOND-STREET.

MDCCXCIV.

THE PREFACE.

THE delay of the following publication has been occafioned by the want of health to prepare it for the prefs, during the winter months. It now goes forward, under the great difadvantages, of having been haftily copied from my notes, amidft frequent profeffional interruptions. Its imperfections I hope will be overlooked, when it is confidered, that my only defign in publifhing thus prematurely, was to obviate as much as poffible, the danger of the difeafe, fhould it unhappily appear in our city in the courfe of the prefent feafon.

In

In the hiftory of the fever, I have introduced an account of the fymptoms and
prognofis, in fuch places as they occurred
moft naturally, without a ftrict regard to
the artificial order of the fchools.

In the detail of the fymptoms, I have
divided the body into different fyftems.
This divifion I have found to accord more
eafily with the principles of medicine which
I have adopted, than the common method
of defcribing them, as they appear in the
animal, natural, and vital functions.

In republifhing an account of the con-
troverfies between the phyficians of Philadelphia, my motives were, to prevent the
revival of certain opinions and modes of
practice, by bringing them forward under
the patronage of refpectable names, and to
juftify in a great meafure, from their influence, the want of univerfal fuccefs, by the

only

only fafe, and proper mode of treating the
yellow fever. I hope I fhall be excufed for
this part of the following work, when it is
perceived, that I have been more minute in
relating my own miftakes, than thofe of
other Phyficians; and that I have connected
no names with the opinions and modes of
practice which I have oppofed, but fuch
as were given to the public by their authors, during the prevalence of the fever.

                    BENJAMIN RUSH.

PHILADELPHIA,
June 14th, 1794.

                    b   Account

Of

Observations

───────────────────────────────────

☞ *The reader will pleafe to correct the following errors :*

In p. 41, line 2.
— p. 49, line 6.
— p. 55, line 9,   } for Dr. Phyfic, read Dr. *Phyfick.*
— p. 119, l. 8,

— p. 144, line 6, infert *fporadic* before cafe.
— p. 144, line 19, infert *prevailed,* inftead of occurred.

AN

ACCOUNT

OF THE

Bilious remitting Yellow Fever,

AS IT *APPEARED* IN

PHILADELPHIA,

IN THE YEAR 1793.

B

AN

ACCOUNT, &c.

B EFORE I proceed to defcribe the fever which is to be the fubject of this Effay, it will be proper to give a fhort account of the difeafes which preceded it.

The ftate of the weather during the firft feven months of the year, and during the time in which the fever prevailed in the city, as recorded by Mr Rittenhoufe, will be inferted immediately after the hiftory of the difeafe.

The MUMPS which made their appearance in December 1792, continued to prevail during the month of January 1793. Befides this diforder, there were many cafes of catarrh in the city,

B 2   brought

brought on chiefly by the inhabitants expofing themfelves for feveral hours on the damp ground in viewing the aerial voyage of Mr Blanchard on the 9th day of the month.

The weather which had been moderate in December and January became cold in February. The mumps continued to prevail during this month with fymptoms fo inflammatory, as to require in fome cafes two bleedings. Many people complained this month of pains and fwellings in the jaws. A few had the fcarlatina anginofa.

The mumps, pains in the jaws, and fcarlatina continued throughout the month of March. I was called to two cafes of pleurify in this month, which terminated in a temporary mania. One of them was in a woman of ninety years of age, who recovered. The blood drawn in the other cafe, (a gentleman from Maryland) was diffolved. The continuance of a tenfe pulfe, induced me notwithftanding to repeat the bleeding. The blood was now fizy. A third bleeding was prefcribed, and my patient recovered. Several cafes of obftinate eryfipelas fucceeded inoculation in children during this, and the next month, one of which proved fatal.

Bloffoms

Blossoms were universal on the fruit-trees, in the gardens of Philadelphia, on the first day of April. The scarlatina anginosa continued to be the reigning epidemic in this month.

There were several warm days in May, but the city was in general healthy. The birds appeared two weeks sooner this spring than usual.

The register of the weather shews, that there were many warm days in June. The scarlatina continued to maintain its empire during this month.

The weather was uniformly warm in July. The scarlatina continued during the beginning of this month, with symptoms of great violence. A son of James Sharswood, aged seven years, had with the common symptoms of this disorder, great pains and swellings in his limbs, accompanied with a tense pulse. I attempted in vain to relieve him by vomits and purges. On the 10th day of the month, I ordered six ounces of blood to be drawn from his arm, which I observed afterwards to be very sizy. The next day he was nearly well. Between the 22d and the 24th days of the month, there died three persons whose respective ages were 80, 92, and 96½. The weather at this time

was

was extremely warm. I have elfewhere taken notice of the fatal influence of extreme heat, as well as cold, upon human life in old people. A few bilious remitting fevers appeared towards the clofe of this month. One of them under my care, ended in a tedious typhus mitior, from which the patient was recovered with great difficulty. It was the fon of Dr Hutchins of the ifland of Barbadoes.

The weather for the firft two or three weeks in Auguft was temperate, and pleafant. The colera morbus, and remitting fevers were now common. The latter were attended with fome inflammatory action in the pulfe, and a determination to the breaft. Several dyfenteries appeared at this time, both in the city and in its neighbourhood. During the latter part of July, and the beginning of this month, a number of the diftreffed inhabitants of St Domingo, who had efcaped the defolation of fire and fword, arrived in the city. Soon after their arrival, the influenza made its appearance, and fpread rapidly among our citizens. The fcarlatina ftill kept up a feeble exiftence among children. The above difeafes were univerfal, but they were not attended with much mortality. They prevailed in different parts of the city, and each feemed to appear occafionally to be the ruling epidemic.

epidemic. The weather continued to be warm and dry. There was a heavy rain on the 25th of the month, which was remembered by the citizens of Philadelphia as the laſt that fell, for many weeks afterwards.

There was ſomething in the heat and drought of the ſummer months, which was uncommon, in their influence upon the human body. Labourers every where gave out (to uſe the country phraſe) in harveſt, and frequently too when the mercury in Fahrenheit's thermometer was under 84°. It was aſcribed by the country people to the calmneſs of the weather, which left the ſweat produced by heat and labour, to dry ſlowly upon the body.

The crops of grain and graſs were impaired by the drought. The ſummer fruits were as plentiful as uſual, particularly the melons, which were of an excellent quality. The influence of the weather upon the autumnal fruits, and upon vegetation in general, ſhall be mentioned hereafter.

I beg pardon for the length of this introduction. Some parts of it, I hope, will not appear uſeleſs in the ſequel of this work.

B 4

I now

I now enter upon a detail of fome folitary cafes
of the epidemic, which foon afterwards fpread
diftrefs through our city, and terror throughout
the United States.

On the 5th of Auguft, I was requefted by Dr
Hodge to vifit his child.   I found it ill with a fever
of the bilious kind, which terminated (with a
yellow fkin) in death on the 7th of the fame
month.

On the 6th of Auguft, I was called to Mrs
Bradford, the wife of Mr Thomas Bradford.   She
had all the fymptoms of a bilious remittent, but
they were fo acute, as to require two bleedings,
and feveral fucceffive dofes of phyfic.   The laft
purge fhe took was a dofe of *calomel*, which operated plentifully.   For feveral days after her re-
recovery, her eyes and face were of a yellow
colour.

On the fame day, I was called to the fon of
Mrs M‘Nair, who had been feized violently
with all the ufual fymptoms of a bilious fever.
I purged him plentifully with falts and creamor
tartar, and took ten or twelve ounces of blood
from his arm.   His fymptoms appeared to yield
to thefe remedies ; but on the 10th of the month

an

an hæmorrhage from the nofe came on, and on the morning of the 12th he died.

On the 7th of this month I was called to vifit Richard Palmer, a fon of Mrs Palmer in Chef-nut-ftreet. He had been indifpofed for feve-ral days with a fick ftomach and vomiting after eating. He now complained of a fever and head-ach. I gave him the ufual remedies for the bilious fever, and he recovered in a few days. On the 15th day of the fame month, I was fent for to vifit his brother William, who was feized with all the fymptoms of the fame diforder. On the 5th day his head-ach became extremely acute, and his pulfe fell to fixty ftrokes in a minute. I fufpected congeftion to have taken place in his brain, and ordered him to lofe eight ounces of blood. His pulfe became more frequent, and lefs tenfe after bleeding, and he recovered in a day or two after-wards.

On the 14th day of this month I was fent for to vifit Mrs Leaming, the wife of Mr Thomas Lea-ming. I fufpected at firft that fhe had the influ-enza, but in a day or two, her fever put on bili-ous fymptoms. She was affected with an uncom-mon difpofition to faint. Her pulfe was languid, but *tenfe*. I took a few ounces of blood from her, and

and purged her with falts, and *calomel.* I afterwards gave her a fmall dofe of laudanum which
difagreed with her. In my note book, I find
I have recorded, that " fhe was the worfe for it."
I was led to make this remark by its being fo very
uncommon, for a perfon who had been properly
bled and purged, to take laudanum in a common bilious fever, without being benefited by it.
She recovered however flowly, and was yellow
for many days afterwards.

On the morning of the 18th of this month, I
was requefted to vifit Peter Afton, in Vine-ftreet,
in confultation with Dr Say. I found him on the
3d day of a moft acute bilious fever. His eyes
were inflamed, and his face flufhed with a deep
red colour. His pulfe feemed to forbid evacuations. We prefcribed the ftrongeft cordials; but
to no purpofe. We found him at 6 o'clock in
the evening, fitting upon the fide of his bed, perfectly fenfible, but without a pulfe, with cold clam-
my hands, and his face of a yellowifh colour. He
died a few hours after we left him.

None of the cafes which I have mentioned,
excited the leaft apprehenfion of the exiftence of a
yellow fever in our city; for I had frequently feen
fporadic cafes in which the common bilious fever
of

of Philadelphia, had put on fymptoms of great malignity, and terminated fatally in a few days, and
now and then with a yellow colour on the fkin,
before, or immediately after death.

On the 19th of this month I was requefted to
vifit the wife of Mr Peter Le Maigre, in Water-
ftreet, between Arch and Race-ftreets, in confultation with Dr Foulke and Dr Hodge. I found
her in the laft ftage of a highly bilious fever. She
vomited conftantly, and complained of great heat
and burning in her ftomach. The moft powerful
cordials, and tonics were prefcribed, but to no purpofe. She died on the evening of the next day.

. Upon coming out of Mrs Le Maigre's room,
I remarked to Dr Foulke and Dr Hodge, that I
had feen an unufual number of bilious fevers, accompanied with fymptoms of uncommon malignity, and that I fufpected all was not right in our
city. Dr Hodge immediately replied, that a fever
of a moft malignant kind had carried off four or
five perfons within fight of Mr Le Maigre's door,
and that one of them had died in twelve hours after the attack of the diforder. This information
fatisfied me that my apprehenfions were well found-
ed. The origin of this fever was difcovered to

me

me at the fame time, from the account which Dr
Foulke gave me of a quantity of damaged coffee
which had been thrown upon Mr Ball's wharf,
and in the adjoining dock, on the 24th of July,
nearly in a line with Mr Le Maigre's houfe, and
which had putrefied there to the great annoyance
of the whole neighbourhood.

After this confultation I was foon able to trace
all the cafes of fever which I have mentioned to
this fource. Dr Hodge lived a few doors above
Mr Le Maigre's, where his child had been expofed to the exhalation from the coffee for feveral
days. Mrs Bradford had fpent an afternoon in a
houfe directly oppofite to the wharf and dock on
which the putrid coffee had emitted its noxious
effluvia, a few days before her ficknefs, and had
been much incommoded by it. Her fifter Mrs
Leaming had vifited her during her illnefs, and
probably caught the fever from her, for fhe perfectly recollected perceiving a peculiar fmell unlike
to any thing fhe had been accuftomed to in a fick
room, as foon as fhe entered the chamber where
her fifter lay. Young Mr M'Nair and Mrs Palmer's two fons had fpent whole days in a compting
houfe, near where the coffee was expofed, and
each of them had complained of having been made
fick

fick by its offenfive fmell, and Mr Afton had frequently been in Water-ftreet near the fource of
the exhalation.

This difcovery of the malignity—extent—and
origin of a fever which I knew to be highly contagious, as well as mortal, gave me great pain.
I did not hefitate to name it, the *Bilious remitting
Yellow Fever.* I had once feen it epidemic in
Philadelphia, in the year 1762. Its fymptoms
were among the firft impreffions which difeafes
made upon my mind. I had recorded fome of
thefe fymptoms. I had likewife recorded its mortality. I fhall here introduce a fhort account of
it from a note book which I kept during my ap-
prenticefhip.

" In the year 1762, in the months of Auguft,
" September, October, November and Decem-
" ber, the bilious yellow fever prevailed in Phi-
" ladelphia, after a *very hot fummer,* and fpread
" like a plague, carrying off daily for fome time,
" upwards of twenty perfons.

" The patients were generally feized with ri-
" gors, which were fucceeded with a violent fever,
" and pains in the head and back. The pulfe
" was full, and fometimes irregular. The eyes

4   were

" were inflamed, and had a yellowifh caft, and a
" vomiting almoft always attended.

" The 3d, 5th and 7th days were moftly criti-
" cal, and the difeafe generally terminated on one
" of them, in life or death.

" An eruption on the 3d or 7th day over the
" body, proved falutary.

" An exceffive heat, and burning about the
" region of the liver, with cold extremities, por-
.." tended death to be at hand."

I have taken notice in my note book, of the
principal remedy which was prefcribed in this
fever by my preceptor in medicine, but this fhall
be mentioned hereafter.

Upon my leaving Mrs Le Maigre's, I exprefled
my diftrefs at what I had difcovered, to feveral of
my fellow citizens. The report of a malignant
and contagious fever being in town, fpread in every direction, but it did not gain univerfal credit.
Some of thefe phyficians who had not feen patients in it, denied that any fuch fever exifted,
and afferted (though its mortality was not denied)
that it was nothing but the common annual remittent

mittent of the city. Many of the citizens, joined the phyficians in endeavouring to difcredit the account I had given of this fever, and for a while, it was treated with ridicule or contempt. Indignation in fome inftances was excited againft me, and one of my friends whom I advifed in this early ftage of the diforder, to leave the city, has fince told me that for that advice, " he had hated me."

My lot in having thus difturbed the repofe of the public mind, upon the fubjeft of general health, was not a fingular one. There are many inftances upon record, of phyficians who have rendered themfelves unpopular, and even odious to their fellow citizens, by giving the firft notice of the exiftence of malignant and mortal difeafes. A phyfician who afferted that the plague was in Meffina in the year 1743, excited fo much rage in the minds of his fellow citizens againft him, as to render it neceffary for him to fave his life by retreating to one of the churches of that city.

In fpite, however, of all oppofition, the report of the exiftence of a malignant and contagious fever in the city, gained fo much ground, that the governor of the ftate directed Dr Hutchinfon, the infpector of fickly veffels, to inquire into the truth

of

of it, and into the nature of the difeafe. In confequence of this order, I received the following
letter from Dr Hutchinfon.

DEAR SIR,

A CONSIDERABLE alarm has taken place,
in confequence of the appearance of an infeftious
diforder in this city; from which the governor has
been induced to direft me to make enquiries relative to the exiftence and nature of fuch diforder. In
executing this duty, I muft rely on the affiftance of
fuch of my medical brethren as may have been called to attend any of the perfons fuppofed to have
been infefted : as I underftand you have had feveral of them under your care, I would be much
obliged to you to communicate to me (as fpeedily
as can be done with convenience to yourfelf) fuch
fafts as you have been able to afcertain relative to
the exiftence of fuch diforder ; in what part of the
city it prevails ; when it was introduced ; and what
was the probable caufe of it.

I am, Sir,

With the greateft refpeft,

AUGUST 24th,
1793.

Dr Benjamin Rufh.

Your obedient fervant,

J. HUTCHINSON.

To

To this letter I wrote the following anfwer a few hours after it came to hand.

DEAR SIR,

A MALIGNANT fever has lately appeared in our city, originating I believe from fome damaged coffee, which putrified on a wharf near Arch-ftreet. This fever was confined for a while to Water-ftreet, between Race and Arch-ftreets; but I have lately met with it in Second-ftreet, and in Kenfington; but whether propagated by contagion, or by the original exhalation, I cannot tell. The difeafe puts on all the intermediate forms of a mild remittent, and a typhus gravior. I have not feen a fever of fo much malignity, fo general, fince the year 1762.

From, dear fir,

Auguft 24th,
1793.

Yours fincerely,

BENJ. RUSH.

A FEW days afterwards, the following publica-cation, by Dr Hutchinfon, appeared in the American Daily Advertifer of Auguft 28th.

C

THE

THE governor having directed an inquiry to afcertain
the facts, refpecting the exiftence of a contagious fever
in the city, and the probable means of removing it, Dr
Hutchinfon, the phyfician of the port, has made the following ftatement upon the fubject, in a letter to Nathaniel Falconer, Efq. health-officer of the port of Philadelphia.

DEAR SIR,

IMMEDIATELY on the receipt of your
letter, with the enclofure from the governor, fta-
ting that a confiderable alarm had taken place, in
confequence of the appearance of an infectious diforder in this city, I endeavoured to take meafures
to afcertain the facts, relative to the exiftence of
fuch difeafe : for this purpofe, I wrote to fuch of
my medical brethren, who had been called on to
attend perfons fuppofed to have been infected ; and
from their anfwers, as well as from my own obfervations, I am convinced that a malignant fever has
lately made its appearance in Water-ftreet and in
Kenfington ; principally in Water-ftrcet between
Arch and Race-ftreets. This part of the city I
examined perfonally on Thurfday and Friday laft,
and found that eaft of Front-ftreet, and between
Arch and Racc-ftreets, fixty-feven perfons were
difeafed, many with the malignant fever. Thirteen of them are fince dead, and numbers remain
ill. For a while this fever was confined to the
above-

abovementioned part of the city, but the diforder is fpreading, and now appears in other places, fo that feveral are affected in other parts of Water-ftreet, fome in Second-ftreet, fome in Vine-ftreet, fome in Carter's-alley, fome in other ftreets; but in moft cafes the contagion can be traced to Water-ftreet. Dr Say, who has attended more in this difeafe than any other phyfician, informs me, that he firft obferved it in Kenfington, on the fifth or fixth of this month; that he did not perceive it in Water-ftreet, until about the twelfth or fifteenth, but that on its appearance in the latter place, the whole neighbourhood was foon affected—He further informs me, that he has at this time upwards of 40 patients, which he fuppofes to be infected; and that he has loft about 20 patients in this difeafe, fince its firft appearance. As far as I have been able to afcertain, the number of perfons who have died altogether of this fever, amounts to 40 or thereabouts *.

The general opinion both of the medical gentlemen, and of the inhabitants of Water-ftreet is, that the contagion originated from fome damaged coffee, or other putrified vegetable and animal matters;

* The regifter of the deaths fhows that it amounted at that time to upwards of 150.

C 2　　　　　and.

and, on enquiry, it appears, that on a few wharfs
above Arch-ftreet, there was not only a quantity of
damaged coffee, which was extremely offenfive, expofed for fome time, but alfo fome putrid hides,
and other putrid animal and vegetable fubftances.
Should, however, Dr Say's opinion be well found-
ed, that he obferved the difeafe in Kenfington previoufly to its appearance in Water-ftreet, this cannot be the original caufe of the contagion.

It does not appear to be an imported difeafe;
for I have heard of no foreigners or failors that
have hitherto been infected; nor has it been found
in any lodging houfes; but it is, on the contrary,
principally confined to the inhabitants of Water-
ftreet, and fuch as have done bufinefs, or had confiderable intercourfe, with that part of the city.
The Difpenfary phyficians tell me, that out of the
large number of fick, now under the care of that
charitable inftitution, they have had but one perfon afflicted with this fever.   In the Pennfylvania
Hofpital, the diforder does not exift.

The difeafe appears differently in different perfons; it puts on all the intermediate forms between
a mild remittent and the worft fpecies of Typhus
Gravior.

                                          I en-

I enclose you a copy of the proceedings of the college of physicians, which contains their recommendation of the means for preventing the future progress of the disease.

I am, with the greatest respect,

Your most obedient servant,

Philadelphia, }
August 27th, 1793, }   J. HUTCHINSON.

The disease continued to spread, and with a degree of mortality that had long been unknown by common fevers.

On the 25th of the month, the college of physicians was summoned by their president to meet, in order to consult about the best methods of treating this fever, and of checking its progress in the city. After some confideration upon the nature of the disease, a committee was appointed to draw up some directions for those purposes ; and the next day the following were presented to the college, and adopted unanimously by them. They were afterwards published in most of the news papers.

Philadelphia, *August* 26th, 1793,

The college of physicians having taken into confideration the malignant and contagious fever that

C 3   now

now prevails in this city, have agreed to recommend to their fellow citizens the following means
of preventing its progrefs.

1ft. That all unneceffary intercourfe fhould be
avoided with fuch perfons as are infected by it.

2d. To place a mark upon the door or window
of fuch houfes as have any infected perfons in it.

3d. To place the perfons infected in the centre
of large and airy rooms, in beds without curtains,
and to pay the ftricteft regard to cleanlinefs, by frequently changing their body and bed linen, alfo
by removing as fpeedily as poffible, all offenfive
matters from their rooms.

4th. To provide a large and airy hofpital, in the
neighbourhood of the city, for the reception of
fuch poor perfons as cannot be accommodated with
the above advantages in private houfes.

5th. To put a ftop to the tolling of the bells.

6th. To bury fuch perfons as die of this fever
in carriages, and in as private a manner as poffible.

7th. To

7th. To keep the ftreets and wharfs of the city as clean as poffible.—As the contagion of the dif- cafe may be taken into the body and pafs out of it, without producing the fever, unlefs it be render- ed active by fome occafional caufe, the following means fhould be attended to, to prevent the conta- gion being excited into action in the body.

8th. To avoid all fatigue of body and mind.

9th. To avoid *ftanding* or *fitting* in the fun ; al- fo in a current of air, or in the evening air.

10th. To accommodate the drefs to the wea- ther ; and to exceed rather in warm than in cool cloathing.

11th. To avoid intemperance, but to ufe fer- mented liquors, fuch as wine, beer, and cyder, in moderation.

The college conceive *fires* to be very ineffectual, if not dangerous means of checking the progrefs of this fever. They have reafon to place more de- pendence upon the burning of *gun-powder.* The be- nefits of *vinegar* and *camphor*, are confined chiefly to infected rooms, and they cannot be ufed too fre- quently upon handkerchiefs, or in fmelling-bottles,

C 4   by

by perfons whofe duty calls them to vifit or attend the fick.

Signed by order of the college,

WILLIAM SHIPPEN, Jun.
Vice Prefident.

SAMUEL P. GRIFFITTS,
Secretary.

From a conviction that the difeafe originated in the putrid exhalations from the damaged coffee, I publifhed in the American Daily Advertifer of Auguft 29th, the following fhort addrefs to the citizens of Philadelphia, with a view of directing the public attention to the fpot where the coffee lay, and thereby of checking the progrefs of the fever as far as it was continued by the original caufe.

" Mr DUNLAP,

" A DOUBT has been expreffed by Dr Hutchinfon, in his letter to the health-officer, whether the malignant fever, which now prevails in our city, originated in an exhalation from fome putrid coffee on a wharf, between Arch and Race-ftreets, *becaufe* it made its firft appearance at Kenfington. Upon

Upon enquiry, it appears that the firſt perſons who died with this fever, about the 5th of the month, in that village, had been previouſly expoſed to the atmoſphere of the wharf, and that three of the crew of the Daniſh ſhip, who are now ill with it at Kenſington, received the ſeeds of the diſeaſe on board their ſhip, while ſhe lay at or near Race-ſtreet wharf. If theſe faɛts could not be aſcertained, it does not follow, that the diſeaſe was not generated by the putrid coffee; for, morbid exhalations, it is well known, produce fevers at the diſtance of two and three miles, where they are not oppoſed by houſes, woods, or a hilly country. This is obvious to all the farmers who live in the neighbourhood of mill-ponds.

" It is no new thing for the effluvia of putrid vegetables to produce malignant fevers. Cabbage, onions, black pepper, and even the mild potatoe, when in a ſtate of putrefaɛtion, have all been the remote cauſes of malignant fevers. The noxious quality of the effluvia from mill-ponds, is derived wholly from a mixture of the putrified leaves and bark of trees, with water.

" It is much leſs common for the effluvia of putrid animal matters to produce fevers. How ſeldom do we hear of them in the neghbourhood of ſlaughter-

flaughter-houfes, or of the work-fhops of fkinners
or curriers?

" Thefe obfervations are intended to ferve two
purpofes : 1ft, To fupport the opinion of Dr
Hutchinfon, that the malignant fever, which has
excited fo general, and fo juft an alarm in our city,
is *not an imported* difeafe ; and, 2dly, To direct the
attention of our citizens to the fpot from whence
this fevere malady has been derived. It will be
impoffible to check it during the continuance of
warm and dry weather, while any of the impure
matter which produced it, remains upon the peftilential wharf."

R."

This publication had no other effect, than to
produce frefh clamours againft the author ; for the
citizens as well as moft of the phyficians of Philadelphia had adopted a traditional opinion, that the
yellow fever could exift among us, only by importation from the Weft Indies.

In confequence, however, of a letter from Dr
Foulke to the Mayor of the city, in which he had decided, in a pofitive manner in favour of the generation of the fever from the putrid coffee ; the mayor
gave orders for the removal of the coffee, and the
cleaning

ation:2aimaimaimaima

cleaning of the wharf and dock. It was faid that meafures were taken for this purpofe; but Dr Foulke, who vifited the place where the coffee lay, has repeatedly affured me, that they were fo far from being effectual, that an offenfive fmell was exhaled from it many days afterwards.

I fhall pafs over for the prefent, the facts and arguments on which I ground my affertion of the generation of this fever in our city. They will come in more properly in the clofe of the hiftory of the difeafe.

The feeds of the fever, whether received into the body, from the putrid effluvia of the coffee, or by contagion, generally excited the difeafe in a few days. I met with feveral cafes in which it acted, fo as to produce a fever on the fame day, in which it was received into the fyftem, and I heard of two cafes in which it excited ficknefs, fainting, and fever, within one hour after the perfons were expofed to it. I met with no inftance in which there was a longer interval than fixteen days, between the contagion being received into the body, and the production of the difeafe.

This poifon acted differently in different confti-tutions, according to previous habits, to the de-

4

grees

grees of predifpofing debililty, or to the quantity
and concentration of the contagion which was applied to the body.

In fome conftitutions the contagion was at once a
remote, a predifpofing, and an exciting caufe of the
difeafe ; hence fome perfons were affected by it,
who had not departed in any inftance from their ordinary habits of living, as to diet, drefs, and exercife. But it was more frequently brought on by
fome predifpofing, or exciting caufe. I fhall briefly
enumerate each of them.

Whatever be the fpecific quality of the matter
which produced the fever, it is certain, that it
acted as a ftimulus upon the whole fyftem. In a
moderate degree, it produced only a quicknefs
and fulnefs of the pulfe, but when it was more
active, it induced that fpecies of debility which
has been happily called *indirect*. It is the reverfe
of *direct* debility, which is produced by the abftraction of natural, and ufual ftimuli from the
body. When the contagion acted with fo much
force, as to induce indirect debility, a fever fometimes followed without the aid of an exciting
caufe, but this was feldom the cafe. In ninety-
nine cafes out of an hundred, which came under
my notice, I could diftinctly trace the formation
of

of the difeafe to fome of the following caufes, acting feparately, or in greater or lefs combination,
and inducing indirect or direct debility upon the
fyftem. The caufes which induced *indirect* debility were,

1. FATIGUE of body or mind, induced by labour,
by walking, riding, watching, or the like. It was
labour which excited the difeafe fo univerfally a-
mong the lower clafs of people. A long walk often
induced it. Few efcaped it after a day, or even a
few hours fpent in gunning. A hard trotting
horfe brought it on two of my patients. Perhaps,
riding on horfeback, and in the fun, was the exciting caufe of the difeafe in moft of the citizens
and ftrangers who were affected by it in their
flight from the city. A fall excited it in a girl,
and a ftroke upon the head excited it in a young
man who came under my care. Many people
were feized with the diforder in confequence of
their exertions on the night of the 7th of September, in extinguifhing the fire which confumed Mr
Dobfon's printing-office, and even the lefs violent
exercife of working the fire engines for the purpofe of laying the duft in the ftreets, added frequently to the number of the fick.

2. HEAT,

2. HEAT, from every caufe, but more efpecially
the heat of the fun, was a very common exciting
caufe of the diforder. It aided the ftimulus of the
contagion in bringing on indirect debility. The regifter of the weather during the latter end of Auguft—the whole of September, and the firft two
weeks in October, will fhew how much the heat
of the fun muft have contributed to excite the difeafe, more efpecially among labouring people.
The heat of common fires, likewife became a frequent caufe of the activity of the contagion, where
it had been received into the body ; hence the
greater mortality of the difeafe among bakers,
blackfmiths, and hatters, than among any other
clafs of people.

3. INTEMPERANCE in eating or drinking. A
plentiful meal, and a few extra-glaffes of wine, feldom failed of exciting the fever. But where the
body was ftrongly impregnated with the contagion,
even the fmalleft deviation from the cuftomary
ftimulus of diet, in refpect to quality or quantity,
roufed the contagion into action. A fupper of
twelve oyfters in one, and only three, in another
of my patients, produced the difeafe. A half an
ounce of meat rendered the contagion active in
a lady, who had lived by my advice for two
weeks

weeks upon milk and vegetables. A fupper of fallad dreffed after the French fafhion, excited it in one of Dr Meafe's patients. It is becaufe men are more predifpofed by their conftitution, and employments, to indirect debility than women, and that young and middle aged perfons are more predifpofed to this fpecies of debility than old people; that more men than women, and more young than old people, were affected by the diforder.

There were feveral exciting caufes of the difeafe, which acted by inducing *direct* debility upon the fyftem. It may appear difficult at firft fight to explain, how caufes fo oppofite in their nature, as *indirect* and *direct* debility fhould produce exactly the fame effect. The difficulty vanifhes when we reflect, that the abftraction of one ftimulus, by accumulating the excitability of the fyftem, encreafes the force of thofe which remain. The contagion when received into the body, was frequently innocent, until it was aided by the addition of a new, or by the abftraction of a cuftomary ftimulus. The caufes which acted in the latter way were,

1. FEAR. This paffion debilitates, only becaufe it abftracts its antagonift paffion of courage.

In

In many people the difeafe was excited by a fudden paroxifm of fear ; but I faw fome remarkable
inftances where timid people efcaped the difeafe,
although they were conftantly expofed to it. Perhaps a moderate degree of fear ferved to balance
the tendency of the fyftem to indirect debility from
the exceffive ftimulus of the contagion, and thereby to preferve it in a ftate of healthy equilibrium.
I am certain that fear did no harm, after the difeafe was formed, in thofe cafes where a morbid
excefs of action, or proftration of the moving
powers from excefs of ftimulus, had taken place.
It was an early difcovery of this fact which led me
not to conceal from my patients the true name of
this fever, when I was called to them on the *day*
of their being attacked by it. The fear, co-ope-
rated with fome of my remedies (to be mentioned hereafter) in reducing the morbid excitement
of the arterial fyftem.

2. GRIEF. It was remarkable that the greateft concentration of the contagion did not produce the difeafe in many cafes in the attendants upon the fick, while there was a hope of
their recovery. The grief which followed the
extinction of hope, by death, frequently produced the difeafe within a day or two afterwards,
and that, not in one perfon only, but often in moft
                                                    of

óf the near relations of the difeafed. But the difeafe was alfo produced by a change in the ftate of
the mind directly oppofite to that which has been
mentioned. Many perfons that attended patients
who recovered, were feized with the diforder a
day or two after they were relieved from the toils
and anxiety of nurfing. The collapfe of the mind
from the abftraction of the ftimulus of hope and
defire, by their ample gratification, probably produced that debility, and lofs of the equilibrium
in the fyftem which favoured the activity of the
contagion.

The effects of both the ftates of mind which
have been defcribed, have been happily illuftrated
by two facts which are recorded by Dr Jackfon.*
He tells us that the garrifons of Savannah and
York Town, were both healthy during the fiege
of thofe towns, but that the former became fickly as foon as the French and American armies re-
treated from before it, and the latter, immediately
after its capitulation.

3. COLD. It will not be neceffary to paufe
here, to prove that cold is a negative quality, and
produced only by the abfence of heat. Its action

* Treatife on the Fevers of Jamaica, page 298.

D   in

in exciting the difeafe, depended upon the diminution of the neceffary and natural heat of the body, and thereby fo far deftroying the equilibrium
of the fyftem, as to enable the contagion to produce exceffive or convulfive motions in the blood
veffels.   The night air, even in the warm month
of September, was often fo cool as to excite the
difeafe where the drefs and bed clothes were not
accommodated to it.   It was excited in one cafe
by a perfon's only wetting his feet in the month
of October, and neglecting afterwards to change
his fhoes and ftockings.   Every change in the
weather, that was fhort of producing froft, evidently encreafed the number of fick people.   This
was obvious after the 18th and 19th of September,
when the mercury fell to 44°, and 45°.   The
hopes of the city received a fevere difappoint-
ment upon this occafion, for I well recollect there
was a general expectation that this change in the
weather would have checked the diforder.   The
fame increafe of the number of fick, was obferved to follow the cool weather which fucceeded
the 6th and 7th of October, on which days the
mercury fell to 43° and 46°.

It was obferved that thofe perfons who were
habitually expofed to the cool air, were lefs liable
to the difeafe than others.   I afcribe it to the *ha-*
                                                    bitual

bitual impreffion of the cool night air upon the bodies of the city watchmen, that only four or five of them out of 25 were affected by the disorder.

After the body had been heated by violent exercife, a breeze of cool air fometimes excited the difeafe in thofe cafes where there had been no change in the temperature of the weather.

4. SLEEP. A great proportion of all who were affected by this fever, were attacked in the night. Sleep induced direct debility, and thereby difpofed the contagion which floated in the blood, to act with fuch force upon the fyftem as to deftroy its equilibrium, and thus to excite a fever. The influence of fleep as a predifpofing, and exciting caufe was often affifted by the want of bed cloaths, fuited to the midnight or morning coolnefs of the air.

5. IMMODERATE EVACUATIONS. The efficacy of moderate purging and bleeding in preventing the difeafe, led fome people to ufe thofe remedies in an excefs, which both predifpofed to the difeafe, and excited it. The morbid effects of thefe evacuations, were much aided by fear, for it was this paffion which perverted the judgment in fuch

D 2

a man-

a manner, as to lead to the exceffive ufe of remedies, which to be effectual, fhould only be ufed
in moderate quantities.

The difeafe appeared with different fymptoms,
and in different degrees, in different people.
They both varied likewife with the weather. In
defcribing the difeafe I fhall take notice of the
changes in the fymptoms, which were produced
by changes in the temperature of the air.

The precurfors, or premonitory figns of this
fever were, coftivenefs, a dull pain in the right
fide, defect of appetite, flatulency, perverted tafte,
heat in the ftomach, giddinefs, or pain in the
head, a dull—watery—brilliant, yellow or red
eye, dim and imperfect vifion, a hoarfenefs, or
flight fore throat, low fpirits, or unufual vivacity,
a moifture on the hands, a difpofition to fweat at
nights, or after moderate exercife, or a fudden
fuppreffion of night fweats. The dull eye, and
the lownefs of fpirits appeared to be the effects of
fuch an excefs in the ftimulus of the contagion as
to induce indirect debility, while the brilliant eye,
and the unufual vivacity, feemed to have been
produced by a lefs quantity of the contagion acting as a cordial upon the fyftem. More or lefs of
thefe fymptoms, frequently continued for two or
three

three days before the patients were confined to their beds, and in fome people they continued during the whole time of its prevalence in the city, without producing the difeafe. I wifh thefe fymptoms to be remembered by the reader. They will form the corner ftone of a fyftem which I hope will either eradicate the diforder altogether, or render it as fafe as an intermitting fever, or as the fmall pox when it is received by inoculation.

Frequent as thefe precurfors of the fever were, they were not univerfal. Many went to bed in good health, and awoke in the night with a chilly fit. Many rofe in the morning after regular and natural fleep, and were feized at their work, or after a walk with a fudden and unexpected attack of the fever. In moft of thefe cafes the difeafe came on with a chilly fit, which afforded by its violence or duration a tolerable prefage of the iffue of the diforder.

Upon entering a fick room where a patient was confined by this fever, the firft thing that ftruck the eye of a phyfician, was the countenance. It was as much unlike that which is exhibited in the common bilions fever, as the face of a wild, is unlike the face of a mild domeftic animal. The eyes were fad, watery, and fo inflamed in

D 3 fome

fome cafes as to refemble two balls of fire. Sometimes they had a moft brilliant or ferocious appearance. The face was fuffufed with blood, or
of a dufky colour, and the whole countenance was
downcaft and clouded. After the 10th of September, when a determination of blood to the
brain became univerfal, there was a preternatural
dilatation of the pupil. Sighing attended in almoft every cafe. The fkin was dry, and frequently of its natural temperature. Thefe were the
principal fymptoms which difcovered themfelves
to the eye, and hand of a phyfician. The anfwers to the firft queftions propofed upon vifiting
a patient, were calculated to produce a belief in
the mind of a phyfician, that the difeafe under
which the patient laboured, was not the prevailing malignant epidemic. I did not for many weeks
meet with a dozen patients, who acknowledged
that they had any other indifpofition than a common cold, or a flight remitting, or intermitting
fever. I was particularly ftruck with this felf deception in many perfons, who had nurfed relations
that had died with the yellow fever, or who had
been expofed to its contagion in families, or neighbourhoods, where it had prevailed for days and
even weeks with great mortality. I fhall hereafter trace a part of this difpofition in the fick to
deceive themfelves, to the influence of certain
publications

publications which appeared foon after the difeafe became epidemic in the city.

In the further hiftory of this fever, I fhall defcribe its fymptoms as they appeared.

I. In the fanguiferous fyftem.

II. In the liver, lungs, and brain.

III. In the alimentary canal ; in which I include the ftomach as well as the bowels.

IV. In the fecretions and excretions.

V. In the nervous fyftem.

VI. In the fenfes and appetites.

VII. In the lymphatic and glandular fyftem.

VIII. Upon the fkin.

IX. In the blood.

After having finifhed this detail, I fhall mention fome general charaƈters of the difeafe, and

D 4   afterwards

afterwards fubdivide it into claffes, according to
its degrees and duration.

I. The BLOOD VESSELS (and not the ftomach
and bowels according to Dr Warren) are the
" feat and throne" of this as well as of all
other fevers. I have publicly taught for feveral years, that a fever is occafioned by a convulfion in the arterial fyftem. When the epidemic,
which we are now confidering, came on with a
full, tenfe, and quick pulfe, this convulfion
was very perceptible ; but it frequently came on
with a weak pulfe ; often without any preternatural frequency or quicknefs, and fometimes fo low
as not to be perceived without prefling the artery
at the wrifts. In many cafes the pulfe intermitted
after the 4th, in fome after the 5th, and in others
after the 14th ftroke. Thefe intermiffions occurred in feveral perfons who were infected, but who
were not confined by the fever. They likewife
continued in feveral of my patients for many days
after their recovery. This was the cafe in particular in Mrs Clymer, Mrs Palmer's fon William, and
in a fon of Mr William Compton. In fome there
was a preternatural flownefs of the pulfe. It beat 44
ftrokes in a minute in Mr B. W. Morris—48 in
Mr Thomas Wharton, Jun. and 64 in Mr William
Saafom,

Sanfom, at a time when they were in the moft imminent danger. Dr Phyfic informed me, that in
one of his patients the pulfe was reduced in frequency to 30 ftrokes in a minute. All thefe
different ftates of the pulfe have been taken notice
of by authors who have defcribed peftilential fevers. * They have been improperly afcribed to
the abfence of fever : I would rather fuppofe that
they are occafioned by the ftimulus of the contagion, acting upon the arteries with too much force
to admit of their being excited into quick and convulfive motions. The remedy which removed it
(to be mentioned hereafter) will render this explanation of its caufe ftill more probable. Milton
defcribes a darknefs, from an excefs of light. In
like manner, we obferve in this fmall intermitting
and flow pulfe, a deficiency of ftrength from an
excefs of force applied to it. In every cafe of it
which came under my notice, it was likewife tenfe
or chorded. This fpecies of pulfe occurred chiefly in the month of Auguft, and in the firft ten
days in September. I had met with it formerly in a fporadic cafe of yellow fever. It was
new to all my pupils. One of them, Mr Wafh-

---

* Vergafca, Sorbait, and Boate in Haller's Biliotheca Medicinæ, Vol. III. alfo by Dr Stubbs in the Philofophical
Tranfactions, and Riverius in his treatife de febre peftilenti.

ington,

ington, gave it the name of the "undifcribable pulfe." It aided in determining the fpecific na- ture of this fever before the common bilious re- mittent difappeared in the city. For a while, I afcribed this peculiarity in the pulfe, more efpeci- ally its *flownefs*, to an affeftion of the brain only, and fufpefted that it was produced, by what I have taken the liberty clfewhere to call the *phrenicula*, or inflammatory ftate of the internal dropfy of the brain, and which I have remarked to be an occa- fional fymptom and confequence of remitting fe- ver. * I was the more difpofed to adopt this opi- nion, from perceiving this flow and intermitting pulfe more frequently in children than in adults. Impreffed with this idea, I requefted Mr Coxe, one of my pupils, to affift me in examining the ftate of the eye. For two days we difcovered no change in it, but on the third day after we began to in- fpeft the eyes, we both perceived a preternatural dilatation of the pupils in different patients ; and we feldom afterwards faw an eye in which it was abfent. In Dr Say it was attended by a fquinting, a fymptom which marks a high degree of a mor- bid affeftion of the brain. Had this flownefs or intermiffion in the pulfe occurred only after figns of inflammation or congeftion had appeared in the

* Medical Inquiries and Obfervations, Vol. II.

brain,

brain, I fhould have fuppofed that it had been derived wholly from that caufe; but I well recollect
having felt it feveral days before I could difcover
the leaft change in the pupil of the eye. I am forced therefore to call in the operation of another
caufe, to affift in accounting for this ftate of the
pulfe, and this I take to be a fpafmodic affection,
accompanied with preternatural dilatation or con-
traction of the heart. Lieutaud mentions this fpecies of pulfe in feveral places, as occurring with an
undue enlargement of this mufcle *. Dr Ferriar
defcribes a cafe, in which a low, irregular, intermitting and hardly perceptible pulfe, attended
a morbid dilatation of the heart. † In a letter
I lately received from Mr Hugh Fergufon, a ftudent of medicine in the college of Edinburgh,
written from Dublin, during the time of a vifit to
his father, and dated September 30th, 1793, I find
a fact which throws additional light upon this fubject. " A cafe (fays my young correfpondent)
where a remarkable intermiffion of pulfe was obferved, occurred in this city laft year. A gentleman of the medical profeffion, middle aged, of a de-
licate habit of body, and who had formerly fuffer-

---

* Hiftoria Anatomica Medica, Vol. II. Obf. 405. 418.
423. 510.

† Medical Hiftories and Reflections, p. 150.

cd

ed phthifical attacks, was attacked with the acute
rheumatifm. Some days after he was taken ill,
he complained of uncommon fulnefs, and a very
peculiar kind of fenfation about the præcordia,
which it was judged proper to relieve by copious
blood-letting. This being done, the uneafinefs
went off. It returned however three or four times,
and was as often relieved by bleeding. During
each of his fits (if I may call them fo), the patient experienced an almoft total remiffion of his
pains in his limbs ; but they returned with equal
or greater violence after blood-letting. During
the fit there was an intermiffion of the pulfe (the
firft time) of no lefs than thirteen ftrokes. It was
when beating full, ftrong, and flow. The third
intermiffion was of nine ftrokes. The gentleman
foon recovered, and has enjoyed good health for
ten months paft. The opinion of fome of his phyficians was, that the heart was affected as a mufcle, by the rheumatifm, and alternated with the
limbs."

I am the more inclined to believe the peculiarity in the pulfe which has been mentioned in the
yellow fever, arofe in part from a fpafmodic affection of the heart, from the frequency of an uncommon palpitation of this mufcle, which I difcovered
in this diforder, more efpecially in old people.
The

The difpofition likewife to fyncope and fighing, which fo often occurred, can be explained upon no other principle than inflammation, fpafm, dilatation, or congeftion in the heart. After the 10th of September this undefcribable or *fulky* pulfe (for by the latter epithet I fometimes called it) became lefs obfervable; and in proportion as the weather became cool, it totally difappeared. It was gradually fucceeded by a pulfe, full, tenfe, quick, and as frequent as in pleurify or rheumatifm. It differed however from a pleuritic or rheumatic pulfe, in imparting a very different fenfation to the fingers. No two ftrokes feemed to be exactly alike. Its action was of a hobbling nature. It was at this time fo familiar to me, that I think I could have diftinguifhed the difeafe by it, without feeing the patient. It was remarkable, that this pulfe attended the yellow fever even when it appeared in the mild form of an intermittent, and in thofe cafes where the patients were able to walk about, or go abroad. It was nearly as *tenfe* in the remiffions and intermiffions of the fever, as it was in the exacerbations. It was an alarming fymptom, and when the only remedy which was effectual to remove it, was neglected, fuch a change in the fyftem was induced, as frequently brought on death in a few days.

This

This change in the pulfe, from extreme lownefs, to fulnefs and activity, appeared to be owing
to the diminution of the heat of the weather,
which by its ftimulus, added to that of the contagion, had induced thofe fymptoms of indirect
debility in the pulfe, which have been mentioned.

The pulfe moft frequently leffened in its fulnefs, and became gradually weak, frequent, and
imperceptible before death, but I met with feveral
cafes in which it was full, active, and even tenfe
in the laft hours of life.

HEMORRHAGIES belong to the fymptoms of
this fever as they appeared in the fanguiferous fyftem. They occurred in the beginning of the diforder chiefly from the nofe and uterus. Sometimes but a few drops of blood diftilled from the
nofe. The menfes were unufual in their quantity,
when they appeared at their ftated periods, but
they often came on a week or two before the ufual
time of their appearance. I faw one cafe of an
hemorrhage from the lungs on the firft day of the
fever, which was miftaken for a common hemop-
tyfis. As the difeafe advanced, the difcharges of
blood became more univerfal. They occurred from
the gums, ears, ftomach, bowels, and urinary paffages. Drops of blood iffued from the inner Can-
thus

thus of the left eye of Mr Jofiah Coates. Dr Wood-houfe attended a lady who bled from the holes in her ears, which had been made by ear rings. Many bled from the orifices which had been made by bleeding, feveral days after they appeared to have been healed, and fome from wounds which had been made in veins in unfuccefsful attempts to draw blood. Thefe laft hemorrhages were very troublefome, and in fome cafes precipitated death.

II. I come now to mention the fymptoms of this fever as they appeared in the LIVER, the LUNGS, and the BRAIN. From the hiftories which I had read of this diforder, I was early led to ex-amine the ftate of the LIVER, but I was furprifed to find fo few marks of hepatic affection. I met with but two cafes in which the patient could lie only on the right fide. Many complained of a dull pain in the region of the liver, but very few complained of that forenefs to the touch, about the pit of the ftomach which is taken notice of by authors, and which was univerfal in the yellow fever in 1762. In proportion as the cool weather advanced, a preternatural determination of the blood took place chiefly to the lungs and brain. Many were affected with pneumonic fymptoms,

and

and fome appeared to die of fudden effufions of
blood or ferum in the lungs. It was an unexpected effufion of this kind which put an end to
the life of Mrs Keppele after fhe had exhibited
hopeful figns of a recovery.

I faw one perfon who recovered from an affection
of the lungs, by means of a copious expectoration
of yellow phlegm and mucus. But the BRAIN was
principally affected with morbid congeftion in this
diforder. It was indicated by the fuffufion of blood
in the face, by the rednefs of the eyes, by a dilatation of the pupils, by the pain in the head, by
the hemorrhagies from the nofe and ears, by the
ficknefs, or vomiting, and by an almoft univerfal
coftive ftate of the bowels. I wifh to imprefs the
reader with thefe facts, for they formed one of the
ftrongeft indications for the ufe of the remedies
which I adopted for the cure of this diforder. It
is difficult to determine the exact ftate of thefe
vifcera in every cafe of bilious and yellow fever.
Inflammation certainly takes place in fome cafes,
and internal hemorrhagies in others; but I believe
the moft frequent affection of thefe vifcera confifts
in a certain morbid accumulation of blood in them,
which has been happily called by Dr Clark an
engorgement or choaking of the blood veffels. I

I   believe

believe further with Dr Clark * and Dr Balfour †, that death in moſt caſes in bilious fevers is the effeꜩ of theſe morbid congeſtions, and wholly un-conneꜩed with direꜩ debility or a ſuppoſed putre-faꜩion in the fluids. It is true the diſſeꜩions of Dr Phyſic and Dr Cathrall diſcovered no morbid appearances in either of the viſcera which have been mentioned, but it ſhould be remembered, that theſe diſſeꜩions were made early in the diſorder. Dr Annan attended the diſſeꜩion of a brain of a patient who died at Buſh-hill ſome days afterwards, and obſerved the blood veſſels to be unuſually turgid. In thoſe caſes where con-geſtion only takes place, it is as eaſy to conceive that all morbid appearances in the brain may ceaſe after death, as that the ſuffuſion of blood in the face ſhould diſappear after the retreat of the blood from the extremities of the veſſels in the laſt mo-ments of life. It is no new thing for morbid affeꜩions of the brain to leave either ſlender or no marks of diſeaſe after death. Dr Quin has given a diſſeꜩion of the brain of a child that died with all the ſymptoms of hydrocephalus inter-nus, and yet nothing was diſcovered in the brain but a ſlight turgeſcence of its blood veſſels. Dr

* Vol. i. p. 168.

† Treatiſe on the Inteſtinal remitting Fever, p. 125.

E   Girdleſtone

Girdleftone fays, no injury appeared in the brains
of thofe perfons who died of the fymptomatic apoplexy, which occurred in a fpafmodic difeafe which
he defcribes in the Eaft Indies; and Mr Clark informs us, that the brain was in a natural ftate
in every cafe of death from puerperile fever, notwithftanding it feemed to be affefted in many
cafes foon after the attack of that diforder*.

I wifh it to be remembered here, that the yellow
fever like all other difeafes is influenced by climate and feafon. The determination of the fluids
is feldom the fame in different years, and I am fure
it varied with the weather in the difeafe which I
am now defcribing. Dr Jackfon fpeaks of the
head being moft affefted in the Weft India fevers
in *dry* fituations. Dr Hillary fays, that there was
an unufual determination of the blood towards the
brain after a *hot* and *dry* feafon in the fevers of
Barbadoes in the year 1753, and Dr Ferriar in his
account of an epidemic jail fever in Manchefter in
1789, 1790, informs us, that as foon as froft fet
in, a delirium became a more frequent fymptom
of that diforder, than it had been in more temperate weather.

III.

* Effay on the Epidemic Difeafe of Lying-in Women, of
the years 1787 and 1788. p. 34.

III. The Stomach and Bowels were affected in many ways in this fever. The difeafe feldom appeared without naufea or vomiting. In fome cafes, they both occurred for feveral days, or a week before they were accompanied by any fever. This was more frequently the cafe, where the difeafe was taken by exhalation from the putrid coffee, than by contagion. Sometimes a pain, known by the name of gaftrodynia, ufhered in the difeafe. The ftomach was fo extremely irritable as to reject drinks of every kind. Sometimes green or yellow bile was rejected on the firft day of the diforder, by vomiting; but I much oftener faw it continue for two days without difcharging any thing from the ftomach, but the drinks which were taken by the patient. If the fever in any cafe came on without vomiting, or if it had been checked by remedies that were ineffectual, to remove it altogether, it generally appeared, or returned, on the 4th or 5th day of the diforder. I dreaded this fymptom on thofe days, for although it was not always the forerunner of death, yet it generally rendered the recovery more difficult and tedious. In fome cafes the vomiting was more or lefs conftant from the beginning to the end of the diforder, whether it terminated in life or death.

The

The vomiting which came on about the 4th or
5th day, was accompanied with a burning pain in the
region of the ftomach. It produced great anxiety
and tofling of the body from one part of the bed
to another. In fome cafes this painful burning
occurred before any vomiting had taken place.
Drinks were now rejected from the ftomach fo
fuddenly as often to be difcharged over the hand
that lifted them to the head of the patient. The
contents of the ftomach (to be mentioned hereafter) were fometimes thrown up with a convulfive
motion, that propelled them in a ftream to a great
diftance, and in fome cafes all over the clothes of
the by-ftanders.

Flatulency was an almoft univerfal fymptom in
every ftage of this diforder. It was very diftreffing in many cafes. It occurred chiefly in the ftomach.

The BOWELS were generally coftive, and in
fome patients, as cbftinately fo, as in the dry
gripes. In fome cafes there was all the pain and
diftrefs of a bilious colic, and in others, the tenef-
mus, and mucous and bloody difcharges of a true
dyfentery. A diarrhœa introduced the difeafe in
in a few perfons, but it was chiefly in thofe who
had been previoufly indifpofed with weak bowels.
                                                    A pain-

A painful tenfion of the abdomen took place in many, accompanied in fome inftances by a dull, and in others, by an acute pain in the lower part of the belly.

The vomiting and coftivenefs in the firft ftage of this fever, I believe were occafioned chiefly by the morbid ftate of the brain. But the vomiting and burning in the ftomach, and the pain in the bowels which occurred on the 4th and 5th days, appeared to be the effects of inflammation induced in part by the effufion of acrid bile into the alimentary canal, and in part by a change in the action of the coats of the ftomach and bowels, induced by effufions of ferum or red blood, fimilar to thofe which take place on the fkin in malignant fevers, and which are known by the name of petechiæ. I am the more difpofed to afcribe a large portion of the inflammation, erofions, and mortifications, which have been obferved after death in the ftomach and bowels in this fever, to the latter caufe, from the difcovery which has been made of petechiæ and carbuncles in the bowels in the plague, exactly fimilar to thofe which are found on the external parts of the body in that diforder*.

* Haller's Biliotheca Medicinæ, vol. iv. p. 375.

IV. I come now to defcribe the ftate of the
SECRETIONS and EXCRETIONS, as they appeared
in different ftages of this fever.

There appeared to be a preternatural fecretion
and excretion of bile. It was difcharged from the
ftomach and bowels in large quantities, and of
very different qualities and colours.

1. On the firft and fecond days of the diforder,
many patients puked from half a pint to nearly a
quart of green or yellow bile. Four cafes came
under my notice in which black bile was difcharged on the *firft* day. Three of thefe patients
recovered. I afcribed their recovery, to the bile
not having as yet acquired acrimony enough to in-
flame, or corrode the ftomach.

2. There was frequently on the 4th or 5th day,
a difcharge of matter from the ftomach, refembling
coffee impregnated with its grounds. This was
always an alarming fymptom. I believed it at
firft to be a modification of vitiated bile, but I was
led afterwards by its refemblance to the urine (to
be defcribed hereafter) to fufpeft that it was produced by a morbid fecretion in the liver, and ef-
fufed from it into the ftomach. Many recovered
who difcharged this coffee-coloured matter.

3. Towards

3. Towards the clofe of the difeafe, there was a difcharge of matter of a deep or pale black colour, from the ftomach. Flakey fubftances frequently floated in the bafon or chamber-pot upon the furface of this matter. It appeared to be bile in a highly acrid ftate, That the bile may become extremely acrid in this ftage of the diforder is evident from feveral obfervations and experiments. Dr Phyfic's hand was inflamed in confequence of its being wetted by bile in this ftate, in diffecting a dead body. Dr Arthaud examined the body of a foldier who died of the yellow fever at the French Cape on the 16th of May 1789, whofe bile imparted a green colour*, to the tincture of radifhes. I am not certain that the black matter, which was difcharged in the laft ftage of this diforder, was always vitiated or acrid bile. It was probably in fome cafes, the matter which was formed in confequence of the mortification of the ftomach./ The matter which was difcharged from carbuncles on the fkin, as I fhall fay hereafter, was always of a dark colour. Several diffections of perfons who have died of the yellow fever, have fhewn abfceffes in the ftomach, not unlike external carbuncles. May not the black matter in fome cafes be derived from thefe internal carbuncle-like abfceffes ?

* Rofier's Journal for Jan. 1790. vol. xxxvi. p. 380.

4. There

4. There was frequently difcharged from the ftomach in the clofe of the difeafe, a large quantity of grumous blood, which exhibited a dark colour on its outfide, refembling that of fome of the matters which have been defcribed, and which I believe was frequently miftaken for what is commonly known by the name of the *black vomiting.* Several of my patients did me the honour to fay, I had cured them, after that fymptom of approaching diffolution had made its appearance; but I am inclined to believe, dark-coloured blood only, or the coffee coloured matter, was miftaken for the matters which conftitute the fatal black vomiting. I except here the black difcharge before mentioned, which took place in three cafes on the firft day of the diforder. This I have no doubt was bile, but it had not acquired its greateft acrimony, and it was difcharged before mortification, or even inflammation could have taken place in the ftomach. Several perfons died without a black vomiting of any kind.

Along with all the difcharges from the ftomach which have been defcribed, there was occafionally a large worm, and frequently large quantities of mucus and tough phlegm.

The

The colour, quality, and quantity of the *fæces* depended very much upon the treatment of the difeafe. Where active purges had been given, the ftools were copious, fœtid, and of a black or dark colour. Where they were fpontaneous, or excited by weak purges, they had a more natural appearance. In both cafes, they were fometimes of a green, and fometimes of an olive colour. Their fmell was more or lefs fœtid, according to the time in which they had been detained in the bowels. I vifited a lady who had paffed feveral days without a ftool, and who had been treated with tonic remedies. I gave her a purge, which in a few hours procured a difcharge of fæces fo extremely fœtid, that they produced fainting in an old woman who attended her. The acrimony of the fæces was fuch as to excoriate the rectum, and fometimes to produce an extenfive inflammation all around its external termination. The quantity of the ftools produced by a fingle purge was in many cafes very great. They could be accounted for only by calling in the conftant, and rapid formation of them, by preternatural effufions of bile into the bowels.

I attended one perfon, and heard of two others, in whom the ftools were as white as in the jaundice. I fufpected in thefe cafes, the bile was fo

impacted

impacted in the gall bladder, or in its ducts, as
not to be difcharged in a fufficient quantity to colour the fœces. Large round worms were frequently difcharged with the ftools.

The *urine* was in fome cafes plentiful, and of a
high colour. It was at times clear, and at other
times turbid. About the 4th or 5th day it fometimes affumed a dark colour, and refembled ftrong
coffee. This colour continued in one inftance for
feveral days after the patient recovered. In fome,
the difcharge was accompanied by a burning pain
refembling that which takes place in a gonorrhœa.
I met with one cafe in which this burning came
on only in the evening, with the exacerbation of
the fever, and went off with its remiffion in the
morning.

A total deficiency of the urine took place in
many people for a day or two, without pain. Dr
Sydenham takes notice of the fame fymptom in
the highly inflammatory fmall pox.* It generally accompanied, or portended great danger. I
fufpected that it was connected in this difeafe, as
in the hydrocephalus internus, with a morbid ftate
of the brain. I heard of one cafe in which there

* Wallis's Edition, Vol. i. p. 197.

was

was a *fuppreffion* of urine, which could not be relieved without the ufe of the catheter.

A young man was attended by Mr Fifher, one of my pupils, who difcharged feveral quarts of limpid urine juft before he died.

Dr Arthaud informs us in the hiftory of the diffection before quoted, that the urine after death imparted a green colour to the tincture of radifhes.

Many people were relieved by copious *fweats* on the firft day of the diforder. They were in fome inftances fpontaneous, and in others, they were excited by diluting drinks, or by ftrong purges. Thefe fweats were often of a yellow colour, and fometimes had an offenfive fmell. They were in fome cafes cold, and attended at the fame time with a full pulfe. In general, the fkin was dry in the beginning as well as in the fubfequent ftages of the diforder. I faw but few inftances of the difeafe terminating like common fevers, by fweat after the third day. I wifh this fact to be remembered by the reader, for it laid part of the foundation of my method of curing this fever.

There

There was in fome cafes a preternatural fecretion and excretion of *mucus* from the glands of
the throat. It was difcharged by an almoft conftant hawking and fpitting. All who had this
fymptom recovered.

The TONGUE was in every cafe moift, and
of a white colour on the firft and fecond days
of the fever. As the difeafe advanced, it affumed a red colour, and a fmooth fhining appearance. It was not quite dry in this ftate.
Towards the clofe of the fever, a dry black
ftreak appeared in its middle, which gradually extended to every part of it. Few recovered after this appearance on the tongue took
place.

V. In the NERVOUS SYSTEM the fymptoms of
the fever were different according as it affected
the brain—the mufcles—the nerves—or the mind.
The fudden and violent action of the contagion,
induced apoplexy in feveral people. In fome, it
brought on fyncope, and in others, convulfions
in every part of the body. The apoplectic cafes
generally proved fatal, for they fell chiefly upon
hard drinkers. Perfons affected by fyncope, or
convulfions, fometimes fell down in the ftreets.
Two cafes of this kind happened near my houfe.
One

One of them came under my notice. He was fuppofed by the bye-ftanders to be drunken, but his countenance, and convulfive motions, foon convinced me that this was not the cafe.

A coma was obferved in fome people, or an obftinate wakefulnefs in every ftage of the difor-der. The latter fymptom moft frequently attended the convalefcence. Many were affected with im-mobility, or numbnefs in their limbs.

Thefe fymptoms were conftant, or temporary, according to the nature of the remedies which were made ufe of, to remove them. They ex-tended to all the limbs, in fome cafes, and only to a part of them in others. In fome, a violent cramp both in the arms, and legs attended the firft attack of the fever. I met with one cafe in which there was a difficulty of fwallowing from a fpafmodic affection of the throat, fuch as occurs in the locked-jaw.

A hiccup attended the laft ftage of this difor-der, but I think lefs frequently than the laft ftage of the common bilious fever. I faw only five cafes of recovery where this fymptom took place.

There was in fome inftances a deficiency of fen-fibility, but in others a degree of it, extending to every

every part of the body, which rendered the application of common rum to the fkin, and even the
leaft motion of the limbs painful.

I was furprifed to obferve the laft ftage of this
fever to exhibit fo few of the fymptoms of the
common typhus or nervous fever. Tremors of
the limbs and twitchings of the tendons were uncommon. They occurred only in thofe cafes in
which there was a predifpofition to nervous difeafes, and chiefly in the convalefcent ftate of the
diforder.

While the mufcles and nerves in many cafes exhibited fo many marks of preternatural weaknefs, in fome, they appeared to be affected with
preternatural excitement. Hence patients in the
clofe of the diforder often rofe from their beds,
walked acrofs their rooms, or came down ftairs,
with as much eafe as if they had been in perfect
health. I loft a patient in whom this ftate of morbid ftrength occurred to fuch a degree, that he
ftood up before his glafs, and fhaved himfelf on
the day in which he died.

The mind fuffered with the morbid ftates of the
brain and nerves. A delirium was a common
fymptom. It alternated in fome cafes with the
exacerbations and remiffions of the fever. In
fome

some, it continued without a remission, until a few hours before death. Many, however, passed through the whole course of the disease without the least derangement in their ideas, even where there were evident signs of a morbid congestion in the brain. Some were seized with maniacal symptoms. In these, there was an apparent absence of fever. Such was the degree of this mania in one man, that he stripped of his shirt, left his bed, and ran through the streets with no other covering than a napkin on his head, at 8 o'clock at night, to the great terror of all who met him. The symptoms of mania occurred most frequently towards the close of the disease, and sometimes continued for many days, and weeks, after all the febrile symptoms had disappeared.

The temper was much affected in this fever. There were few, in whom it did not produce great depression of spirits. This was the case in many, in whom pious habits had subdued the fear of death. In some the temper became very irritable. Two cases of this kind came under my notice, in persons who in good health, were distinguished for uncommon sweetness of disposition and manners.

I observed in several persons the operations of the understanding to be unimpaired, throughout the

the whole courfe of the fever, who retained no remembrance of any thing that paffed in their ficknefs. My pupil Mr Fifher furnifhed a remarkable example of this correctnefs of underftanding with a fufpenfion of memory. He neither faid, nor did any thing during his illnefs, that indicated the leaft derangement of mind, and yet he recollected nothing that paffed in his room, except my vifits to him. His memory awakened upon my taking him by the hand on the morning of the 6th day of his diforder, and congratulating him upon his efcape from the grave.

In fome, there was a weaknefs, or total defect of memory for feveral weeks after their recovery. Dr Woodhoufe informed me that he had met with a woman who after fhe had recovered, could not recollect her own name.

Perhaps it would be proper to rank that felf-deception with refpect to the nature and danger of the difeafe which was fo univerfal, among the inftances of derangement of mind.

The pain which attended the diforder was different according as the fyftem was affected by direct or indirect debility. In thofe cafes in which the fyftem funk under the violent impreffion of the contagion, there was little or no pain. In

4   proportion

proportion as the fyftem was relieved from this oppreffion it recovered its fenfibility. The pain in the head, was acute and diftreffing. It affected the eye balls in a peculiar manner. A pain extended in fome cafes from the back of the head, down the neck. The ears were affected in feveral perfons with a painful fenfation, which they compared to a ftring drawing their two ears together through the brain. The fides, and the regions of the ftomach, liver and bowels, were all, in different people, the feats of either dull or acute pains. The ftomach towards the clofe of the diforder was affected with a burning or fpafmodic pain of the moft diftreffing nature. It produced in fome cafes great anguifh of body and mind. In others it produced cries and fhrieks which were often heard on the oppofite fide of the ftreets to where the patients lay. The back fuffered very much in this diforder. The ftouteft men complained, and even groaned under it. An acute pain extended in fome cafes from the back, to one or both thighs. The arms and legs fympathized with every other part of the body. One of my patients, upon whofe limbs the difeafe fell, with its principal force, faid that his legs felt as if they had been fcraped with a fharp inftrument. The fympathy of friends with the diftreffes of the fick, extended to a fmall part of their mifery, when it did not include their fufferings from pain.

F   One

One of the deareft friends I ever loft by death, declared in the height of her illnefs, that " no one knew the pains of a yellow fever, but thofe who felt them."

VI.   The *fenfes* and *appetites* exhibited feveral marks of the univerfal ravages of this fever upon the body.   A deafnefs attended in many cafes, but it was not often as in the nervous fever, a favourable fymptom.   A dimnefs of fight, was very common in the beginning of the difeafe. Many were affected with temporary blindnefs.   In fome there was a lofs of fight in confequence of gutta ferena, or a total deftruction of the fubftance of the eye.   There was in many perfons a forenefs to the touch, which extended all over the body. I have often obferved this fymptom to be the forerunner of a favourable iffue of a nervous fever, but it was lefs frequently the cafe in this diforder.

The *thirft* was moderate or abfent in fome cafes, but it occurred in the greateft number of perfons whom I faw in this fever.   Sometimes it was very intenfe.   One of my patients who fuffered by an exceffive draught of cold water, declared juft before he died, that " he could drink up the Delaware."   It was always an alarming fymptom, when this thirft came on in this extra-

vagant

vagant degree in the laſt ſtage of the diſorder. In the beginning of the fever, it generally abated upon the appearance of a moiſt ſkin. Water, was preferred to all other drinks.

The *appetite* for food was impaired in this, as in all other fevers, but it returned much ſooner than is common after the patient began to recover. Coffee was reliſhed in the remiſſions of the fever, in every ſtage of the diſorder. So keen was the appetite for ſolid, and more eſpecially for animal food, after the ſolution of the fever, that many ſuffered from eating aliment that was improper from its quality or quantity. There was a general diſreliſh for wine, but malt liquors were frequently grateful to the appetite.

Many people retained a reliſh for tobacco much longer after they were attacked by this fever, and acquired a reliſh for it much ſooner after they began to recover, than are common in any other febrile diſeaſe. I met with one caſe in which my patient, who was ſo ill as to require two bleedings, continued to chew tobacco through every ſtage of his fever.

The convaleſcence from this diſorder was mark-ed in ſome inſtances, by a ſudden revival of the

venereal

venereal appetite. Several weddings took place in
the city between perfons who had recovered from
the fever. Twelve took place among the convalefcents in the hofpital at Bufh-hill. I wifh I
could add, that the paffion of the fexes for each
other, among thofe fubjeɑs of public charity, was
always gratified only in a lawful way. Delicacy
forbids a detail of the fcenes of debauchery which
were praɑifed near the hofpital in fome of the
tents, which had been appropriated for the reception of convalefcents. It is not peculiar to the
yellow fever to produce this morbid excitability
of the venereal appetite. It was produced in a
much higher degree by the plague which raged in
Meffina in the year 1743.

VII. The *lymphatic* and *glandular fyftem* did
not efcape without fome figns of the infeɑion of
this difeafe. I met with three cafes of fwellings
in the inguinal, two in the parotid, and one in the
cervical glands: all thefe patients recovered without
a fuppuration of their fwellings. They were extremely painful in one cafe in which no rednefs
or inflammation appeared. In the others, there
was confiderable inflammation, and but little pain.

In one of the cafes of inguinal buboes, the whole
force of the difeafe feemed to be colleɑed into the
lymphatic

lymphatic fyftem. The patient walked about, and had no fever nor pain in any part of his body, except in his groin. In another cafe which came under my care, a fwelling and pain extended from the groin along the fpermatic cord into one of the tefticles. Thefe glandular fwellings were not peculiar to our late epidemic. They occurred in the yellow fever of Jamaica as defcribed by Dr Williams, and always with a happy iffue of the diforder*. A fimilar concentration of the contagion of the plague in the lymphatic glands, is taken notice of by Dr Patrick Ruffel.

VIII. The SKIN exhibited many marks of this fever. It was preternaturally warm in fome cafes, but it was often preternaturally cool. In fome there was a diftreffing coldnefs in the limbs for two or three days. The yellow colour from which this fever has derived its name, was not univerfal. It feldom appeared where purges had been given in fufficient dofes. The yellownefs rarely appeared before the third, and generally about the fifth or feventh day of the fever. Its early appearance always denoted great danger. It fometimes appeared firft on the neck and breaft, inftead of the eyes. In one of my patients it difcovered itfelf firft be-

---

* Effay on the Bilious or Yellow Fever, p. 35.

hind

hind one of his ears, and on the crown of his head,
which had been bald for feveral years. The remiffions and exacerbations of the fever feemed to
have an influence upon this colour, for it appeared
and difappeared altogether, or with fainter or deep-
er fhades of yellow, two or three times in the
courfe of the diforder. The eyes feldom efcaped
a yellow tinge ; and yet I faw a number of cafes
in which the difeafe appeared with uncommon malignity and danger, without the prefence of this
fymptom. Two very different caufes have been
fuppofed to produce this yellow colour of the fkin.
By fome it has been attributed to the diffolution
of the blood ; but I fhall fay hereafter, that the
blood was feldom diffolved in this fever. The yellow colour, moreover, occurred in thofe cafes where
the blood exhibited an inflammatory cruft, and it
continued in many perfons for five or fix weeks
after their recovery. From thefe facts it is evident, that the yellownefs was in all cafes the effect
of an abforption and mixture of bile with the
blood.

There was a clay-coloured appearance in the
face in fome cafes, which was very different from
the yellow colour which has been defcribed. It
occurred in the laft ftage of the fever, and in no
inftance did I fee a recovery after it.

                                      There

There were eruptions of various kinds on the ſkin, each of which I ſhall briefly deſcribe.

1. I met with two caſes of an eruption on the ſkin, reſembling that which occurs in the ſcarlet fever. Dr Hume ſays, pimples often appear on the pit of the ſtomach in the yellow fever of Jamaica. I examined the external region of the ſtomach in many of my patients, without diſcovering this ſymptom.

2. I met with one caſe, in which there was an eruption of watery bliſters, which after burſting, ended in deep, black ſores.

3. There was an eruption about the mouth in many people, which ended in ſcabs, ſimilar to thoſe which take place in the common bilious fever. They always afforded a proſpect of a favourable iſſue of the diſeaſe.

4. Many perſons had eruptions which reſembled moſchetto bites. They were red and circumſcribed. They appeared chiefly on the arms, but they ſometimes extended to the breaſt. Like the yellow colour of the ſkin, they appeared and diſappeared two or three times in the courſe of the diſorder.

F 4

5. Pe-

5. Petechiæ were common in the latter ſtage of the fever. They ſometimes came on in large, and at other times in ſmall red blotches ; but they foon acquired a dark colour. In moſt, caſes they were the harbingers of death.

6. Several caſes of carbuncles, ſuch as occur in the plague, came under my notice. They were large and hard ſwellings on the limbs, with a black apex, which upon being opened, diſcharged a thin, dark-coloured, bloody matter. From one of theſe malignant ſores, an hemorrhage took place, which precipitated the death of the amiable widow of Dr John Morris.

7. A large and painful anthrax on the back ſuc-ceeded a favourable iſſue of the fever in the Rev. Dr Blackwell.

8. I met with a woman who ſhewed me the marks of a number of ſmall boils on her face and neck, which accompanied her fever.

Notwithſtanding this diſpoſition to cutaneous eruptions in this diſorder, it was remarkable that bliſters were much leſs diſpoſed to mortify than in the common nervous fever. I met with only one caſe in which a deep-ſeated ulcer followed the application

plication of blifters to the legs. Such was the in-
fenfibility of the fkin in fome people, that blifters
made no impreffion upon it.

IX. How far the *blood* may be confidered as the
vehicle of the contagion, it is not my bufinefs at
prefent to inquire; nor fhall I in this place mention the different appearances it exhibited when
drawn from a vein. It has been fuppofed to un-
dergo a change from a healthy to a putrid ftate;
and m'any of the fymptoms of the fever which
have been defcribed, particularly the hemorrhagies
an.d erupüns on the fkin, have been afcribed to
this fuppfied putrefaction of the blood. It would
be eafio multiply arguments to prove, that no
ci thing as putrefaction can take place in the
blood; and that the fymptoms which have been
fuppofed to prove its exiftence, are all effects
of a fudden, violent, and rapid inflammatory action, or preffure upon the blood-veffels; and hence
the external and internal hemorrhagies. The petechiæ on the furface of the fkin depend upon the
fame caufe. They are nothing but effufions of ferum or red blood, from a rupture or preternatural
dilatation of the capillary veffels *. The fmell

* See Wallis's edition of Sydenham, Vol. I. p. 165. Vol.
II. p. 52, 94, 98, 350. De Haen's Ratio Medendi, Vol.
II. p. 162. Vol. IV. p. 172. Gaubii Pathologia, § 498,
and

emitted from perfons affected by this difeafe was far from being of a putrid nature ; and if this had been the cafe, it would not have proved the exi-ftence of putrefaction in the blood ; for a putrid fmell is often difcharged from the lungs, and from the pores in fweat, which is wholly unconnected with a putrid, or perhaps any other morbid ftate of the blood. There are plant which difcharge an odor, which conveys to the nofe a fenfation like that of putrefaction ; and yet thefe plants exift at the fame time, in a ftate of the moft healthy vege'-tation : nor does the early putrid mell of a body which perifhes with this fever, prve a putrid change to have taken place in the bod before death. All animals which die fuddenlynd with-out lofs of blood, are difpofed to a fpeec ntre-faction. This has long been remarked in an.ls that have been killed after a chace, or by ligh, ning. The poifonous air called *famiel*, which is defcribed by Chardin, produces, when it deftroys life, inftant putrefaction. The bodies of men who die of violent paffions, or after ftrong convulfions, or even after great mufcular exertion, putrefy in a few hours after death. The healthy ftate of

and Dr Sybert's inaugural differtation, entitled " An at-tempt to Difprove the doctrine of the Putrefaction of the Blood in Living Animals," publifhed in Philadelphia in 1793.

the

the body depends upon a certain ftate of arrange-
ment in the fluids. A derangement of thefe fluids
is the natural confequence of the violent and rapid motions, or of the undue preffure upon the folids, which have been mentioned. It occurs in
every cafe of death from indirect debility, whether it be induced by the exceffive ftimulus of contagion, by the volatile vitriolic acid which is fuppofed to conftitute the deftructive famiel wind, or
by violent commotions excited in the body by external or internal caufes. The practice among
fifhermen in fome countries, of breaking the heads
of their fifh as foon as they are taken out of the water, in order to retard their putrefaction, proves the
truth of the explanation I have given of its caufe,
foon after death. The fudden extinction of life in
the fifh, prevents thofe convulfive or violent motions which induce fudden *diforganization* in their
bodies. It was remarkable that putrefaction took
place moft fpeedily after death from the yellow
fever, where the commotions of the fyftem were
not relieved by evacuations. In thofe cafes where
purges and bleeding had been ufed, putrefaction
did not take place fooner after death than is common in any other febrile difeafe, under equal circumftances of heat and air.

There is a fact mentioned by Dr Ferriar, from
Dr Hamilton, late profeffor of anatomy at Glaf-
gow,

gow, which may feem at firft fight to militate
againft the facts I have mentioned. He fays that
he had obferved bodies which were brought into
the diffecting room, that had petechiæ on them,
were longer in putrefying than any others. The
fevers of which the poor (the common fubjects
of diffection) die, are generally of the low nervous kind. Great *direct* debility is the charac-
teriftic of thefe fevers. The petechiæ which occur in them, appear in the laft ftage of this direct
debility. They are the effect, not of too much
impetus in the blood, as in the yellow fever, but
of a defect or total abfence of it in the laft hours
of life. The flow progrefs of the body to putrefaction after death, in the inftances mentioned
by Dr Hamilton, feems to depend upon the fame
caufe as that to which I have afcribed it in thofe
cafes of death from the yellow fever, in which e-
vacuations had been ufed, viz. *direct* debility.
In the former cafes this flownefs of putrefaction is
induced by nature—in the latter by art. The
effects of debility from both caufes are, notwithftanding, the fame.

Thus have I defcribed the fymptoms of this fever. From the hiftory I have given, it appears
that it counterfeited nearly all the acute and
chronic difeafes, to which the human body is fubject. An epitome, both of its fymptoms and its theory,

ory, is happily delivered by Dr Sydenham in the following words. After defcribing the epidemic cough, pleurify, and peripneumony of 1675, he adds, " But in other epidemics, the fymptoms are fo flight from the difturbance raifed in the blood by the morbific particles contained in the mafs, that nature being in a manner *oppreffed*, is rendered unable to produce *regular* fymptoms that are fuitable to the difeafe ; and almoft all the phænomena that happen are *irregular*, by reafon of the entire *fubverfion* of the animal œconomy ; in which cafe the fever is often *depreffed*, which of its own nature, would be very high. Sometimes alfo fewer figns of a fever appear than the nature of the difeafe requires, from a tranflation of the malignant caufe, either to the nervous fyftem, to fome other parts of the body, or to fome of the juices not contained in the blood; whilft the morbific matter is yet turgid" *.

The difeafe ended in death in various ways. In fome it was fudden ; in others it came on by gradual approaches. In fome the laft hours of life were marked with great pain, and ftrong convulfions ; but in many more, death feemed to infinuate itfelf into the fyftem, with all the gentlenefs of

---

* Wallis's edition, Vol. I. p. 344.

natural

natural fleep. Mr Powell expired with a fmile on his countenance. Dr Griffitts informed me that Dr Johnfon exhibited the fame fymptom in the laft hours of his life. This placid appearance of the countenance, in the act of dying, was not new to me. It frequently occurs in difeafes which affect the brain and nerves. I loft a patient three years ago in the gout, who not only fmiled, but laughed, a few minutes before he expired.

I proceed now to mention fome peculiarities of the fever which could not be brought in under any of the foregoing heads.

In every cafe of this diforder which came under my notice, there were evident remiffions, or inter-miffions of the fever, or of fuch fymptoms as were fubftituted for fever. I have long confidered with Mr Senac, a *tertian* as the only original type of all fevers. The bilious yellow fever indicated its defcent from this parent diforder. I met with many cafes of regular tertians in which the pa-tients were fo well on the intermediate days as to go abroad. It appeared in this form in Mr Van Berkel the minifter of the United Netherlands. Nor was this mild form of the fever devoid of danger. Many died who neglected it as a trifling diforder, or who took the common remedies for

intermit-

intermittents to cure it. It generally ended in a remittent before it deftroyed the patient. The tertian type difcovered itfelf in fome people after the more violent fymptoms of the fever had been fubdued, and continued in them for feveral weeks. It changed from a tertian to a quartan type in Mr Thomas Willing, nearly a month after his recovery from the more acute and inflammatory fymptoms of the diforder.

It is nothing new for a malignant fever to appear in the form of a tertian. It is frequently the garb of the plague. Riverius defcribes a tertian fever which proved fatal on the third day, which was evidently derived from the fame exhalation which produced a continual malignant fever. *

The remiffions were more evident in this, than in the common bilious fever. They generally occurred in the forenoon. It was my misfortune to be deprived by the great number of my patients, of that command of time which was neceffary to watch the exacerbations of this fever under all their various changes, as to time, force, and duration. From all the obfervations that were fuggefled by

* De Febre Peftilenti, vol. xi. p 93.

vifits,

vifits, at hours that were feldom left to my choice,
I was led to conclude, that the fever exhibited in
different people all that variety of forms which
has been defcribed by Dr Cleghorn in his account
of the tertian fever of Minorca. A violent exacerbation on even days was evidently attended
with more danger than on odd days. The fame
thing was obferved by Dr Mitchell in the Yellow
Fever of Virginia in the year 1741. " If (fays
he) " the exacerbations were on equal days, they
" generally died in the third paroxyfm, or the
" 6th day, but if on unequal days, they recovered
" on the 7th."

The deaths which occurred on the 3d, 5th,
and 7th days, appeared frequently to be the effects
of the commotions or depreffion, produced in the
fyftem on the 2nd, 4th, and 6th days.

The remiffion on the third day, was frequently
fuch as to beget a belief that the difeafe had run
its courfe, and that all danger was over. A violent attack of the fever on the 4th day removed
this deception, and if a relaxation had taken place
in the ufe of proper remedies on the 3d day,
death frequently occurred on the 5th or the feventh.

I   The

The termination of this fever in life, and death, was much more frequent on the 3d, 5th, 7th, 9th and 11th days, than is common in the mild remitting fever. Where death occurred on the even days, it feemed to be the effect of a violent paroxifm of the fever, or of great vigour of con-ftitution, or of the force of medicines which pro-tracted fome of the motions of life beyond the clofe of the odd days which have been mentioned.

I think I obferved the fever to terminate on the third day more frequently in Auguft, and during the firft ten days in September, than it did after the weather became cool. In this, it refembled the common bilious remittents of our city, alfo the fimple tertians defcribed by Dr Cleghorn *. The danger feemed to be in proportion to the tendency of the difeafe to a fpeedy crifis, hence more died in Auguft in proportion to the number who were affected than in September or October, when the difeafe was left to itfelf. But, however ftrange after this remark it may appear, the dif-eafe yielded to the remedies which finally fubdued it, more fpeedily and certainly upon its firft ap-pearance in the city, than it did two or three weeks afterwards.

* Difeafes of Minorca, p. 185.

G   The

The difeafe continued for fifteen, twenty, and even thirty days in fome people. Its duration was much influenced by the weather, and by the ufe or neglect of certain remedies (to be mentioned hereafter) in the firft ftage of the diforder.

It has been common with authors to divide the fymptoms of this fever into three different ftages. The order I have purfued in the hiftory of thofe fymptoms, will render this divifion unneceffary. It will I hope be more ufeful to divide the patients affected with the diforder into three claffes.

The *firft* includes thofe in whom the ftimulus of the contagion, produced the fymptoms of indirect debility, fuch as coma, languor, fighing, a difpofition to fyncope, and a weak, or flow pulfe.

The *fecond* includes thofe in whom the contagion acted with lefs force, producing great pain in the head, and other parts of the body; delirium, vomiting, heat, thirft, and a quick, tenfe, or full pulfe, with obvious remiffions or intermiffions of the fever.

The *third* clafs includes all thofe perfons in whom the ftimulus of the contagion acted fo feebly as not to confine them to their beds or houfes.

This

This clafs of perfons affected by the yellow fever, was very numerous. Many of them recovered without medical aid, or by the ufe of domeftic prefcriptions; many of them recovered in confequence of a fpontaneous diarrhœa, or plentiful fweats; many were faved by moderate bleeding, and purging; while fome died, who conceived their complaints to be occafioned by a common cold, and neglected to take proper care of themfelves, or to ufe the neceffary means for their recovery. It is not peculiar to the contagion of the yellow fever to produce this feeble operation upon the fyftem. It has been obferved in the fouthern ftates of America, that in thofe feafons in which the common bilious fever is epidemic " no body is quite well," and that what are called in thofe ftates " inward fevers" are univerfal. The fmall-pox even in the natural way, does not always confine the patient; and thoufands pafs through the plague without being confined to their beds or houfes. Dr Hodges prefcribed for this clafs of patients in his parlour in London in the year 1665, and Dr Patrick Ruffel did the fame from a chamber window fifteen feet above the level of the ftreet at Aleppo. Notwithftanding the mild form the plague put on in thefe cafes, it often proved fatal according to Dr Ruffel. I have introduced thefe facts chiefly with a view of prepa-

ring

ring the reader to reject the opinion that we had
two species of fever in the city at the same time;
and to shew that the yellow fever appears in a
more simple form than with " strongly marked"
characters; or in other words, with a yellow skin,
and a black vomitting.

It was remarkable that this fever always found
out the weak part of every constitution it attacked.
The head, the lungs, the stomach, the bowels,
and the limbs, suffered more or less, according as
they were more or less debilitated by previous
inflammatory, or nervous diseases, or by a mixture of both, as in the gout.

I have before remarked, that the influenza, the
scarlatina, and a mild bilious remittent, prevailed
in the city, before the yellow fever made its appearance. In the course of a few weeks they all
disappeared, or appeared with symptoms of the
yellow fever; so that after the first week of September, it was the solitary epidemic of the city.

The only case like influenza which I saw after the
5th of September, was in a girl of 14 years of
age, on the 13th of the month. It came on with
a sneezing and cough. I was called to her on
the third day of her disorder. The instant I felt

her

her pulfe, I pronounced her difeafe to be the yellow fever. Her father was offended with this opinion, although he lived in a highly infected neighbourhood, and objected to the remedies I prefcribed for her. In a few days fhe died. In the courfe of ten days, her father and fifter were infected, and both died I was informed, with the ufual fymptóms of the yellow fever.

It Has been an axiom in medicine, time immemorial, that no two contagious fevers of unequal force can exift long together in the fame place. As this axiom feems to have been forgotten by many of the phyficians of Philadelphia, and as the ignorance or neglect of it, led to that contrariety of opinion and practice, which unhappily took place in the treatment of the diforder, I hope I fhall be excufed by thofe phyficians to whom this fact is as familiar as the moft fimple law of nature, if I fill a few pages with proofs of it, from practical writers.

Thucydides long ago remarked that the plague chafed all other difeafes from Athens, or obliged them to change their nature, by affuming fome of its fymptoms.

G 3 Dr

Dr Sydenham makes the fame remark upon
the plague in London in 1665. Dr Hodges in
his account of the fame plague, fays that " at the
rife of the plague all other diftempers, went into
it, but at its declenfion, that it degenerated into
others, as inflammations, headach, quinfies, dyfenteries, fmall-pox, meafles, fevers, and he&ics,
wherein the plague yet predominated*."

During the prevalence of the plague in Grand
Cairo, no fporadic difeafe of any kind makes its
appearance. The fame obfervation is made by
Sauvage in his account of the plague at Alais in
the province of Languedoc†.

The fmall-pox though a difeafe of lefs force than
the plague, has often chafed it from Conftantinople, probably from its infecting at a greater diftance
than the plague. But this exclufive prevalence
of a fingle epidemic is not confined to the plague
and fmall-pox. Dr Sydenham's writings are full
of proofs of the dominion of febrile difeafes over
each other : Hence after treating upon a fympto-

* Dr Hodges Account of the Plague in London, p. 26.

† Sed hoc obfervatu dignum fuit, omnes alios morbos
acutos, durante pefte filuiffe, et omnes morbos acutos e pef-
tis genere fuiffe. Nofologia Methodica, vol. i. p. 416.

matic

matic pleurify, which fometimes accompanied a
flow fever in the year 1675, and which had probably been injudicioufly treated by fome of thofe
phyficians who prefcribe for the name of a difeafe,
he delivers the following aphorifm, " whoever in
the cure of fevers, hath not always in view, the
conftitution of the year, inafmuch as it tends to
produce fome particular epidemic difeafe, and
likewife to reduce all the cotemporary difeafes to
its own form and likenefs, proceeds in an uncertain and fallacious way*." It appears further
from the writings of this excellent phyfician, that
where the monarchy of a fingle difeafe was not
immediately acknowledged, by a fudden retreat
of all cotemporary difeafes, they were forced to
do homage to it, by wearing its livery. It would
be eafy to multiply proofs of this affertion, from
the numerous hiftories of epidemics which are to
be found in his works. I fhall mention only one
or two of them. A continual fever accompanied
by a dry fkin, had prevailed for fome time in the
city of London. During the continuance of this
fever, the regular fmall-pox made its appearance.
It is peculiar to the fmall-pox when of a diftinct
nature, to be attended by irregular fweats before
the eruption of the pock. The continual fever

* Vol. i. p. 340.

now

now put on a new fymptom. It was attended by fweats in its firft ftage; exactly like thofe which attended the eruptive fever of the fmall-pox*. This defpotifm of a powerful epidemic, extended itfelf to the moft trifling indifpofitions. It even blended itfelf, Dr Sydenham tells us, with the commotions excited in the fyftem by the fuppreffion of the lochia, as well as with the common puerperile fever †. Dr Morton, has left teftimonies behind him in different parts of his works, which eftablifh, in the moft ample manner, the truth of Dr Sydenham's obfervations. Dr Huxham defcribes the fmall-pox as blending fome of its fymptoms with thofe of a flow fever at Plymouth in the year 1729‡. Dr Cleghorn mentions a conftitution of the air at Minorca, fo highly inflammatory, " that not only tertian fevers, but even a common hurt or bruife required more plentiful evacuations than ordinary."§ Riverius informs us in his hiftory of a peftilential fever that prevailed in France, that " it united itfelf with phrenitis, angina, pleurify, peripneumony, hepatitis, dyfentery, and many other difeafes ||."

* Vol. i. p. 352.
† Vol. ii. p. 164. fee alfo p. 1. p. 109, 122, 204, 212, 233, 274, 355, 358-9, and 436.
‡ De Aere et morb. epidem. p. 33, 34.
§ Page 285. || De Febre Peftilenti, vol. ii. p. 95.

The

The bilious remitting fever which prevailed in Philadelphia in 1780, chafed away every other febrile difeafe; and the fcarlatina anginofa which prevailed in our city in 1783 and 1784, furnifhed a ftriking proof of the influence of epidemics over each other. In the account which I publifhed of this difeafe, in the year 1789, there are the following remarks. " The intermitting fever which made its appearance in Auguft, was not loft during the month of September. It continued to prevail, but with feveral peculiar fymptoms. In many perfons it was accompanied by an eruption on the fkin, and a fwelling of the hands and feet. In fome it was attended with fore throat, and pains behind the ears. Indeed fuch was the prevalence of the contagion which produced the fcarlatina anginofa, that many hundred people complained of fore throats, without any other fymptom of indifpofition. The flighteft exciting caufe, and particularly cold, feldom failed of producing the diforder *."

I fhall mention only one more authority in favour of the influence of a fingle epidemic upon difeafes. It is taken from Mr Clark's effay on the epidemic difeafe of lying-in women, of the

* Medical Inquiries and Obfervations, Lond. edit. Vol. I. p. 122.

years

years 1787 and 1788. " There does not appear to be any thing in a parturient ftate, which can prevent women from being affected by the general caufes of difeafe at that time ; and fhould they become ill, their complaints will probably partake of the nature of the reigning epidemic*." I have faid that the fever fometimes put on the fymptoms of dyfentery, pleurify, rheumatifm, colic, palfy, and even of the locked jaw. That thefe were not original difeafes, but fymptomatic affections only of the reigning epidemic, will appear from other hiftories of bilious fevers. Dr Balfour tells us in his account of the inteftinal remitting fever of Bengal †, that it often appeared with fymptoms of dyfentery, rheumatifm, and pleurify. Dr Cleghorn and Dr Lind mention many cafes of the bilious fever appearing in the form of a dyfentery. Dr Clark afcribes the dyfentery, the diarrhœa, the colic, and even the palfy, to the fame contagion which produced the bilious fever in the Eaft Indies ‡ ; and Dr Hunter, in his treatife upon the difeafes of Jamaica, mentions the locked jaw as one of its occafional fymptoms.

* Page 28.
† Page 132.
‡ Obfervations on the Difeafes in long Voyages to the Eaft Indies, Vol. I. p. 13, 14, 48, 151. Vol. II. p. 99, 318. and 320.

Even

Even the different grades of this fever, from the mildeſt intermittent to the moſt acute continual fever, have been diſtinctly traced by Lanciſſi to the fame marſh exhalation *.

However irrefragably theſe numerous facts and authorities eſtabliſh the aſſertion of the prevalence of but one powerful epidemic at a time, the propoſition will receive freſh ſupport, from attending to the effects of two impreſſions of unequal force made upon the ſyſtem at the fame time: only one of them is felt: hence the gout is ſaid to cure all other diſeaſes. By its ſuperior pain it deſtroys ſenſations of a leſs painful nature. The ſmall-pox and meaſles have ſometimes exiſted together in the body; but this has, I believe, ſeldom occurred, where one of them has not been the predominating diſeaſe †. In this reſpect, this combination of epidemics only conforms to the general law which has been mentioned.

I beg pardon for the length of this digreſſion. I did not introduce it to expoſe the miſtakes of thoſe phyſicians who found as many diſeaſes in our city,

* Lib. II. Cap. V.
† Hunter on the Venereal Diſeaſe, introduction, p. 3.

as

as the yellow fever had fymptoms, but to vindi-
cate myfelf from the charge of innovation, in having uniformly and unequivocally afferted, after
the firft week in September, that the yellow fever
was the only febrile difeafe which prevailed in the
city. I fhall hereafter mention fome facts upon
the fubject of the extent of the contagion, which
will add fuch weight to the affertion, as to render
the difbelief of it, as much a mark of a deficiency
of reafon, as it is of reading and obfervation.

Science has much to deplore from the multipli-
cation of difeafes. It is as repugnant to truth in
medicine, as polytheifm is to truth in religion.
The phyfician who confiders every different affection of the different fyftems in the body, or every
affection of different parts of the fame fyftem, as
diftinct difeafes, when they arife from one caufe,
refembles the Indian or African favage, who confiders water, dew, ice, froft, and fnow, as diftinct
effences : while the phyfician who confiders the
morbid affections of every part of the body, (however diverfified they may be in their form or degrees) as derived from one caufe, refembles the
philofopher, who confiders dew, ice, froft, and
fnow, as different modifications of water, and as
derived fimply from the abfence of heat.

Humanity

Humanity has likewife much to deplore from this paganifm in medicine. The fword will probably be fheathed for ever, as an inftrument of death, before phyficians will ceafe to add to the mortality of mankind, by prefcribing for the names of difeafes.

The facts I have delivered upon this fubject will admit of a very important application to the cure, not only of the yellow fever, but of all other acute and dangerous epidemics. I fhall hereafter affign a final caufe for the law of epidemics which has been mentioned, which will difcover an union of the goodnefs of the Supreme Being with one of the greateft calamities of human life.

All ages were affected by this fever, but perfons between fourteen, and forty years of age, were moft fubject to it. Many old people had it, but it was not fo fatal to them, as to robuft perfons in middle life. It affected children of all ages. I met with a violent cafe of the diforder, in a child of four months, and a moderate cafe of it, in a child of only ten weeks old. The latter had caught it from its mother. It had a deep yellow fkin. Both thefe children recovered.

The

The proportion of children who fuffered by
this fever may be conceived from a fingle fact.
Seventy five perfons were buried in the grave-
yard of the Swedifh Church in the months of
Auguft, September, and October, twenty four of
whom were children. They were buried chiefly
in September and October; months, in which children, generally enjoy good health in our city.

Men were more fubject to the difeafe than women. Pregnancy feemed to expofe women to it.

The refugees from the French Weft-Indies,
univerfally efcaped it. This was not the cafe with
the natives of France, who had been fettled in
the city.

It is nothing new, for epidemics to affect perfons of one nation, and to pafs by perfons of other
nations in the fame city or country. At Nimu-
guen in the year 1736, Deigner informs us that
the French people, (two old men excepted), and
the Jews, efcaped a dyfentery which was univerfal among perfons of all other nations. Ramazini
tells us that the Jews at Modena, efcaped a tertian
fever which affected nearly all the other inhabitants of the town. Shenkius fays that the Dutch
and

and Italians efcaped a plague which prevailed for two years in one of the towns of Switzerland, and Dr Bell, in an inaugural differtaion publifhed at Edinburgh in 1779, remarks that the jail fever which attacked the foldiers of the Duke of Buccleugh's regiment, fpared the French prifoners who were guarded by them. It is difficult to account for thefe facts. However numerous their caufes may be, a difference in diet which is as much a diftinguifhing mark of nations as drefs, or manners, will probably be found to be one of them.

From the accounts of the yellow fever which had been publifhed by many writers, I was led to believe that the negroes in our city would efcape it. In confequence of this belief, I publifhed the following extract from Dr Lining's hiftory of the yellow fever as it had four times appeared in Charlefton in South-Carolina.

For the American Daily Advertifer.

" I T has been remarked, that the *black people* have in no one inftance been infected with the malignant fever which now prevails in our city. The late Dr Lining, of South Carolina, long ago made the fame remark. " There is
fomething

fomething very fingular (fays the Doctor) in the conftitution of the Negroes which renders them not liable to this fever; for though many of them were as much expofed as the nurfes to the infection, yet I never knew of one inftance of this fever among them, though they are equally fubject with the white people to the bilious fever *."

The only defign of this remark is, to fuggeft to our citizens the fafety and propriety of employing black people to nurfe and attend perfons infected by this fever; alfo, to hint to the black people, that a noble opportunity is now put into their hands, of manifefting their gratitude to the inhabitants of that city, which firft planned their emancipation from flavery, and who have fince afforded them fo much protection and fupport, as to place them, in point of civil and religious privileges, upon a footing with themfelves."

A day or two after this publication, the following letter from the Mayor of the city, to Mr Claypoole the printer of the Mail, appeared in his paper.

* Effays and Obfervations, Phyfical and Literary. Vol. xi. page 409.

" SIR,

" SIR,

" IT is with peculiar fatisfaction that I communicate to the public, through your paper, that the AFRICAN SOCIETY, touched with the diftreffes which arife from the prefent dangerous diforder, have voluntarily undertaken to furnifh nurfes to attend the afflicted: and that by applying to ABSALOM JONES and WILLIAM GRAY, both members of that fociety, they may be fupplied.

September 6th, ⎱   MATTH. CLARKSON,
    1793. ⎰   Mayor."

It was not long after thefe worthy Africans undertook the execution of their humane offer of fervices to the fick, before I was convinced I had been miftaken. They took the difeafe, in com- mon with the white people, and many of them died with it. I think I obferved the greateft num- ber of them to ficken after the mornings and evenings became cool. A large number of them were my patients. The difeafe was lighter in them, than in white people. I met with no cafe of hemorrhage in a black patient. '

The tobacconifts, and perfons who ufed to- bacco did not efcape the difeafe. I obferved fnuff- takers to be more devoted to their boxes than ufual, during the prevalence of the fever.

H   I have

I have remarked formerly that fervant maids fuffered much by the difeafe. They were the only patients I loft in feveral large families. I afcribe their deaths to the following caufes :

1*ft*. To the great indirect debility induced upon their fyftems by fatigue in attending their mafters and miftreffes, or their children. Indirect debility, according to its degrees and duration feems to have had the fame effect upon the mortality of this fever, that it has upon the mortality of an inflammation of the lungs. When it is moderate and of fhort duration, it predifpofes only to a common pneumony, but when it is violent and protracted, in its degrees and duration, it predifpofes to a pulmonary confumption.

2*dly*. To their receiving large quantities of contagion into their bodies, and in a moft concentrated ftate by being obliged to perform the moft menial offices for the fick, and by wafhing, as well as removing infected linen, and the like.

3*dly*. To their being left more alone in confined or diftant rooms, and thereby fuffering from depreffion of fpirits, or the want of a punctual fupply of food and medicines.

There

There did not appear to be any advantage from fmelling vinegar, tar, camphor, or volatile falts, in preventing the diforder. Bark and wine were equally ineffeftual for that purpofe. I was called to many hundred people who were infected after ufing one or more of them. Nor did the white-wafhing of walls fecure families from the aftion of the contagion. I am difpofed to believe garlick was the only fubftance that was in any degree ufe-ful, in preventing the diforder. I met with feve-ral perfons who chewed it conftantly, and who were much expofed to the contagion, without being infefted. All other fubftances feemed to do harm by begetting a falfe confidence in the mind, to the exclufion of more rational preferva-tives. I have fufpected further, that fuch of them as were of a volatile nature. helped to fpread the difeafe by affording a vehicle for the contagion through the air.

There was great mortality in all thofe families who lived in wooden houfes. Whether this arofe from the fmall fize of thefe houfes, or from the want of cleanlinefs of the people who occupied them, or from the contagion becoming more ac-cumulated, by adhering to the wood, I am unable to determine. Perhaps it was the effeft of the co-operation of all three of thofe caufes.

I have

I have faid formerly that intemperance in drink-ing predifpofed to the difeafe; but there were fe-veral inftances of perfons having efcaped it who were conftantly under the influence of ftrong drink. The ftimulus of ardent fpirits, probably predominated over the ftimulus of the contagion, and thus excited an artificial fever which defended the fyftem from that which was epidemic.

I heard of fome fea-faring people who lived on board their veffels who efcaped the difeafe. The fmell of the tar was fuppofed to have preferved them; but from its being ineffeftual in other cafes, I was led to afcribe their efcape to the infefted air of the city being diluted by a mixture with the pure air that came from the water.

Many people who were infefted in the city, were attacked by the difeafe in the country, but they propagated it in very few inftances, even to perfons who flept in the fame room with them.

Dr Lind informs us that many perfons efcaped the yellow fever which prevailed in Penfacola in the year 1765, by retiring to the fhips which lay in the harbour, and that when the difeafe had been taken, the pure air of the water changed it
into

into an intermitting fever *. The fame changes have frequently been produced in malignant fevers, by fending patients infected with them from the foul air of a city, into the pure air of the country.

Perfons confined in the Houfe of Employment, in the Hofpital, and in the Jail, were preferved from the fever. The airy and remote fituation of thofe buildings, was probably the chief means of their prefervation. Perhaps they derived additional fecurity from their fimple diet, their exemption from hard labour, and from being conftantly fheltered from heat and cold.

Several families who fhut up their front and back doors and windows, and avoided going out of their houfes except to procure provifions, efcaped the diforder.

I have taken fome pains to afcertain whether any clafs of tradefmen efcaped the fever, or whether there was any fpecies of labour which protected from it. The refult of my inquiries is as follows : Three butchers only out of nearly one hundred who remained in the city, died with the diforder. Many of them attended the markets

* Difeafes of Warm Climates, p. 169.

H 3 every

every day. Two painters, who worked at their
bufinefs during the whole time of the prevalence
of the fever, and in expofed fituations, efcaped it.
Out of forty fcavengers who were employed in
collecting and carrying away the dirt of the ftreets,
only one caught the fever and died. Very few
grave-diggers, compared with the number who
were employed in that bufinefs, were infected ; and
it is well known, that fcarcely an inftance was
heard of perfons taking the difeafe, who were
conftantly employed in digging cellars. The fact
is not new that grave-diggers efcape the contagion of malignant fevers. It is taken notice of by
Dr Clark. There feems to be fomething in the
frefh earth which attracts or deftroys by mixture,
contagion of every kind. Clothes infected by the
fmall-pox are more certainly purified by being buried under ground, than in any other way. Even
poifons are rendered inert, by the action of the
earth upon them. Dogs have long ago eftablifhed
this fact, by fcratching a hole in the ground, and
burying their limbs or nofes in it, when bitten by
poifonous fnakes. The practice I have been told,
has been imitated with fuccefs by the fettlers upon
new lands in feveral parts of the United States.

was more infected than other parts of the city. The reverfe of this affertion was true in feveral cafes, owing probably to the line of communication of the contagion being broken by the abfence of houfes, and to its being diluted and weakened by its mixture with the air of the grave-yards; for this air was pure, compared with that which ftagnated in the ftreets.

It was faid further, that the difeafe was propagated by the inhabitants affembling on Sundays for public worfhip; and as a proof of this affertion, it was reported, that the deaths were more numerous on Sundays than on other days; occafioned by the contagion received on one Sunday, producing death on the fucceding firft day of the week. The regifter of the deaths fhows that this was not the cafe. I am difpofed to believe that fewer people fickened on Sundays, than on any other day of the week; owing to the general reft from labour, which I have before faid was one of the exciting caufes of the difeafe. From fome facts to be mentioned prefently, it will appear probable, that places of public worfhip, in confequence of their fize, as well as of their being fhut up during the greateft part of the week, were the freeft from contagion of any houfes in the city. It is agreeable to difcover in this, as well as in all other cafes

H 4   of

of public and private duty, that the means of
health, and moral happinefs are in no one inftance
oppofed to each other.

There were for feveral weeks two fources of
infection, viz. exhalation, and contagion. The exhalation infected at the diftance of three and four
hundred yards; while the contagion infected only
acrofs the ftreets. The more narrow the ftreet,
the more certainly the contagion infected. Few
efcaped it in alleys. After the 15th of September, the atmofphere of every ftreet in the city was
loaded with contagion; and there were few citizens in apparent good health, who did not exhibit one or more of the following marks of its
prefence in their bodies.

1. A yellownefs in the eyes, and a fallow colour upon the fkin.

2. A preternatural quicknefs in the pulfe. I
found but two exceptions to this remark, out of a
great number of perfons whofe pulfes I examined.
In one of them it difcovered feveral preternatural
intermiffions in the courfe of a minute. This
quicknefs of pulfe occurred in the negroes, as
well as in the white people. I met with it in a
woman who had had the yellow fever in 1762.

In

In two women, and in one man above 70, the pulfe beat upwards of 90 ftrokes in a minute. This preternatural ftate of the pulfe, during the prevalence of a peftilential fever in perfons in health, is taken notice of by Reverius *.

3. Frequent and copious difcharges by the fkin of yellow fweats. In perfons who were much expofed to the contagion, thefe fweats fometimes had an offenfive fmell, refembling that of the wafhings of a gun.

4. A fcanty difcharge of high coloured or turbid urine.

5. A deficiency of appetite, or a greater degree of it than was natural.

6. Coftivenefs.

7. Wakefulnefs.

8. Head-ach.

9. A preternatural dilatation of the pupils.— This was univerfal. I was much ftruck in obfer-

* "Pulfus fanorum pulfibus fimiles admodum, periculofi." *De Febre Peftilenti,* p. 114.

ving

ving the pupil in one of the eyes of a young man who called upon me for advice, to be of an oblong figure. Whether it was natural, or the effect of the contagion acting on his brain, I could not determine.

It will be thought lefs ftrange, that the contagion fhould produce thefe changes in the fyftems of perfons who refided conftantly in the city, when I add, that many country people who fpent but a few hours in the ftreets in the day, in attending the markets, caught the difeafe, and fickened and died after they returned home; and that others, whom bufinefs compelled to fpend a day or two in the city during the prevalence of the fever, but who efcaped an attack of it, declared that they were indifpofed during the whole time, with languor or head-ach.

I was led to obferve and record the above effects of the contagion upon perfons in apparent good health, by a fact I met with in Dr Mitchell's hiftory of the yellow fever in Virginia in the year 1741. In that fever, blood drawn from a vein was always diffolved. The fame ftate of the blood was obferved in many perfons who had been expofed to the contagion, who difcovered no other fymptom of the difeafe.

A wo-

A woman whom I had formerly cured of a mania, who lived in an infected neighbourhood, had
a frefh attack of that diforder, accompanied by an
unufual menftrual flux. I afcribed both thefe
complaints to the action of the contagion upon her
fyftem.

Citizens thus impregnated with the contagion,
communicated it in feveral inftances to their country friends. The difeafe produced in this way was
very light, amounting in all the cafes that came
under my notice, to little more than a ficknefs at
ftomach or vomiting.

The fmell of the contagion, as emitted from a
patient in a clean room, was like that of the fmall-
pox, but in moft cafes of a lefs difagreeable nature. Putrid fmells in fick rooms were the effects of a mixture of the contagion with fome fil-
thy matters. In fmall rooms, crouded in fome inftances with four or five fick people, there was an
effluvia that produced giddinefs, ficknefs at ftomach, a weaknefs of the limbs, faintnefs, and in
fome cafes a diarrhœa. I met with a fetid breath
in one patient, which was not the effect of that
medicine which fometimes produces it.

The contagion adhered to all kinds of cloathing, and feemed to be propagated by them. It
was

was in no inftance communicated by means of paper ; a circumftance which contributed both to
leffen and encreafe the diftrefs produced by the difeafe, by enabling the citizens to keep up an intercourfe by letters with their country friends.

The ftate of the atmofphere during the whole
month of September, and the firft two weeks in
October favoured the accumulation of the contagion in the city.

The regifter of the weather, fhews how little
the air was agitated by winds during the above
time. In vain were changes in the moon expected to alter the ftate of the air. The light
of the morning, mocked the hopes that were
raifed by a cloudy fky in the evening. The fun
ceafed to be viewed with pleafure. Hundreds
fickened every day beneath the influence of his
rays; and even where they did not excite the difeafe, they produced a languor in the body unknown to the oldeft inhabitant of the city, at the
fame feafon of the year.

A meteor was feen at two o'clock in the morning on or about the twelfth of September. It fell
between Third-ftreet and the Hofpital, nearly in
a line with Pine-ftreet. Mofchetoes (the ufual
attendants of a fickly autumn) were uncommonly
nume-

numerous. Here and there a dead cat added to the impurity of the air of the ftreets; for many of thofe animals perifhed with hunger in the city, in confequence of fo many houfes being deferted by the inhabitants who had fled into the country.

It appears further, from the regifter of the weather, that there was no rain between the 25th of Auguft and the 15th of Oftober, except a few drops, hardly enough to lay the duft of the ftreets on the 9th of September, and the 12th of Oftober. In confequence of this drought, the fprings and wells failed in many parts of the country. The duft in fome places extended two feet below the furface of the ground. The paftures were deficient, or burnt up. There was a fcarcity of autumnal fruits in the neighbourhood of the city. But while vegetation drooped or died from the want of moifture in fome places, it revived with preternatural vigor from unufual heat in others. Cherry-trees bloffomed, and apple, pear, and plum-trees bore young fruit in feveral gardens in Trenton, thirty miles from Philadelphia, in the month of Oftober.

However inoffenfive uniform heat, when agitated by gentle breezes may be, there is, I believe, no record of a dry, warm and ftagnating air, having

ving exifted for any length of time without producing difeafes. Hippocrates in defcribing a peftilential fever, fays the year in which it prevailed,
was without a breeze of wind*. The fame ftate
of the atmofphere for fix weeks, is mentioned in
many of the hiftories of the plague which prevailed in London in 1665. Even the fea air itfelf
becomes unwholefome by ftagnating; hence Dr
Clark informs us, that failors become fickly after
long calms in Eaft India voyages†. Sir John
Pringle delivers the following aphorifm from a
number of fimilar obfervations upon this fubject.
" When the heats come on foon, and continue
throughout autumn, not moderated by winds, or
rains, the feafon proves fickly, diftempers appear
early, and are dangerous‡."

Who can review this account of the univerfal
diffufion of the contagion of this difeafe, its univerfal effects upon perfons apparently in good
health, and its accumulation and concentration,
in confequence of the calmnefs of the air, and be
lieve, that it was poffible for a febrile difeafe to

* " Sine aura, ufque annus fuit."   *Epid.* 3.

† Vol. i. p. 5.

‡ Difeafes of the Army, p. 5. of the 7th London Edition.

I   exift

exift at that time in our city that was not derived from this contagion?

The Weft India writers upon the yellow fever have faid, that it is feldom taken twice, except by perfons who have fpent fome years in Europe or America in the interval between its firft and fecond attack. I directed my inquiries to this queftion, and I now proceed to mention the refult of them. I met with five perfons during the prevalence of the difeafe, who had had it formerly; two of them in the year 1741, and three in 1762, who efcaped it in 1793, although they were all more or lefs expofed to the contagion. One of them felt a conftant pain in her head while the difeafe was in her family. Four of them were aged, and of courfe lefs liable to be acted upon by the contagion, than perfons in early or middle life. Mr Thomas Shields furnifhed an unequivocal proof that the difeafe could be taken after an interval of many years. He had it in the year 1762, and narrowly efcaped from a violent attack of it laft year. Cafes of reinfection were very common during the prevalence of this fever. They occurred moft frequently, where the firft attack had been light. But they fucceeded attacks that were fevere in Dr Griffitts, Dr Meafe, my pupil Mr

Mr Coxe, and feveral others, whofe cafes came under my notice.

I have before remarked, that the contagion fometimes excited a fever as foon as it was taken into the body, but that it often lay there from one to fixteen days, before it produced the difeafe. How long it exifted in the body after a recovery from the fever, I could not tell, for perfons who recovered were in moft cafes expofed to the action of the contagion from external fources. The pre-ternatural dilatation of the pupils was a certain mark of the continuance of fome portion of the contagion in the fyftem. In one perfon who was attacked with the fever on the night of the 9th of October, the pupils did not contract to their natural dimenfions, until the 7th of November.

Having defcribed the effects of the contagion upon the body, I proceed now to mention the changes induced upon it by death.

Let us firft take a view of it as it appeared foon after death. Some new light may perhaps be thrown upon the proximate caufe of the difeafe, by this mode of examining the body.

My

My information upon this fubject was derived from the attendants upon the fick, and from the two African citizens who were employed in burying the dead, viz. Richard Allen and Abfalom Jones. The coincidence of the information I received from different perfons, fatisfied me that all that I fhall here relate, is both accurate and juft.

A deep yellow colour appeared in many cafes within a few minutes after death. In fome, the fkin became purple, and in others black. I heard of one cafe in which the body was yellow above, and black below its middle. In fome, the fkin was as pale, as it is in perfons who die of common fevers. A placid countenance was obferved in many, refembling that which occurs in an eafy and healthful fleep.

Some were ftiff within one hour after death. Others were not fo, for fix hours afterwards. This fudden ftiffnefs after death, Dr Valli informs us, occurred in perfons who died of the plague in Smyrna in the year 1784*.

Some grew cold foon after death, while others retained a confiderable degree of heat for fix hours, more efpecially on their backs.

* Experiments on Animal Electricity, p. 90.

A ftream

A ftream of tears appeared on the cheeks of a young woman, which feemed to have flowed after her death.

Some putrefied in a fhort time after their diffolution, but others had no fmell for twelve, eighteen and twenty hours afterwards. This abfence of fmell occurred in thofe cafes in which evacuations had been ufed without fuccefs in the treatment of the difeafe.

Many difcharged large quantities of black matter from the bowels, and others blood from the nofe, mouth and bowels after death. The frequency of thefe difcharges, gave rife to the practice of pitching the joints of the coffins which were ufed to bury the dead.

The morbid appearances of the internal parts of the body as they appear by diffection after death, from the yellow fever, are different in different countries, and in the fame countries in different years. I confider them all as effects only of a ftimulus acting upon the whole fyftem, and determined more or lefs by accidental circumftances, to particular vifcera. Perhaps the ftimulus of the contagion determines the fluids more violently in moft cafes to the liver, ftomach, and bowels, and thereby difpofes them more than other

parts

parts to inflammation and mortification, and to
fimilar effufions and eruptions with thofe which
take place on the fkin. There can be no doubt
of the contagion acting fpecifically upon the liver,
and thereby altering the qualities of the bile. I
tranfcribe with great pleafure the following account of the ftate of the bile in a female flave of
forty years of age from Dr Mitchell's hiftory of
the yellow fever, as it prevailed in Virginia in
the years 1737 and 1741, inafmuch as it was part
of that clue which led me to adopt one of the
remedies on which much of the fuccefs of my
practice depended.

" The gall bladder (fays the Doctor) appeared
outwardly of a deep yellow, but within was full
of a black ropy coagulated atrabilis, which fort
of fubftance obftructed the pori biliarii, and duc-
tus choledochus. This atrabilis was hardly fluid,
but upon opening the gall bladder, it retained its
form, and fhape, without being evacuated, being
of the confiftence of a thin extract, and within,
glutinous and ropy, like foap when boiling. This
black matter feemed fo much unlike bile, that I
doubted if there were any bile in the gall-bladder.
It more refembled bruifed or mortified blood, evacuated from the mortified parts of the liver, fur-
rounding it, although it would ftain a knife or
probe thruft into it of a yellow colour, which with

l 2   its

its ropy confiſtence, ſeemed more peculiar to a bilious humour."

The ſame appearance of the bile was diſcovered in ſeveral other ſubjects diſſected by Dr
Mitchell.

The liver in the abovementioned ſlave, was turgid and plump on its outſide, but on its concave
ſurface, two thirds of it were of a deep black colour, and round the gall-bladder, it ſeemed to be
mortified and corrupted.

The duodenum was lined on its inſide near the
gall bladder with a viſcid ropy bile, like that
which has been deſcribed.   Its villous coat was lined with a thick fur or ſlime, which when ſcraped
or pealed off, the other vaſcular and muſcular
coats of the gut, appeared red and inflamed.

The omentum was ſo much waſted, that nothing but its blood-veſſels could be perceived.

The ſtomach was inflamed both on its outſide
and inſide.   It contained a quantity of bile of the
ſame conſiſtence, but of a blacker colour than that
which was found in the gall bladder.   Its villous
coat like that of the duodenum, was covered with
fuzzy and ſlimy matter.   It moreover appeared to
be

be diftended or fwelled. This peculiarity in the inner coat of the ftomach was univerfal in all the bodies that were opened, of perfons who died of this difeafe.

The lungs inftead of being collapfed, were inflated as in infpiration. They were all over full of black or livid fpots. On thefe fpots were to be feen fmall veficlss or blifters, like thofe of an eryfipelas or gangrene, containing a yellow humour.

The blood-veffels in general feemed empty of blood, even the vena cava and its branches; but the vena portarum was full and diftended as ufual. The blood feemed *collected* in the *vifcera*; for upon cutting the lungs or found liver or fpleen, they bled freely.

The brain was not opened in this body, but it was not affected in three others whofe brains were examined.

Dr Mackittrick, in his inaugural differtation publifhed at Edinburgh in the year 1766 " De febre Indiæ occidentalis, Maligna Flava," or upon the yellow fever of the Weft Indies, fays, that in fome of the patients who died of it, he found the

liver

liver fphacelated, the gall bladder full of black
bile, and the veins turgid with black fluid blood,
In others he found the liver no ways enlarged,
and its "texture only vitiated." The ftomach,
the duodenum, and ilium, were remarkably inflamed in all cafes. The pericardium contained a
vifcid yellow ferum, and in a larger quantity than
common. The urinary bladder was a little inflamed. The lungs were found.

Dr Hume in defcribing the yellow fever of Jamaica, informs us, that in feveral dead bodies
which he opened, he found the liver enlarged and
turgid with bile, and of a pale yellow colour. In
fome he found the ftomach and duodenum inflamed. In one cafe he difcovered black fpots in
the ftomach, of the fize of a crown piece. To
this account he adds, " that he had feen fome fubjects opened, on whofe ftomachs *no marks of inflammation* could be difcovered ; and yet thefe had
exceffive vomiting."

Dr Lind has furnifhed us with an account of
the ftate of the body after death in his fhort hiftory of the yellow fever, which prevailed at Cadiz
in the year 1764. " The ftomach, (he fays) me-
fentery, and inteftines were covered with gangre-
nous fpots : there were ulcers on the orifice of the
ftomach,

ftomach, and the liver and lungs were of a putrid colour and texture *."

To thefe accounts of the morbid appearances of the body after death from the yellow fever, I fhall only add the account of feveral diffections which was given to the public in Mr Brown's Gazette, during the prevalence of our late epidemic, by Dr Phyfic and Dr Cathrall.

" BEING well affured of the great importance of diffections of morbid bodies in the inveftigation of the nature of difeafes, we have thought it of confequence that fome of thofe, dead of the prefent prevailing malignant fever, fhould be examined; and without enlarging on our obfervations, it appears at prefent fufficient to ftate the following facts.

" 1ft. That the brain in all its parts has been found in a natural condition.

" 2d. That the vifcera of the thorax are perfectly found. The blood, however, in the heart and veins is fluid, fimilar in its confiftence, to the blood of perfons who have been hanged, or deftroyed · by electricity.

* Difeafes of Warm Climates, p. 125.

I 4   " 3d.

" 3d. That the ftomach, and beginning of the duodenum are the parts that appear moft difeafed. In two perfons who died of the difeafe on the 5th day, the villous membrane of the ftomach, efpecially about its fmaller end, was found highly inflamed ; and this inflammation extended through the pylorus into the duodenum, fome way.—The inflammation here, was exactly fimilar to that induced in the ftomach by acrid poifons, as by arfenic, which we have once had an opportunity of feeing in a perfon deftroyed by it.

" The bile in the gall-bladder was quite of its natural colour, though very vifcid.

" In another perfon who died on the 8th day of the difeafe, feveral fpots of extravafation were difcovered between the membranes, particularly about the fmaller end of the ftomach, the inflammation of which had confiderably abated. Pus was feen in the beginning of the duodenum, and the villous membrane at this part was thickened.

" In two other perfons who died at a more advanced period of the difeafe, the ftomach appeared fpotted in many places with extravafations, and the inflammation difappeared. It contained, as did alfo the inteftines, a black liquor, which had been
vomited

vomited and purged before death.   This black liquor appears clearly to be an altered fecretion from the liver; for a fluid in all refpects of the fame qualities was found in the gall-bladder. This liquor was fo acrid, that it induced confiderable inflammation and fwelling on the operator's hands, which remained fome days.   The villous membrane of the inteftines in thefe laft two bodies was found inflamed in feveral places.

" The liver was of its natural appearance, excepting in one of the laft perfons, on the furface of which a very few diftended veins were feen : all the other abdominal vifcera were of a healthy appearance.

" The external furface of the ftomach as well as of the inteftines, was quite free from inflammation ; the veins being diftended with blood, which appeared through the tranfparent peritoneum, gave them a dark colour.

" The ftomach of thofe whe died early in the difeafe was always contracted ; but in thofe who died at a more advanced period of it, where extravafations appeared, it was diftended with air."

P. S. PHISICK,
J. CATHRALL."

I have

I have before remarked that thefe diffcctions were made early in the diforder, and that **Dr** Annan attended a diffection of a body at Bufh-hill fome time afterwards, in which an unufual turgefcence appeared in the veffels of the brain.

Thus far have I delivered the hiftory of the yellow fever as it affected the human body with ficknefs and death.   I fhall now mention a few of thofe circumftances of public and private diftrefs which attended it.   I have before remarked, that the firft reports of the exiftence of this fever were treated with neglect or contempt.   A ftrange apathy pervaded all claffes of people.   While I bore my fhare of reproach for " terrifying our citizens with imaginary danger," I anfwered it by lamenting " that they were not terrified enough."   The publication from the college of phyficians foon diffipated this indifference and incredulity.   Fear or terror now fat upon every countenance.   The difeafe appeared in many parts of the town, remote from the fpot where it originated ; although in every inftance it was eafily traced to it.   This fet the city in motion.   The ftreets and roads leading from the city were crouded with families flying in every direction for fafety to the country. Bufinefs began to languifh.   Water-ftreet between Market and Race-ftreets became a defart.
The

The poor were the firſt victims of the fever. From the ſudden interruption of buſineſs, they ſuffered for a while from poverty, as well as diſeaſe. A large and airy houſe at Buſh-hill about a mile from the city, was opened for their reception. This houſe, after it became the charge of a committee appointed by the citizens on the 14th of September, was regulated and governed with the order and cleanlineſs of an old and eſtabliſhed hoſpital. An American and French phyſician had the excluſive medical care of it after the 22d of September.

The contagion after the ſecond week in September, ſpared no rank of citizens. Whole families were confined by it. There was a deficiency of nurſes for the ſick, and many of thoſe who were employed were unqualified for their buſineſs. There was likewiſe a great deficiency of phyſicians from the deſertion of ſome, and the ſickneſs and death of others. At one time, there were only three phyſicians who were able to do buſineſs out of their houſes, and at this time, there were probably not leſs than 6,000 perſons ill with the fever.

During the firſt three or four weeks of the prevalence of the diſorder, I ſeldom went into a

houſe

houfe the firft time, without meeting the parents
or children of the fick in tears. Many wept aloud
in my entry, or parlour, who came to afk for advice for their relations.   Grief, after awhile de-
fcended below weeping, and I was much ftruck
in obferving that many perfons fubmitted to the
lofs of relations and friends, without fhedding a
tear, or manifefting any other of the common
figns of grief.

A chearful countenance was fcarcely to be feen
in the city for fix weeks.   I recollect once in entering the houfe of a poor man, to have met a
child of two years old that fmiled in my face.   I
was ftrangely affected with this fight (fo difcordant
to my feelings and the ftate of the city) before I
recollected the age and ignorance of the child.   I
was confined the next day by an attack of the
fever, and was forry to hear upon my recovery,
that the father and mother of this little creature
died, a few days after my laft vifit to them.   ·

The ftreets every where difcovered marks of the
diftrefs that pervaded the city.   More than one
half the houfes were fhut up, although not more
than one third of the inhabitants had fled into the
country.   In walking for many hundred yards, few
perfons were met, except fuch as were in queft of
                                    a phyfician,

a phyfician, a nurfe, a bleeder, or the men who buried the dead. The hearfe alone kept up the remembrance of the noife of carriages or carts in the ftreets. Funeral proceffions were laid afide. A black man, leading, or driving a horfe, with a corpfe on a pair of chair wheels, with now and then half a dozen relations or friends following at a diftance from it, met the eye in moft of the ftreets of the city at every hour of the day, while the noife of the fame wheels paffing flowly over the pavements, kept alive anguifh and fear in the fick and well, every hour of the night *.

* In the life of Thomas Story a celebrated preacher among the Friends, there is an account of the diftrefs of the city in its infant ftate from the prevalence of the yellow fever in the autumn of 1699, nearly like that which has been defcribed I fhall infert the account in his own words. " Great was the fear that fell on all flefh. I faw no lofty or airy countenance, nor heard any vain jefting to move men to laughter. Every face gathered pale-nefs, and many hearts were humbled, and countenances fallen, and funk, as fuch that waited every moment to be fummoned to the bar, and numbered to the grave." The fame author adds that fix, feven, and fometimes eight died of this fever in a day for feveral weeks. His fellow tra-veller and companion in the miniftry Roger Gill, difco-vered upon this occafion an extraordinary degree of Chrif-tian philanthropy. He publicly offered himfelf in one of the meetings of the Society as a facrifice for the people,

and

But a more ferious fource of the diftrefs of the city arofe from the diffentions of the phyficians, about the nature and treatment of the fever. It was confidered by fome, as a modification of the influenza, and by others as the Jail fever. Its various grades, and fymptoms were confidered as fo many different difeafes, all originating from different caufes. There was the fame contrariety in the practice of the phyficians that there was in their principles. The newfpapers conveyed accounts of both to the public, every day. The minds of the citizens were diftracted by them, and hundreds fuffered and died from the delays which were produced by an erroneous opinion of a plurality of difeafes in the city, or by indecifion in the choice, or a want of confidence in the remedies of their phyfician.

The fcience of medicine is related to every thing, and the philofopher as well as the Chriftian will be gratified by knowing the effects of a great and mortal epidemic upon the morals of a people. It was fome alleviation of the diftrefs

and prayed that " God would pleafe to accept of his life for them, that a ftop might be put to the contagion." He died of the fever a few days afterwards.

produced

produced by it, to obferve its influence upon the obligations of morality and religion. It was re-marked during this time, by many people that the name of the Supreme Being was feldom profaned either in the ftreets, or in the intercourfe of the citizens with each other. Two robberies only, and thofe of a trifling nature, occured in nearly two months, although many hundred houfes were ex-pofed to plunder, every hour of the day and night. Many of the religious focieties met two or three times a week, and fome of them every evening, to implore the interpofition of heaven to fave the city from defolation. Humanity and charity kept pace with devotion. The public have already feen accounts of their benevolent exercifes in other publications. It was my lot to witnefs the uncom-mon activity of thofe virtues upon a fmaller fcale. I faw little to blame, but much to admire and praife in perfons of different profeffions, both fexes, and of all colours. It would be foreign to the defign of this work, to draw from the obfcurity which they fought, the many acts of humanity and charity, of fortitude, patience, and perfeve-rance which came under my notice. They will be made public, and applauded elfewhere.

But the virtues which were excited by our ca-lamity, were not confined to the city of Philadel-phia.

phia. The United States wept for the diftreffes of their capital. In feveral of the ftates, and in many cities, and villages, days of humiliation and prayer were fet apart to fupplicate the Father of mercies in behalf of our afflicted city. Nor was this all. From nearly every ftate in the Union, the moft liberal contributions of money, provifions, and fuel, were poured in for the relief and fupport of fuch as had been reduced to want, by the fuf-penfion of bufinefs, as well as by ficknefs, and the death of friends.

The number of deaths between the firft of Au-guft and the ninth of November, amounted to four thoufand and forty four. I fhall here infert a regifter of the number which occurred on each day, beginning on the firft of Auguft and ending on the ninth of November. By comparing it with the regifter of the weather, it will fhew the influence of the latter on the difeafe. Several of the deaths in Auguft were from other acute dif-orders, and a few in the fucceeding months were from fuch as were of a chronic nature.

K   Auguft

August		died.			died.
August	1	9	Brought forward		325
	2	8	September	1	17
	3	9		2	18
	4	10		3	11
	5	10		4	23
	6	3		5	20
	7	12		6	24
	8	5		7	18
	9	11		8	42
	10	6		9	32
	11	7		10	29
	12	5		11	23
	13	11		12	33
	14	4		13	37
	15	9		14	48
	16	7		15	56
	17	6		16	67
	18	5		17	81
	19	9		18	68
	20	7		19	61
	21	8		20	67
	22	13		21	57
	23	10		22	76
	24	17		23	68
	25	12		24	96
	26	17		25	87
	27	12		26	52
	28	22		27	60
	29	24		28	51
	30	20		29	57
	31	17		30	63
		325			1768

Septem-

		died.			died.
Brought forward		1768	Brought forward		3318
October	1	74	October	21	59
	2	66		22	82
	3	78		23	54
	4	58		24	38
	5	71		25	35
	6	76		26	23
	7	82		27	13
	8	90		28	24
	9	102		29	17
	10	93		30	16
	11	119		31	21
	12	111	November	1	13
	13	104		2	21
	14	81		3	15
	15	80		4	15
	16	70		5	14
	17	80		6	11
	18	59		7	15
	19	65		8	8
	20	55		9	6
		3318	Total,		3881*

From this table it appears that the principal mortality was in the second week of October. A general expectation had obtained, that cold weather was as fatal to the contagion of this fever as

* In the above accounts there is a deficiency of returns from several grave-yards of 163.

heavy

heavy rains. The ufual time for its arrival had come, but the weather was ftill not only moderate, but warm. In this awful fituation, the ftouteft hearts began to fail. Hope fickened, and defpair fucceeded diftrefs in almoft every countenance. On the *fifteenth* of October it pleafed God to alter the ftate of the air. The clouds at laft dropped health in fhowers of rain, which continued during the whole day, and which were fucceeded for feveral nights afterwards by cold and froft. The effects of this change in the weather, appeared firft in the fudden diminution of the fick, for the deaths continued for a week afterwards to be numerous, but they were of perfons who had been confined before, or on the day in which the change had taken place in the weather.

The appearance of this rain was like a dove with an olive branch in its mouth, to the whole city. Public notice was given of its beneficial effects in a letter fubfcribed by the mayor, of Philadelphia, who acted as prefident of the committee, to the mayor of New York. I fhall infert the whole of this letter. It contains, befides the above information, a record of the liberality of that city, to the diftreffed inhabitants of Philadelphia.

K 2   " SIR,

" Sir,

" I am favoured with your letter of the 12th inftant, which I have communicated to the Committee for the relief of the poor and afflicted of this city.

" It is with peculiar fatisfaction that I execute their requeft, by making in their name, on behalf of our fuffering fellow-citizens, the moft grateful acknowledgements, for the feafonable benevolence of the Common-Council of the city of New-York. Their fympathy is balm to our wounds.

" We acknowledge the divine interpofition, whereby the hearts of fo many around us have been touched with our diftrefs, and have united in our relief.

" May the almighty difpofer of all events be gracioufly pleafed to protect your citizens from the dreadful calamity with which we are now vifited; whilft we humbly kifs the rod, and improve by the difpenfation.

" The part, fir, which you perfonally take in our afflictions, and which you have fo pathetically ex-preffed in your letter, excites in the breafts of the

4   Committee

Committee the warmeſt ſenſations of fraternal affection.

" The refreſhing rain which fell the day before
yeſterday, though light, and the cool weather
which hath ſucceeded, appear to have given a
check to the prevalence of the diſorder; of this
we have ſatisfactory proofs; as well in the de-
creaſe of the funerals, as in the applications for
removal to the hoſpital.

" I have at your requeſt, this day drawn upon
you, at ſight, in favour of the Preſident and Di-
rectors of the Bank of North America, for the
ſum of five thouſand dollars, the benevolent dona-
tions of the Common-Council of the city of New-
York.

" With ſentiments of the greateſt eſteem and
regard,

I am, Sir,

Philadelphia, } Your moſt obedient humble ſervant,
Oct. 17, 1793. }

MATTH. CLARKSON."

Richard Varick, Mayor of }
the city of New-York. }

It

It is no new thing for bilious fevers of every defcription, to be checked, or fubdued by *wet* and *cold* weather.

The yellow fever which raged in Philadelphia in 1699, and which is taken notice of by Thomas Story in his Journal, ceafed about the latter end of October, or the beginning of November. Of this there are fatisfactory proofs in the regifter of the interments in the Friends burying-ground, and in a letter dated November 9th, Old Style, 1699, from Ifaac Norris to one of his correfpondents, which his grand-fon Mr Jofeph P. Norris, politely put into my hands, with feveral others, which mention the difeafe, and all written in that memorable year in Philadelphia. The letter fays, "It has pleafed God to put a ftop to our fore vifitation, and town and country are now generally healthy." The fame difeafe was checked by wet and cold weather in the year 1741. Of this there is a proof in a letter from Dr Franklin to one of his brothers, who ftopped at Burlington, on his way from Bofton to Philadelphia on account of the fever, until he was affured by the Doctor, that a thunder guft which had cooled the air, had rendered it fafe for him to come into the city*. Mr

* From a fhort note in the regifter of the interments in the Friend's burying-ground, it appears, that the fever this

Lynford Lardner in a letter to one of his Englifh friends, dated September 24, 1747, Old Style, after mentioning the prevalence of the fever in the city, fays " the weather is now much cooler, and thofe under the diforder revive. The fymptoms are lefs violent, and the fever gradually abates."

I have in vain attempted to procure an account of the time of the commencement of cold weather, in the autumn of 1762. In the fhort hiftory of the fever of that year, which I have inferted from my note book, I have faid that it continued to prevail in the months of November and December. The regifter of the interments in the Friends burying-ground in thofe months, confirms that account. They were nearly as numerous in November and December, as in September and October. Viz. in September 22, in October 27, in November 19, and in December 26.

year made its firft appearance in the month of June. The following is a copy of that note. " 12th of the 6th month (O. S.) 1741, a malignant yellow fever now fpreads much." Befides that note, there is the following: " 25th of the 7th month (O. S.) 1741, many who died of the above diftemper, were perfons lively, and ftrong, and in the prime of their time.

K 4   The

The bilious remitting fever of 1780, yielded to cool weather, accompanied by rain, and an easterly wind *.

Sir John Pringle will furnish ample satisfaction, to such of my readers as wish for more proofs of the efficacy of heavy rains, and cold weather, in checking the progress and violence of autumnal remitting fevers†.

From the 15th of October, the disease not only declined, but assumed more obvious inflammatory symptoms. It was, as in the beginning, more necessarily fatal where left to itself, but it yielded more certainly to art, than it did a few weeks before. The duration of it was now more tedious, than in the warmer weather.

There were a few cases of yellow fever in November, and December, after the citizens who had retired to the country, returned to the city.

I heard of only three persons who returned to the city being infected with the disorder; so com-

* Medical Inquiries and Observations, London Edition, p. 106.

† P. 5, 56, 180, and 323.

pletely

pletely was the contagion deſtroyed in the courſe
of a few weeks.

In conſequence of a proclamation by the Governor, and a recommendation by the Clergy of
Philadelphia, the 12th of December was obſerved
as a day of thankſgiving throughout the ſtate, for
the extinction of the diſorder in the city.

It was eaſy to diſtinguiſh in walking the ſtreets,
the perſons who had returned from the country
to the city, from thoſe who had remained in it
during the prevalence of the fever. The former
appeared ruddy, and healthy, while the latter appeared of a pale or ſallow colour.

It afforded a ſubject of equal ſurpriſe and joy to
behold the ſuddenneſs with which the city recovered its former habits of buſineſs. In the courſe
of ſix weeks after the diſeaſe had ceaſed, nothing
but freſh graves, and the black dreſſes of many
of the citizens, afforded a public trace of the diſtreſs which had ſo lately prevailed in the city.

The month of November, and all the winter
months which followed the autumnal epidemic,
were in general healthy. A catarrh affected a
number

number of people in November. I fufpected it to
be the influenza which had revived from a dor-
mant ftate ; and which had not fpent itfelf when
it yielded to the predominance of the yellow fever. This opinion derives fome fupport from a
curious fact related by the late Mr Hunter of the
revival of the fmall-pox in a patient, in whom it
had been fufpended for fome time by the meafles*. The few fevers which prevailed in the
winter were highly inflammatory. The fmall-
pox in the natural way was in feveral inftances
confluent; and in one or two fatal. I was
prepared to expect this inflammatory diathefis in the fevers of the winter ; for I had been
taught by Dr Sydenham, that the difeafes which
follow a great and mortal epidemic, partake more
or lefs of its general character. But the difeafes
of the winter had a peculiarity ftill more extraordinary ; and that was, many of them had feveral
of the fymptoms of the yellow fever, particularly
a puking of bile, dark-coloured ftools, and a yellow eye. Mr Samuel D. Alexander, a ftudent of
medicine from South Carolina, who was feized
with a pneumony about Chriftmas, had with a
yellow eye, a dilated pupil, and a hard pulfe

* Introduction to a Treatife on the Venereal Difeafe,
p. 3, of the American edition.

which

which beat only 50 ftrokes in a minute. His blood was fuch as I had frequently obferved in the yellow fever, Dr Griffitts informed me, that he attended a patient on the 9th of January in a pneumony, who had an univerfal yellownefs on his fkin. I met with a cafe of pneumony on the 20th of the fame month, in which I obferved the fame degrees of rednefs in the eyes that were common in the yellow fever. My pupil Mr Coxe, loft blood in an inflammatory fever, on the 18th of February, which was diffolved. Mr James In-nis, the brewer, had a deep yellow colour in his eyes, on the fourth day of a pneumony, on the 27th of the fame month ; and Mr Magnus Miller had the fame fymptom of a fimilar diforder, on the 16th of March. None of thefe bilious and ano-malous fymptoms of the inflammatory fevers of the winter and fpring furprifed me. I had been ear-ly taught by Dr Sydenham, that the epidemics of autumn often infinuate fome of their fymptoms in-to the winter difeafes which follow them. Dr Cleghorn informs us, that " the pleurifies which fucceeded the autumnal tertians in Minorca, were accompanied by a vomiting and purging of green or yellow bilious matters *.

* Page 273.

It

It belongs to powerful epidemics to be followed by fome difeafes after they difappear, as well as to run into others at their firft appearance. In the former cafe it is occafioned by a peculiar ftate of the body, created by the epidemic conftitution of the air, not having been changed by the weather which fucceeded it.

The weather in March refembled that of May ; while the weather in April refembled that of March in common years. A rafh prevailed in many families in April, accompanied in a few cafes by a fore throat. It was attended with an itching, a rednefs of the eyes, and a flight fever in a few inftances. The fmall-pox by inoculation in this month was more mortal than in former years, However unimportant thefe facts may appear at this time, future obfervations may perhaps con- nect them with a fimilar conftitution of the air which produced our late autumnal epidemic.

The appearance of bilious fymptoms in the dif- eafes of the winter, excited apprehenfions in feve- ral inftances of the revival of the yellow fever. The alarms though falfe, ferved to produce vigi- lance and induftry in the corporation, in airing and purifying fuch houfes and articles of furniture

as

as belonged to the poor ; and which had been neglected in the autumn, after the ceasing of the dif-
cafe.

The modes of purifying houfes, beds, and
cloihes were various. Fumigations of nitre and
aromatic fubftances were ufed by fome people.
Burying infected articles of furniture under
ground, and baking them in ovens, were ufed by
others. Some deftroyed all their beds and clothing that had been infected, or threw them into
the Delaware. Many white-wafhed their walls,
and painted the wood-work of their houfe. Is
did not conceive the contagion required all, or
any of thofe means to deftroy it. I believed *cold*
and *water* to be fufficient for that purpofe. I
therefore advifed keeping the windows of infected
rooms open night and day, for a few days ; to
have the floors and walls of houfes well wafhed ;
and to expofe beds and fuch articles of houfehold
furniture as might be injured by wafhing, upon
the bare earth for a week or two, taking care to
turn them every day. I ufed no other methods
of deftroying the accumulated contagion in my
houfe and furniture, and experience fhowed that
they were fufficient. Thofe branches of my family who had been abfent during the prevalence
of the fever (amounting to eleven in number) returned

turned to the city on the 22d of November, and occupied the houfe and beds which had been highly infected, without fuffering a moment's indifpofition from it. The weather of the winter favoured the complete deftruction of the contagion. It was alternately moderate and cold ; by which means the contagion, if accidentally revived by the former, was more effectually deftroyed by the latter ftate of the air.

It is poffible a portion of the contagion may exift in clothes or bedding, under fuch circumftances of warmth, as to be excited into action in the courfe of the approaching fummer and autumn ; but it cannot fpread without a correfponding conftitution of the atmofphere. A trunk full of infected clothes, the property of Mr James Bingham, who died of the yellow fever in one of the Weft India iflands about 40 years ago, was opened fome months after they were received by his friends, by a young man who lived in his brother's family. This young man took the difeafe, and died ; but without infecting any of the family : nor did the difeafe fpread afterwards in the city.

The father of Mr Jofeph Pafchall was infected with the yellow fever of 1741, by the fmell of a
bed

bed in paffing through Norris's Alley, in the latter end of December, after the difeafe had left the
city. He died on the 25th of the month, but
without reviving the fever in the city, or even infecting his family.

In a letter from Dr Senter of Newport, dated
January 7th, 1794, I find the following fact, which
I fhall communicate in his own words. It is introduced to fupport the principle, that the yellow
fever cannnot fpread in any country without
the concurrence of a predifpofing conftitution of
air. " This place (fays the Doctor) has traded
formerly very much to the Weft India iflands, and
more or lefs of our people have died there every
feafon, when the difeafe prevails in thofe parts.
Clothes of thefe unfortunate people have been repeatedly brought home to their friends, without
any accident happening to them."

It is not peculiar to the contagion of the yellow
fever to require the concurrence of a morbid conftitution of the air to excite it into action. The contagion of the plague perifhed twice in the city of
Larnica, without fpreading, from the abfence of
that neceffary ftate of the air, in the year 1759*.

* P. Ruffel, p. 4.

Several

Several perfons it is faid died of the yellow fever in the fummer and autumn of 1763, the year
after it had been epidemic in our city. I witneffed
the fymptoms which immediately preceded the
death of one of them. Whether the difeafe in
this cafe was produced by a revival of the contagion, or by miafmata generated in the city, I am
unable to determine.

Dr Mitchell informs us, that the difeafe appeared in Virginia in the fpring of 1742, after the autumn of 1741. In this cafe the contagion was
probably kept alive during the winter by the want
of cleanlinefs in the negro-quarters ; and perhaps
by moderate weather.

Thefe are the only facts which fupport the fears of
the return of the difeafe to our city, in the courfe
of the prefent year. To aid our hopes, that this
will not be the cafe, I have great pleafure in adding, that it has never occurred in fucceffive years
either in this city or in Charlefton ; in one of
which there are records of its having been five,
and in the other four times epidemic.

I feel with my reader the fatigue of this long
detail of facts, and equal impatience with him, to
proceed to the hiftory of the treatment of the fever ;

ver ; but I muft beg leave to detain him a little longer from that part of the work, while I refume the fubject of the origin of the fever. It is an interefting queftion, as it involves in it the means of preventing a return of the diforder.

Soon after the fever left the city, the governor of the ftate addreffed a letter to the College of Phyficians, requefting to know their opinion of its origin ; if imported; from what place; at what time; and in what manner. The defign of this inquiry was to procure fuch information as was proper to lay before the legiflature, in order to improve the laws for preventing the importation or generation of infectious difeafes, or to enact new ones, if neceffary for that purpofe. To the governor's letter, the College of Phyficians fent the following anfwer:

" SIR,

" I T has not been from a want of refpect to yourfelf, nor from inattention to the fubject, that your letter of the 30th ult. was not fooner anfwered ; but the importance of the queftions propofed, has made it neceffary for us to devote a confiderable portion of time and attention to the fubject, in order to arrive at a fafe and juft conclufion.

L   " No

" No inftance has ever occurred of the difeafe
called the *yellow fever*, having been generated in
this city, or in any other parts of the United
States, as far as we know ; but there have been
frequent inftances of its having been imported,
not only into this, but into other parts of North
America, and prevailing there for a certain period
of time ; and from the rife, progrefs, and nature
of the malignant fever, which began to prevail
here about the beginning of laft Auguft, and extended itfelf gradually over a great part of the
city, we are of opinion that this difeafe was imported into Philadelphia, by fome of the veffels
which arrived in the port after the middle of July.
This opinion we are further confirmed in by various accounts we have received from unqueftiona-
ble authorities.

Signed by order of the College of Phyficians,

November 26th, ⎫ JOHN REDMAN, PRESIDENT.
1793.   ⎭

To the Governor of Pennfylvania.

Three members of the College diffented from
the report contained in this letter. They were
Dr Redman the Prefident of the College, Dr
Foulke, and Dr Leib.

I am

I am forry to meet my brethren upon every queftion of our late epidemic in a field of controverfy.
In the prefent they will have a great advantage over
me, for the prejudices of the citizens of Philadelphia are in their favour. Loathfome and dangerous
difeafes have been confidered by all nations as of
foreign extraction. The venereal difeafe and the
leprofy have no native country, if we believe all the
authors who have written upon their origin. Prof-
per Alpinus, derives the almoft yearly plagues of
Cairo from Syria, and Dr Warren flattered the
people of Barbadoes, by an attempt to perfuade
them, that the yellow fever of the Weft Indies,
was originally imported from Siam. This principle of referring the origin of the evils of life,
from ourfelves to others, is univerfal. It difcovered itfelf in paradife, and it is every where, an
effential feature in the character of man.

I have afferted in the introduction to the hiftory
of this fever, that I believed it to have been generated in our city; I fhall now deliver my reafons
for that belief.

1. The yellow fever in the Weft Indies and in
all other countries where it is endemic, is the off-
fpring of vegetable putrefaction. Heat, exercife,
and intemperance in drinking, (fays Dr Lind) *dif-*

pofe

pofe to this fever in hot climates, but they do not produce it, without the concurrence of a remote caufe. This remote caufe exifts at all times, in fome fpots of the Iflands, but in other parts of even the fame iflands, where there are no marfh exhalations, the difeafe is unknown. I fhall not wafte a moment in enquiring into the truth of Dr Warren's account of the origin of this fever. It is fully refuted by Dr Hillary, and it is treated as chimerical by Dr Lind. They have very limited ideas of the hiftory of this fever who fuppofe it to be peculiar to the Eaft or Weft Indies. It was generated in Cadiz after a hot and dry fummer in 1764, and in Penfacola in 1765*. The tertian fever of Minorca, when it attacked Englifhmen put on the ufual fymptoms of the yellow fever†. In fhort, this difeafe, appears according to Dr Lind, in all the fouthern parts of Europe, after hot, and dry weather‡.

2. The fame caufes (under like circumftances) muft always produce the fame effects. There is nothing in the air of the Weft Indies above other hot countries, which difpofes it to produce a yellow fever. Similar degrees of heat, acting upon

* Lind on the Difeafes of Hot Climates, p. 56 and 124.
† Cleghorn, page 176.
  Difeafes of Hot Climates, page 123.

dead

dead and moift vegetable matters, are capable of producing it, together with all its various modifications, in every part of the world. In fupport of this opinion, I fhall tranfcribe part of a letter from Dr Miller, of the Delaware ftate.

" Dover, *Nov.* 5, 1793.

DEAR SIR,

        SINCE the middle of laft July, we have had a Bilious Colic epidemic in this neighbourhood which exhibits phænomena very fingular in this climate ; and fo far as I am informed, unprecedented in the medical records, or popular traditions of this country. To avoid unneceffary details, it will fuffice at prefent to obferve, that the difeafe on this occafion, has affumed not only all the effential characters, but likewife all the violence, obftinacy and malignity defcribed by the Eaft and Weft Indian practitioners. If any difference can be obferved, it feems here to manifeft higher degrees of ftubbornnefs and malignity, than we ufually meet in the hiftories of tropical writers. In the courfe of the difeafe, not only extreme conftipation, frequent vomiting, and the moft excruciating pains of the bowels and limbs, harrafs the unhappy patient; but to thefe fucceed paralyfis, convulfions, &c. and almoft always un-

L 3   common

common mufcular debility,—oppreffion of the præcordia, &c. are the confequence of a fevere attack. Bile difcharged in enormous quantities, conftantly affumes the moft corrupted and acrimonious appearances, commonly æruginous in a very high degree, and fometimes quite atrabilious.

" The inference I mean to draw from the phæ-nomena of this difeafe, as it appears in this neigh-bourhood, and which I prefume will alfo apply to your epidemic, is THIS, that from the uncommon protraction and intenfenefs of our fummer and autumnal heats, but principally from the unufual drought; we have had fince the middle of July, a near approach to a TROPICAL feafon, and that of confequence we ought not to be furprized if tropical difeafes, even of the moft malignant na-ture, are ENGENDERED amongft us."

To the above information it may be added, that the dyfentery which prevailed during the late au-tumn in feveral of the villages of Pennfylvania, was attended with a malignity and mortality, un-known before in any part of the ftate. I need not paufe to remark that this dyfentery arofe from putrid exhalation, and that it is like the bilious colic, only a modification of one original genus of bilious fever.

But

But further, a malignant fever refembling that which was epidemic in our city, prevailed during the autumn in many parts of the United States, viz. at Lynn in Maffachufetts, at Weatherfield and Coventry in Connecticut, at New Galloway in the ftate of New York, on Walkill and on Penfocken creeks in New Jerfey, at Harrifburgh, and Hummelftown in Pennfylvania, in Caroline county in Maryland, on the South branch of the Potowmac in Hardie county, alfo in Lynchburgh and in Alexandria in Virginia, and in feveral counties in North Carolina.   In none of thefe places was there a fufpicion of the difeafe being imported from abroad, or conveyed by an intercourfe with the city of Philadelphia.

It is no objection to the inference which follows from thefe facts, that the common remitting fever was not known during the above period in the neighbourhood of this city, and in many other parts of the ftate, where it had ufually appeared in the autumnal months.   There is a certain combination of moifture with heat, which is effential to the production of the remote caufe of a bilious fever. Where the heat is fo intenfe, or of fuch long duration as wholly to diffipate moifture, or when the rains are fo great as totally to overflow the

L 4   marfhy

marſhy ground, or to waſh away putrid maſſes of matter, no fever can be produced.

Dr Dazilles, in his treatiſe upon the diſeaſes of the Negroes in the Weſt Indies, informs us, that the RAINY feaſon is the moſt healthy at Cayenne, owing to the neighbouring moraſſes being DEEPLY overflowed—whereas at St Domingo, a DRY fea-ſon is moſt productive of diſeaſes; owing to its favouring thoſe degrees of moiſture which pro-duce morbid exhalations. Theſe facts will explain the reaſon why, in certain ſeaſons, places which are naturally healthy in our country, become ſickly, while thoſe places which are naturally ſickly, eſcape the prevailing epidemic. Previouſly to the diſſipation of the moiſture from the putrid maſſes of vegetable matters in our ſtreets, and in the neighbourhood of the city, there were (as ſeveral practitioners can teſtify) many caſes of mild remit-tents, but they all diſappeared about the firſt week in September.

It is worthy of notice, that the yellow fever pre-vailed in Virginia in the year 1741, and in Charleſ-ton in South Carolina in the year 1699, in both which years, it prevailed in Philadelphia. Its pre-valence in Charleſton is taken notice of in a

letter

letter dated November 18th, O. S. 1699, from Ifaac Norris to one of his correfpondents. The letter fays, that " 150 perfons had died in Charlef-ton in a few days," that " the furvivors fled into the country," and that " the town was thinned to a very few people." Is it not probable, from the prevalence of this fever twice in two places in the fame years, that it was produced (as laft year) by a general conftitution of air, co-operating with miafmata, which favoured its generation in differ-ent parts of the continent? But again, fuch was the flate of the air in the fummer of 1793, that it predifpofed other animals to difeafes, befides the human fpecies. In fome parts of New Jerfey, a diforder prevailed with great mortality among the horfes, and in Virginia among the cows, during the laft autumn. The urine in both was yellow.— Large abfceffes appeared in different parts of the body in the latter animals, which when opened, difcharged a yellow ferous fluid. From the colour of thefe difcharges, and of the urine, the difeafe got the name of the *yellow water*.

trid and offenfive, infomuch that the inhabitants
of the houfes in Water and Front Streets, who
were near it, were obliged in the hotteft weather
to exclude it, by fhutting their doors and windows.
Even perfons, who only walked along thofe ftreets,
complained of an intolerable fœtor, which upon
enquiring, was conftantly traced to the putrid coffee. It fhould not furprife us, that this feed, fo
inoffenfive in its natural ftate, fhould produce, after its putrefaction a violent fever. The records
of medicine furnifh inftances of fimilar fevers being produced, by the putrefaction of many other
vegetable fubftances. Fourteen men out of fixteen, perifhed by a malignant fever, a few years
ago, at the ifland of Tortola, from the effluvia generated by fome putrefied potatoes, which were
taken out of the hold of a Liverpool veffel.
" The effluvia (fays Dr Zimmerman) from a little
heap of flax, has been known to occafion a malignant fever, which proved fatal to the family, in
which it firft began, and afterwards fpread its *contagion* through a whole country." Dr Rodgers
in his treatife upon the difeafes of Cork, mentions
a malignant fever which fwept away a great number of the ftudents of Wadham College in Oxford, " The fingularity of the cafe (adds the Doctor) engaged all the gentlemen of the faculty, in
a ferious inquiry into the caufes of fo remarkable

an

an effect, and all agreed that the *contagious* infection arose from the putrefaction of a vaft quantity of cabbages thrown into a heap out of the feveral gardens near the College." Lancifli relates, that one end of the city of Rome was nearly defolated by the effluvia of fome rotted hemp, which lay in the neighbourhood of the city. The fame author remarks, that " fevers often prevail at Conftantinople, which owe their origin to the hemp which is brought from Cairo, and which is put wet into the public granaries, and fuffered to ferment during the fummer. It is afterwards fold, and the feeds of thofe difeafes are afterwards fpread among the people." Many other facts might be adduced of radifhes, turnips, garlic, and fundry other vegetables, generating by putrefaction, fevers, fimilar to thofe which have been mentioned.

4. The rapid progrefs of the fever from Water-ftreet, and the courfes through which it travelled into other parts of the city, afford a ftrong evidence that it was at firft propagated chiefly by exhalation from the putrid coffee. It is remarkable that it paffed firft through thofe alleys, and ftreets which were in the courfe of the winds that blew acrofs the dock and wharf where the coffee lay, and that perfons were affected at a much greater diftance from Water-ftreet by that means, than

was

was afterwards known by means of the contagion which was generated by infected perfons.

5. Many perfons who had worked, or even vifited in the neighbourhood of the exhalation from the coffee, early in the month of Auguft, were indifpofed afterwards with ficknefs, puking, and yellow fweats, long before the air of Water-ftreet was fo much impregnated with the contagion, as to produce fuch effects; and feveral patients whom I attended in the yellow fever declared to me, or to their friends, that their indifpofitions began exactly at the time they inhaled the offenfive effluvia of the coffee.

6. The firft cafes of the yellow fever have been clearly traced to the failors of the veffel who were firft expofed to the effluvia of the coffee. Their ficknefs commenced with the day on which the coffee began to emit its putrid fmell. The difeafe fpread with the encreafe of the poifonous exhalation. A journeyman of Mr Peter Brown's, who worked near the corner of Race and Water-ftreets, caught the difeafe on the 27th of July. Elizabeth Hill, the wife of a fifherman was infected by only failing near the peftilential wharf, about the firft of Auguft, and died at Kenfington on the 14th of the fame month. Many other names might be
mentioned

mentioned of perfons who fickened during the laft week in July or the firft week in Auguft, who afcribed their illneffes to the fmell of the coffee. From three of thofe perfons who came under my notice, the difeafe was evidently propagated by contagion : from one of them, to nearly a whole family, and from another to a girl of eight years old, who was led by curiofity to examine the yellow colour which it was faid had appeared in the face of the infected perfon, after death.

7. It has been remarked that this fever did not fpread in the country, when carried there by perfons who were infected, and who afterwards died with it. This I conceive was occafioned, in part by the contagion being deprived of the aid of miafmata from the putrid matter which firft produced it in our city, and in part, by its being diluted, and thereby weakened by the pure air of the country. During four times in which it prevailed in Charlefton, in no one inftance, according to Dr Lining, was it propagated in any other part of the ftate.

8. It is very remarkable that in the hiftories of the diforder which have been preferved in this country, it has *fix* times appeared about the firft

or

or middle of Auguft, and declined, or ceafed
about the middle of October—viz. in 1732, 1739,
1745, and 1748 in Charlefton; in 1791 in New-
York, and in 1793 in Philadelphia. This frequent occurrence of the yellow fever at the ufual
period of our common bilious remittents, cannot
be afcribed to accidental coincidence, but muft be
refolved in moft cafes into the combination of more
active miafmata with the predifpofition of a tropical feafon. In fpeaking of a tropical feafon, I
include that kind of weather in which rains and
heats are alternated with each other, as well as
that, which is uniformly warm.

9. Several circumftances attended the late epidemic, which do not occur in the Weft-India yellow fever. It affected children as well as adults
in common with our annual bilious fevers. In
the Weft Indies Dr Hume tells us it never attacked any perfon under puberty. It had, moreover,
many peculiar fymptoms (as I have already fhewn)
which are not to be met with in any of the hiftories of the Weft-India yellow fever.

10. Why fhould it furprife us to fee a yellow
fever generated amongft us? It is only a higher
grade of a fever which prevails every year in
our

our city, from vegetable putrefaction. It conforms in the difference of its degrees of violence,
and danger to feafon, as well as climate, and in
this refpect it is upon a footing with the fmall-pox,
the meafles, the fore-throat, and feveral other difeafes. There are few years pafs, in which a plethoric habit, and more active but limited miafmata, do not produce Sporadic Cafes of true yellow fever in Philadelphia. It is very common in
South and North Carolina and in Virginia, and
there are facts which prove, that not only ftrangers,
but native individuals, and in one inftance, a whole
family, have been carried off by it in the ftate of
Maryland. It proved fatal to one hundred perfons in the city of New-York in the year of 1791,
where it was evidently generated by putrid exhalation. The yellow colour of the fkin, has unfortunately too often been confidered as the charac-
teriftic mark of this fever, otherwife many other
inftances of its prevalence might be difcovered, I
have no doubt in every part of the United States.
I wifh with Dr Mofely, the term *yellow*, could be
abolifhed from the titles of this fever, for this colour is not only frequently abfent, but fometimes
occurs in the mildeft bilious remittents. Dr Haller in his pathology, defcribes an epidemic of this
kind in Swifferland, in which this colour generally
attended, and I have once feen it almoft univerfal

in

in a common bilious fever which prevailed in the
American army in the year 1776.

If any thing could furprife me after reading the
report of the College of Phyficians that our late
fever was imported, in fpite of every poffible evidence to the contrary, it would be the opinion
which was delivered publicly by fome leading
members of the College, that no fever produced
by vegetable putrefaction and exhalation, had ever
been contagious.   It is fcarcely poffible to open a
practical book upon medicine, without meeting
with facts which eftablifh a contrary opinion.
The fevers generated by putrid cabbage, mentioned by Dr Rodgers, and by putrid flax mentioned by Dr Zimmerman, were both contagious.
Dr Lind afcribes the yellow fever every where to
marfh or putrid vegetable exhalations; and this
fever, we know, fpreads by contagion.   Dr Lind,
Jun. eftablifhes the contagious nature of the marfh
fever which prevailed in Bengal in the year 1762.
I fhall tranfcribe his words upon this fubject.
" Although marfh miafmata (fays he) firft bring
on the difeafe, yet contagion prefently fpreads it,
and renders it more epidemic.   Thus the Drake
Indiaman continued free from the diforder for
two weeks together, when fhe had no communication with other fhips ; whereas as foon as the
                                                    diforder

diforder was brought on board, many were feized with it within a few days in fuch a manner as to leave no room to entertain the leaft doubt concerning its peftilential nature*."

Dr Clark mentions a contagious malignant fever from marfh miafmata, which prevailed at Prince's Ifland in the year 1771, and which afterwards infected the crew of the Grenville Indiaman †. The contagious peftilential fever in France, fo accurately defcribed by Riverius, was produced by an exhalation from putrid vegetables, particularly hemp and flax ‡. Even intermittents, the moft frequent and the moft numerous offspring of marfh exhalation, are contagious. Of this there are many proofs in practical authors. Bianchi defcribes an intermittent which was highly contagious at Wolfenbuttle in the year 1666 §. Dr Clark mentions a number of cafes in which this mild fpecies of fever was propagated by contagion. Dr Cleghorn has eftablifhed the contagious nature of intermittents by many facts. After mentioning numerous inftances of their ha-

* Page 35, 36.
† Obfervations on the Difeafes of Long Voyages to hot countries, vol. i. p. 123, 124.
‡ De Febre Peftilenti, vol. ii. p. 97.
§ Hiftor. Hepat. p. 745.

M   ving

ving fpread in this way, he fays, " Thefe tertians
have as good a right to be called contagious as
the meafles, fmall-pox, or any other difeafe*."
The United States, in common with other countries, have in many places exhibited proofs of the
contagious nature of fevers, produced by putrid
vegetable exhalations. The yellow fever which
the citizens of New York wifely admit to have
been generated in their city from vegetable putrefaction in the year 1791, fpread by contagion †.
The bilious fever which prevailed in Philadelphia
in the year 1778, was evidently contagious ; fo
were the bilious fevers which prevailed during the
laft autumn in Weathersfield, Harrifburgh, and
on the fouth branch of the Potowmac. I hope
I fhall be excufed by the phyficians of other ftates
(if this publication fhould fall into their hands)
for having employed a fingle page in combating
an error which is fo obvious to common obfervation. My only defign in expofing it, is to prevent
a repetition of its fatal influence in the only city
in the world in which it has ever been believed or
propagated.

* Page 132.

† Addoms's Inaugural Differtation on the Malignant
Fever which prevailed in New York, during the months of
Auguft, September, and October, in 1791, p. 7.

I am

I am far however from denying that this difeafe has not fometimes been imported into our country. From the authority of Dr Lind, it appears that this has once been the cafe in Philadelphia. In this refpeét it is upon a footing with the plague, which is both an imported and a generated difeafe, in the cities of the Eaft. I am difpofed however to believe that the inftances of the yellow fever being imported are very few, compared with thofe of its being generated in our country. What makes this opinion probable is, that neither Great Britain nor Ireland have ever, to my knowledge, been infeéted by this fever, notwithftanding their long and frequent commercial intercourfe with the Weft India iflands. The fummers in each of thofe countries, though feldom *hot* enough to generate a contagious yellow or bilious fever, are notwithftanding *warm* enough to favour the propagation of an imported contagion of that diforder. The jail fever which has more than once been introduced into our city in crowded fhips from Holland, I fufpeét has been fometimes miftaken for the yellow fever of the Weft Indies. But I have another reafon for difcrediting fome of the accounts of the importation of this fever, which have been handed down to us by former generations, and that is, the manner in which the College of Phyficians decided upon the queftion of the origin of

the

the difeafe now under confideration. The governor of the ftate requefted in his letter to them,
to know whether it was imported ; if it were,
from what *place*, at *what time*, and in *what manner*. The report of the College of Phyficians
takes no notice of either of thofe queftions. In
vain did Dr Foulke call upon the college to be
more definite in their anfwer to the governor's
letter. They had faithfully fought for the information required, but to no purpofe. The character of their departed brother Dr Hutchinfon,
for capacity and vigilance in his office, as infpector of fickly veffels, was urged without effect as
an argument againft the probability of the difeafe
being imported. Public report had derived it
from feveral different iflands ; had chafed it from
fhip to fhip, and from fhore to fhore ; and finally
conveyed it at different times into the city, alternately by dead and living bodies ; and from
thefe tales, all of which when inveftigated, were
proved to be without foundation, the College
of Phyficians compofed their letter. It would
feem from this conduct of the College as if medical fuperftition had changed its names, and that in
accounting for the origin of peftilential fevers, ce-
leftial, planetary, and demoniacal influence, had
only yielded to the term—*importation.*

Let

Let not the reader reject the opinion I have delivered, becaufe it is oppofed by fo great a majority of the phyficians of Philadelphia. A fingle phyfician fupported an opinion of the exiftence of the plague at Meffina in the year 1743, in oppofition to all the phyficians (33 in number) of that city. They denied the difeafe in queftion to exift, becaufe it was not accompanied by glandular fwellings. Time fhewed that they were all miftaken, and the plague, which might, probably have been checked at its firft appearance by their united efforts, was by means of their ignorance, introduced with great mortality into every part of the city. This difpofition of phyficians to limit the fymptoms of feveral other difeafes, cannot be fufficiently lamented. The frequent abfence of a yellow colour in our late epidemic, led to miftakes which coft the city of Philadelphia feveral hundred lives.

The report of the College of Phyficians has ferved to confirm me in an opinion, that the plagues which occafionally defolated moft of the countries in Europe in former centuries, and which were always faid to be of foreign extraction, were in moft inftances of domeftic origin. Between the years 1006 and 1680, the plague was epidemic 52 times all over Europe. It prevailed 14 times in

M 3   the

14th century. The ftate of Europe in this long
period, is well known. Idlenefs, a deficiency of
vegetable aliment, a camp life from the frequency
of wars, famine, an uncultivated and marfhy foil,
fmall cabins, and the want of clcanlinefs in drefs,
diet, and furniture, all concurred to generate peftilential difeafes. The plagues which prevailed
in London every year from 1593 to 1611, and
from 1636 to 1649, I fufpeEt were generated in
that city. The diminution of plagues in Europe,
more efpecially in London, appears to have been
produced by the great change in the diet and manners of the people ; alfo by the more commodious
and airy forms of the houfes of the poor, among
whom the plague *always* makes its firft appearance. It is true, thefe plagues were faid by authors to have been imported either direEtly or in-
direEtly from the Levant ; but the proofs of fuch
importation were in moft cafes as vague and deficient, as they were of the Weft India origin of
our late epidemic. The peftilential fevers which
have been mentioned, have been defcribed by authors, by the generic name of the plague ; but
fome of them appear to have originated from putrid vegetable exhalations, and to have refembled
in moft of their fymptoms, the Weft India and
North American yellow fever.

I am aware that the opinion and facts which I have stated upon the origin of the late epidemic, are not popular with our citizens, but I did not dare to conceal them ; for I am perfuaded a knowledge and belief of them, involve in their confequences, the lives of millions that are yet unborn.

Commerce can no more be endangered than Religion, by the publication of philofophical truth. On the contrary it muft fuffer moft by the adoption of the traditional error which I have endeavoured to refute, for while the caufe of a malignant fever is obvious to the fenfes, it will be eafy to guard againft it; but while it is believed that the difeafe may be imported, and no body know, from what *place*, at what *time*, and in *what manner*, we fhall not only be carelefs in the midft of filth and danger, but our city will always hold its character for health by a timid and precarious tenure. I am the more difpofed to expect forgivenefs from my fellow citizens for this attempt to ferve them, by the recollection of the fudden change in the health of our city which followed the arching the offenfive dock between Front and Third ftreets in the year 1782. By advifing that meafure (in which I ftood nearly alone) I incurred the cenfure of feveral valuable citizens. The bills of mortality however foon fhewed that the mea-

M 4

fure

fure was right, and I have fince feen with great
pleafure the extraordinary healthinefs of our city,
afcribed by indifferent people, to that, among
other caufes.

The climate of our country can no more fuffer
than the commerce of our city, by this inveftigation; for it fixes the late fever, and all the other
malignant fevers of the United States, upon putrid
vegetable exhalation. Without the matrix of
putrid vegetable matters, there can no more be a
bilious or yellow fever generated amongft us, than
there can be vegetation without earth—water or
air. To afcribe our late difeafe therefore to the
exclufive influence of the atmofphere, is a reflec-
tion upon our climate which is equally unphilofo-
phical and unjuft.

Let it only be clearly proved, and boldly afferted, that a bilious yellow fever has been, and may
be generated in our country, under the circumftances before mentioned, and the return of it, as
alfo of common bilious and intermitting fevers may
every where be prevented by a due attention to
the cleanlinefs of the wharfs and fuburbs, as
well as the ftreets of our cities, and towns; by
draining and cultivating marfhy grounds in their
neighbourhood, and in the neighbourhood of
                                        farm

farm houfes,—and where the laft cannot be done, by fheltering them from the current of vegetable exhalations, by means of a body of trees that are of fpeedy growth. In this manner, malignant and deadly fevers have been banifhed from moft of the cities in Europe.

I have hinted in the courfe of this hiftory, at the refemblance which the yellow fever bears to the plague. Before I difmifs this part of my fubject, I fhall briefly enumerate the circumftances, and fymptoms, which belong to them in common; and afterwards mention thofe which are peculiar to each of them. The utility of this digreffion will, I hope appear hereafter, when I come to deliver the hiftory of the *cure* of the yellow fever.— The principles which fuggefted and directed it, will apply alike to both difeafes.

The circumftances and fymptoms in which the plague, and the yellow fever (as it lately appeared in our city) refemble each other, are as follow:

In being accompanied and encreafed by warm weather.

In affecting thofe people moft generally who follow occupations which expofe them to be much heated.

heated. The bakers were great fufferers by the plagues at Aleppo, defcribed by Dr P. Ruffel.

In affecting perfons who are fuddenly debilitated by fear or grief.

In affecting all ages ; alfo the poor more than the rich; men more than women; and perfons of robuft, more than thofe of weakly habits.

In attacking with, and without premonitory fymptoms.

In being excited by intemperance, and labour.

In being accompanied by a full, tenfe, depreffed, regular, or an intermitting pulfe.

In being accompanied by hemorrhagies. Thefe are lefs frequent in the plague than in the yellow fever.——Abortions are alike common in both difeafes.

The following fymptoms of our late yellow fever occur likewife in the plague.

Inflammation of the brain.

Inflam-

Inflammation, mortifications, and carbuncles in the alimentary canal and ftomach.

Coftivenefs or diarrhœa. Copious fweats in the beginning of the difeafe which afford relief.— A difcharge of a blackifh liquor from the ftomach by vomiting, in the clofe of the difeafe.

A moift white tongue, in its beginning, and a dry black tongue in its laft ftage.

Abfence of heat and thirft in fome cafes.

Convulfions, fyncope, great depreffion of fpirits, exquifite pain, fo as to excite fcreamings in the fick. Delirium and a temporary lofs of memory after recovery.

A red or a brilliant eye, and great venereal ex‑citability in the convalefcent ftate of the difeafe.

Buboes, and an exclufive affection of the lym‑phatic glands.

Maculæ, or red fpots refembling flea bites, wa‑tery veficles, or blifters which end in mortifica‑tions, petechiæ, anthrax, and carbuncles.

Sizy,

Sizy, denfe, or diffolved blood.

The plague appears in the forms of quotidian,
tertian, and quartan fevers. It has different
grades, alfo different durations, from one day to
two, three and four weeks. It is moft fatal at its
firft appearance. Convulfive twitchings of the
tendons are lefs common in the plague, than in
the nervous fever. It chafes away, or unites with
all other febrile difeafes.

I have before remarked, that during the prevalence of the plague, fome foreigners efcape the
contagion.

The contagion of the plague infects the atmofphere of a whole city, and is propagated without
contact with the fick. Many people difcover
marks of the prefence of this contagion in their
bodies, who are in apparent good health; a difpofition to fweat is very common in fuch perfons.
The difeafe is fometimes propagated by contact
by means of this fweat, when it affects the hands.

Perfons infected with the contagion of the
plague, communicate it before they are fenfible
of their being affected by it. The contagion is
excited at different times, from the moment it is

received

received into the body, until the 16th day afterwards.

Perfons who have had the plague, are capable
of re-infection.

Brutes, as cats and dogs are affected in fome
inftances, with fymptoms of the plague, particularly buboes.

Perfons confined in Seraglios in Eaftern countries, and in Monafteries in Catholic countries,
alfo grave diggers, very often efcape the plague.

The bodies of perfons who die of the plague
become ftiff in fome inftances immediately after
death.   Tears likewife often appear on their
cheeks.

Cold weather checks the plague, but not fo
uniformly as it does the yellow fever.

The difeafes which fucceed the plague, appear
with more or lefs of its fymptoms.

It will appear hereafter that the cure of the
yellow fever, accorded in feveral particulars, with
that of the plague.

The

The circumftances and fymptoms in which the plague *differs* from the yellow fever are as follow :

A vomiting is lefs common in the plague, than in the yellow fever. Bile is lefs frequently dif- charged, and the ftools are lefs fœtid, and offenfive.

There are fmall horny fwellings upon the breaft and limbs in the plague which did not occur in the yellow fever. They are called *tokens.*

The contagion of the plague does not infect at fo great a diftance, as the contagion of the yel- low fever.

It affects more univerfally, than the yellow fe- ver, and (with a few exceptions) it is more mor- tal when left to itfelf.

It fometimes prevails in cold weather. It pre- vails likewife in a greater variety of ftates of the atmofphere.

The body is of its ufual, or of a greenifh co- lour after death.

The plague is of animal origin. It is derived in fome inftances from dead animal matters. The

plagues

plagues which laid wafte the Roman Empire in the reign of Juftinian, are afcribed by Mr Gibbon, to fwarms of putrifying locufts.   But the moft frequent fource of the plague is from human miafmata, rendered peftilential, by famine, grief, the want of cleanlinefs, and by a number of perfons crouded together in fmall rooms, or houfes.

The yellow fever has been confounded with the jail or hofpital fever.   I fhall briefly enumerate the circumftances and fymptoms in which they agree and difagree.

The *firft* are as follow :

The jail-fever affects perfons who are debilitated by grief, fear, or intemperance.

The pulfe is fometimes intermitting in this fever.   This is taken notice of by Dr Ferriar.

There are marks of congeftion in the brain, without any figns of inflammation in it after death. There are likewife in this fever great depreffion of fpirits, fighing, delirium, palfy, and a debilitated ftate of the memory after recovery.   This occurs more frequently, and in a greater degree, after the jail, than after the yellow fever.

The

The eye is fometimes red, and fometimes dull in this fever. There is frequently an abfence of thirft.

There is in the jail fever in its worft ftate, a fuppreffion or great heat in the urine.

Buboes, petechiæ, pain along the fpermatic cord, a fwelling of one tefticle, ulcers in the throat, and abfceffes in different parts of the body, have all occurred occafionally in this fever.

The circumftances and fymptoms in which the jail fever *differs* from the yellow fever, are as follow :

It affects perfons who have been previoufly weakened by other difeafes, or who are of weakly habits.

The pulfe is feldom full or tenfe, but generally weak and quick.

The tongue foon lofes its whitenefs and moif-ture, and affumes when dry, a dark colour.

The ftomach is feldom difordered. The bowels are either in their natural ftate, or a diarrhœa at-tends.

I

tends. The ſtools are ſeldom bilious, or preternaturally fœtid.

There are great twitchings in the tendons, and
tremors in the tongue, and limbs.

Intermiſſions and remiſſions of the fever are ſeldom, or ſcarcely perceptible.

It prevails alike in the winter, ſpring, and autumn. It is moderated, or checked by warm
weather, provided patients are placed in ſituations
in which they can breathe a ſufficient quantity of
freſh air.

It is leſs contagious and mortal than the yellow
fever.

It is derived from human miaſmata produced
under inferior degrees of all thoſe circumſtances,
which favour the generation of the plague. It is,
to the plague in its degree, what the common
bilious, is, to the yellow fever.

There is a camp fever deſcribed by ſome authors, which is derived from a mixture of marſh
and human miaſmata. Its ſymptoms are com-

N   pounded

pounded of thofe which belong to the bilious, and jail fevers.

I fhall not attempt to diftinguifh the yellow, from the common bilious fever. They are only different grades of the fame difeafe. The following, appears to be the natural order of a fcale of fuch fevers as are derived from marfh miafmata.

1. The yellow fever.

2. The common bilious remitting fever.

3. The intermitting fever.

4. The febricula of authors, or what are called " inward fevers," in the fouthern ftates. Different degrees of *force* in the remote caufe, in conjunction with a difference in the fenfible qualities of the air, frequently produce all thofe grades of bilious or marfh fever in different feafons, and fometimes, in the fame feafon. The encreafe, or abftraction of accidental ftimuli, likewife often change thefe different ftates of bilious fever into each other. Thus, what are called inward fevers have often been excited by means of a ride, or a long walk, into an intermittent; an intermittent

has

has been changed by the premature ufe of the bark into a remitting fever, and a common remittent, has, by improper regimen or violent exercife, been excited into a yellow fever. The danger in each cafe, is determined by the force of the miafmata, and the ftate of the air.

In contemplating the immenfe proportion of human mifery, which is produced by peftilential difeafes, we are naturally led to inquire whether their approaches are not indicated by fome unufual figns in the operations of nature. What is called inftinct in many animals, has repeatedly taught them to forefee, and to avoid many natural evils; and if reafon has not taught man to do the fame, it is probably becaufe its exercifes have not been directed to thofe fubjects.

I have endeavoured to difcover whether any thing uncommon occurred in the operations of nature in the atmofphere, or in the animal and vegetable kingdoms in the courfe of the winter and fummer, which preceded our late epidemic. The refult of my inquiries is as follows.

The winter of 1793 was unufually moderate. It was fuppofed this had an influence upon the weather which favoured the generation and pro-

N 2 pagation

pagation of the difeafe. I fhould have been difpofed to admit this opinion, had moderate winters
in Pennfylvania been uniformly fucceeded by fickly autumns. Livy records that a peftilential fever
in Rome was preceded by an unufually *cold* winter *.

The wild pidgeons were common during the
winter of 1793 in many parts of Pennfylvania.
But they have occafionally appeared in great
flocks in our ftate in former winters, without having been the harbingers of a fickly autumn.

Dr P. Ruffel fays, that uncommon and violent
difeafes generally preceded the plague at Aleppo.
Dr Sydenham informs us, that acute inflammatory
fevers were the forerunners of the plague in London in 1665. I fufpect that uncommon circumftances attending certain difeafes, either as to their
violence or time of appearance, will be found to
fuggeft a prelude to a fickly autumn in all countries. The fcarlatina anginofa I have remarked
was attended with an uncommon degree of inflammatory diathefis, in the month of July. Dr Porter informed me that he had been called to feveral cafes of dyfentery, attended with fymptoms of

* Riverius, vol. ii. p. 98.

great

great malignity, in the neighbourhood of Frank-
fort, in the months of July and Auguſt. Dr Señ-
ter informed me in a letter dated the 26th of November, 1793, that " during the laſt two ſummer
months, fevers and fluxes were more obſtinate
than he had ever known them, at Newport in
Rhode Iſland." My pupil Mr Nathaniel Potter,
in a letter from Caroline county, in Maryland,
dated November 1ſt, 1793, gave me the following information. " On my arrival at this place,
on the firſt of Auguſt, I was informed by gentlemen of the faculty, that the dyſentery had prevailed from the firſt of June to the fifteenth of
July, with conſiderable mortality. From obſer-
vations and communications from different people in this county, I did not heſitate to prediſt
a ſickly autumn; for it is an invariable maxim
here, both among phyſicians and farmers, that if
the wheat be damaged by ruſt or blaſt, a contagious dyſentery is ſoon to follow; and the ſooner in
the ſummer the dyſentery appears, the more violent
and mortal will be the diſeaſes of the autumn."

Theſe communications, though ſhort and few,
will be uſeful if they ſerve to lead phyſicians to
obſerve and record hereafter the diſeaſes which
precede univerſal and mortal epidemics.

N 3   There

There can be no doubt of a warm fummer, whether it be wet or dry, having often preceded malignant autumnal fevers. Mr Norris in a letter to one of his friends, dated the 24th of Auguft, O. S. fays that " the fummer of 1699 was the hotteft he had ever felt, and that feveral had died in the harveft fields with the violence of the heat." It appears from another of Mr Norris's letters, dated the 12th of Auguft, O. S. that the yellow fever made its firft appearance in that month. The yellow fevers of 1762 and 1793, were both preceded by warm fummers.

I have one more remark to mention upon this fubject, which was communicated to me by a gentleman who had refided occafionally in fouthern and tropical countries. He informed me that he had obferved in the month of July, feveral weeks before the yellow fever became general, a peculiar and univerfal fallownefs of complexion in the faces of the citizens of Philadelphia, fuch as he had obferved to precede the prevalence of malignant bilious fevers in hot climates. Dr Dick informed me that he had obferved the fame appearance in the faces of people in Alexandria, accompanied in fome cafes by a yellownefs in the eyes, during the laft fummer, and fome time before vio-

lent

lent bilious fevers became epidemic upon the banks of the Potowmac.

With thefe obfervations I take leave of the hif-tory of our late epidemic fever. A few of its fymptoms which have been omitted in the hiftory, will be included in the method of cure; for they were difcovered or produced by the remedies which were ufed for that purpofe.

Th:

☞ *The following Page begins an account of the
ſtates of the thermometer and weather, from
the firſt of January to the firſt of Auguſt, and
of the ſtates of the barometer, thermometer,
winds, and weather, from the firſt of Auguſt to
the ninth of November, 1793. The times of ob-
ſervation for the firſt three months are at 7 in
the morning, and 2 in the afternoon; for the
next five months they are at 6 in the morning,
and 3 in the afternoon. From the firſt of October to the ninth of November, they are as in
the firſt three months.*

D.	Therm. 7h	2h	Weather.	Therm. 7h	2h	Weather.
1	27	30	Cloudy.	9	26	Fair, hazey.
2	30	41	Fair, cloudy.	25	34	Rain, ditto.
3	30	33	Cloudy, rain.	33	37	Cloudy, fair.
4	38	41	Rain, cloudy.	25	46	Cloudy, fair.
5	35	42	Fair, cloudy.	36	44	Cloudy, ditto.
6	33	47	Cloudy, fair.	35	46	Cloudy, rain.
7	33	51	Fair, fair.	36	40	Cloudy, fair.
8	32	49	Fair, ditto.	28	44	Cloudy, ditto.
9	33	48	Hazey, fair.	42	50	Rain, fair.
10	38	51	Fair, ditto.	38	40	Cloudy, fair.
11	35	48	Fair, clouds.	19	27	Fair, cloudy.
12	31	42	Fair, ditto.	20	28	Snow, cloudy.
13	28	42	Fair, do.	22	31	Cloudy, snow.
14	25	27	Hail, snow, sleet.	27	39	Cloudy, fair.
15	32	37	Clouds, mist,	18	40	Fair, ditto.
16	37	39	Rain, ditto.	29	42	Cloudy, ditto.
17	37	45	Rain, snow, fair.	44	48	Rain, ditto.
18	32	52	Fair, ditto.	39	49	Cloudy, fair.
19	37	48	Fair, do.	31	41	Cloudy, rain.
20	33	47	Hazey, cloudy.	52	53	Rain, fair.
21	36	47	Cloudy, fair.	37	49	Fair, ditto.
22	27	32	Fair, ditto.	29	34	Fair, do.
23	22	37	Fair, do.	22	34	Snow, cloudy.
24	30	39	Cloudy, do.	54	59	Rain, cloudy.
25	30	41	Fair, hazey.	34	35	Cloudy, ditto.
26	31	—	Fair.	35	43	Rain, mist.
27	23	38	Fair, cloudy, snow.	43	43	Rain, cloudy.
28	35	45	Cloudy, fair.	14	26	Fair, ditto.
29	29	37	Fair, ditto.			
30	22	23	Snow, hail.			
31	25	32	Cloudy, fair.			

March, 1793.   April, 1793.

Therm. D.	7h	2h	Weather.	Therm. 7h	2h	Weather.
1	20	58	Fair, ditto.	45	70	Cloudy, fair.
2	31	51	Hazey, cloudy.	47	71	Fair, ditto.
3	48	63	Rain, fair.	56	80	Fair, do.
4	43	61	Hazey, ditto.	51	72	Cloudy, fair.
5	51	52	Rain, fair.	53	61	Cloudy, rain.
6	32	50	Fair, ditto.	60	76	Misty, fair.
7	36	62	Fair, do. clouds.	51	65	Fair, do.
8	54	60	Cloudy, rain.	46	74	Fair, do.
9	26	41	Fair, ditto.	55	71	Fair, cloudy.
10	29	51	Fair, do.	50	56	Fair, do.
11	43	55	Rain, do.	37	63	Fair, do.
12	40	43	Cloudy, do.	54	62	Cloudy, rain, fair.
13	38	39	Cloudy, fair.	49	62	Fair, do.
14	26	44	Fair, do.	50	70	Fair, do.
15	32	59	Fair, do.	45	55	Rain, cloudy.
16	52	62	Cloudy, fair.	46	62	Cloudy, fair.
17	51	72	Cloudy, fair.	48	67	Fair, clouds, fair.
18	58	69	Hazey, cloudy.	52	66	Cloudy, fair.
19	53	59	Fair, do.	52	75	Fair, do.
20	42	61	Fair, do.	52	49	Rain, cloudy.
21	41	43	Rain, cloudy.	44	47	Cloudy, ditto.
22	31	47	Fair, do.	43	46	Rain, cloudy.
23	35	57	Fair, do.	42	63	Fair, do.
24	37	50	Fair, do.	44	68	Fair, do.
25	35	59	Fair, do.	45	65	Cloudy, cloudy.
26	47	54	Cloudy, rain.	53	57	Cloudy, rain.
27	43	51	Fair, cloudy.	47	46	Rain, do.
28	33	45	Fair, clouds, fair.	44	54	Rain, cloudy.
29	34	57	Fair, do.	40	59	Fair, do.
30	41	58	Cloudy, fair.	40	65	Fair, do.
31	42	61	Cloudy, fair.			

May, 1793. June, 1793.

D.	7h	2h	Weather.	7h	2h	Weather.
1			oggy, cloudy.	53	61	Rain, fhowery.
2		73	Fog, clouds, fair.	54	64	Clouds, fhowers.
3			Rain, do.	55	62	Cloudy, rain, fair,
4		8?	Fair, do.	54	60	Rain, do. cloudy.
5	55	36	Cloudy, do.	58	72	Cloudy, fair, rain.
6	47		loudy, fair.	—	71	Cloudy, rain,
7	5?	68	Cloudy, fair.	68	78	Fair, do.
8	59	78	Cloudy, fair.	65	—	Fair, do.
9	61	70	Foggy,	70	88	Fog, fair.
10	55	71	Rain,	74	90	Fair, do.
11	55	75	Cloudy, fair.	76	90	Fair, do.
12	61	76	Cloudy, rain.	75	88	Fair, fhowers.
13	57	78	Fair, do.	74	81	Cloudy, rain.
14	59	83	Fair, cloudy.	63	77	Fair, do.
15	60	71	Fair, do.	63	82	Fair, hazey.
16	50	69	Fair, do.	67	85	Fair, do.
17	48	74	Fair, do.	74	89	Fair, fhowers.
18	61	81	Cloudy, fair.	73	88	Fair, do.
19	65	85	Fair, rain.	77	91	Fair, do.
20	65	87	Fair, do.	79	88	Fair, rain, fair.
21	68	86	Fair, do. clouds.	75	85	Cloudy, rain.
22	72	80	Clouds, gufts.	58	78	Cloudy, fair,
23	94	79	Cloudy, fair.	58	78	Fair, do.
24	58	75	Fair, do.	60	79	Fair, do,
25	52	70	Fair, cloudy.	67	74	Cloudy, rain.
26	61	66	Rain, do.	66	69	Cloudy, rain.
27	68	84	Cloudy, fair.	68	80	Cloudy, fair.
28	70	68	Fair, clouds, rain.	71	85	Cloudy, fair.
29	57	62	Cloudy, rain, clouds.	77	88	Cloudy, do.
30	54	57	Cloudy, rain.	74	90	Fair, do.
31	54	60	Clouds, do.			

JULY, 1793.

Days	Barometer 6 A.M.	Barometer 3 P.M.	Therm. 6 A.M.	Therm. 6 P.M.	Wind 6 A.M.	Wind 3 P.M.	Weather.
1	30 0	29 9	77	88	W	W	fair.
2	29 8	29 7	77	81	W		fair, showers.
3	29 9	30 0	74	80	E	E	cloudy,
4	30 1	30 0	70	83	E	SW	cloudy, fair, rain.
5	30 0	29 9	76	90	NW	SW	fair, do.
6	29 9	29 9	78	91	SW	SW	cloudy, thunder.
7	29 9	30 0	73	88	NE	NW	fair, clouds.
8	30 1	30 1	72	85	E	E	cloudy, fair.
9	30 0	29 8	73	81	S	SW	cloudy, do.
10	30 0	30 0	70	84	W	NW	fair, do.
11	30 0	30 0	74	88	NW	NW	fair, clouds.
12	30 1	30 2	70	84	N	N	fair, do.
13	30 1	30 0	68	83	NW	NW	fair, do.
14	30 0	30 0	65	80	N	Calm	fair, hazey.
15	30 0	29 9	66	75	SW	SW	cloudy, do.
16	29 8	29 7	70	83	W	W	rain, fair.
17	29 8	29 9	68	81	NW	NW	fair, do.
18	30 0	30 0	66	86	W	SW	fair, do.
19	29 9	29 9	75	85	SW	W	fair, cloudy, rain.
20	30 0	30 0	72	87	W	NW	fair, do. shower.
21	30 1	30 1	70	86	NW	NW	fair, do.
22	30 0	30 0	72	87	SW	SW	fair, do.
23	30 0	30 0	73	91	SW	SW	fair, cloudy.
24	29 9	29 9	75	89	Calm	W	cloudy, fair.
25	30 1	30 1	71	83	NW	NNW	fair, do.
26	30 2	30 2	63	82	N	NE	fair, do.
27	30 2	30 1	64	81	S calm	S	fair, cloudy.
28	30 1	30 0	72	85	Calm	NNE	cloudy, fair.
29	30 1	30 1	74	85	SSE	NE	cloudy, do. rain.
30	30 1	30 0	73	86	S	SW	cloudy, fair.
31	29 9	29 8	76	80	SSW	SW	cloudy, rain, fair.

AUGUST,

AUGUST, 1793.

	Barometer.		Therm.		Wind.		Weather.	
	6 A.M.	3 P.M.	6 A.M.	3 P.M.	6 A.M.	3	6 A.M.	3 P.M.
1	29 95	30 0	65	77	WNW	NW	cloudy,	fair,
2	30 1	30 1	63	81	NW	SW	fair,	fair,
3	30 6	29 95	62	82	N	NNE	fair,	fair,
4	29 97	30 0	65	87	S	SW	fair,	fair,
5	30 5	30 1	73	90	SSW	SW	fair,	fair,
6	30 2	30 0	77	87	SW	W	cloudy,	fair,
7	30 12	30 1	68	83	NW	W	fair,	fair,
8	30 1	29 95	69	86	SSE	SSE	fair,	rain,
9	29 8	29 75	75	85	SSW	SW	cloudy,	fair,
10	29 9	29 9	67	82	W	SW	fair,	fair,
11	30 0	30 0	70	84	SW	WSW	cloudy,	cloudy,
12	30 0	30 0	70	87	W	W	fair,	fair,
13	30 5	30 0	71	89	SW	W	fair,	fair,
14	30 0	29 95	75	82	SW	SW	fair,	rain,
15	30 0	30 1	72	75	NNE	NE	fair.	cloudy,
16	30 1	30 1	70	83	NNE	NE	fair,	fair,
17	30 1	30 0	71	86	SW	SW	fair,	fair,
18	30 1	30 1	73	89	calm	SW	fair,	fair,
19	30 1	30 0	72	82	N	N	fair,	cloudy,
20	30 1	30 12	69	82	NNE	NNE	fair,	fair,
21	30 15	30 25	62	83	N	NNE	fair,	fair,
22	30 3	30 35	63	86	NE	SE	fair,	fair,
23	30 25	30 15	63	85	calm	S	fair,	fair,
24	30 1	30 1	73	81	calm	calm	cloudy,	rain,
25	30 1	30 1	71	66	NE	NE	rain,	gr. rain
26	30 15	30 2	59	69	NE	NE	cloudy,	cloudy,
27	30 2	30 2	65	73	NE	NE	cloudy,	cloudy,
28	30 2	30 15	67	80	S	calm	cloudy,	clearin.
29	30 16	30 15	72	86	calm	SW	cloudy,	fair,
30	30 1	30 1	74	87	calm	SW	fair,	fair,
31	30 0	30 0	74	84	SW	NW	rain,	fair.

SEPTEMBER

SEPTEMBER, 1793.

	Barometer.			Therm.		Wind.		Weather.	
	6 A. M.	3 P. M.		6 A. M.	3 P. M.	6 A. M.	3 P. M.	6 A. M.	3 P. M.
1	30 0	29 30		71	86	calm	SW	fog,	fair,
2	29 75	29 8		73	86	SW	SW	fair,	fair,
3	80 0			60		NW	N	fair,	fair,
4	30 15	30 15		55	75	W	W	fair.	fair,
5	30 15	30 1		62	80	SE	S	fair,	cloudy,
6	29 97	29 95		70	89	WSW	W	fair,	cloudy,
7	30 0	30 0		65	77	WNW	NW	fair,	fair,
8	30 1	30 1		64	70	calm	calm	cloudy,	cloudy,
9	30 0	30 0		66	80	SE	NW	rain,	fair,
10	30 0	30 0		64	72	N	NNE	fair,	cloudy,
11	30 1	30 0		62	72	NNE	N	cloudy,	fair,
12	29 96	29 9		58	76	NW	NNW	fair,	fair,
13	29 95	30 0		57	72	NW	N	fair,	fair,
14	30 0	30 5		58	79	NW,	NW	fair,	fair,
15	30 0	29 97		65	80	N	S	fair,	fair.
16	29 9	29		70	84	S	SW	cloudy,	fair,
17	29 8	29 85		66	67	N	N	cloudy,	cloudy,
18	30 3			44		N		fair,	
19	30 4	30 35		45	70	calm	SW	fair,	fair,
20	30 3	30 15		54	69	calm	SE	hazey,	hazey,
21	30 0	29 0		59	78	calm		cloudy,	fair,
22	30 0	30 0		63	83	calm		cloudy,	fair,
23	30 1	30 1		62	81	calm	SE	cloudy,	cloudy,
24	30 2	30 2		65	70	NE	ENE	cloudy,	fair,
25	30 15	30 0		61	68	NE	NE	cloudy,	cloudy,
26	29 8	29 7		58	79	N	N	cloudy,	fair,
27	29 7			64		NW	NW	cloudy,	fair,
28	30 5	30 15		54	73	NW	NW	fair,	fair,
29	30 3	30 3		56	74	NE	ENE	cloudy,	fair,
30	30 35	30 3		57	75	calm	SW	foggy,	fair.

OCTOBER,

OCTOBER, 1793.

	Barometer.		Therm.		Winds.		Weather.	
	7 A. M.	2 P. M.	7 A. M.	2 P. M.	7 A. M.	2 P. M.	7 A. M.	2 P. M.
1	30 15	30 5	64	80	SW	SW	cloudy,	fair.
2	29 9	30 5	70	72	W	NNW	cloudy,	fair,
3	30 2	30 15	50	72	W	SW	fair,	fair,
4	29 75	29 7	59	72	SW	W	cloudy,	cloudy,
5	30 0	30 1	58	66	N	N	fair,	fair,
6	30 3	30 3	43	66	NE	W	fair,	fair,
7	30 45		46		calm		fair,	
8	30 6	30 6	53	68	N	N	fair,	fair,
9	30 5	30 4	53	70	NW	NW	fair,	fair,
10	30 2	30 2	49	74	E	NW	fair,	fair,
11	30 0	29 85	51	74	W	W	fair,	fair,
12	26 6	29 55	58	64	SW	NW	rain,	rain,
13	29 85	29 9	49	69	NW	NW	fair,	fair,
14	30 5	30 0	52	76	SW	SW	calm,	fair,
15	29 75	29 8	56	54	SW	N	fair,	rain,
16	30 0	30 c	37	53	NNW	N	fair,	fair,
17	30 1	30 1	37	60	NE	NE	fair,	fair,
18	30 1	30 1	41	62	NW	NW	fair,	fair,
19	30 0	29 9	51	66	N	N	cloudy,	fair,
20	30 0	30 c	44	54	NW	N	fair,	fair,
21	30 0	30 2	49	59	N	NW	fair,	fair,
22	29 6	29 5	51	65	NW	NW	fair,	fair,
23	29 8	29 8	47	60	W	W	fair,	fair,
24	30 3	30 4	36	59	W	NW	fair,	fair,
25	30 4	30 3	46	71	S	S	cloudy,	do.h-w.
26	30 2	30 2	60	72	calm	SW	cloudy.	cloudy,
27	30 3	30 3	44	44	NNE	NNE	cloudy,	cloudy,
28	30 2	30 1	34	37	N	N	cloudy,	cloudy,
29	29 85	29 85	28	44	NNW	NW	fair,	fair,
30	30 1	30 1	28	49	calm	SW	hazey,	hazey,
31	30 15	30 2	42	45	calm	NNE	cloudy,	rain,

NOVEMBER,

NOVEMBER, 1793.

Barometer.				Therm.		Winds.		Weather.	
	7 A. M.		2 P. M.	7 A. M.	2 P. M.	7 A. M.	2 P. M.	7 A. M.	2 P. M.
1	30	1	30	1 40	41	NNE	NE	rain,	cloudy,
2	30	3	30	25 32	49	NNE	NE	fair,	fair,
3	30	1	30	0 43	56	calm	SW	cloudy,	cloudy,
4	29	8	29	9 55	67	SW	SW	cloudy,	fair,
5	30	15	30	1 50	64	NE	NE	rain,	rain,
6	29	8	29	65 63	67	S	S	cloudy,	cloudy,
7	29	8	29	8 44	64	calm	SW	fair,	fair,
8	29	8	29	85 43	56	SSW	SW	fair,	fair,
9	29	9	29	95 42	64	SW	SW	fair,	fair,

Of

Of the Method of Cure.

IN the introduction to the hiſtory of the fever, I mentioned the remedies which I uſed with ſucceſs, in ſeveral caſes which occurred in the beginning of Auguſt. I had ſeen, and re-corded in my note book, the efficacy of gentle purges in the yellow fever of 1762; but finding them unſucceſsful after the 20th of Auguſt, and obſerving the diſeaſe to aſſume uncommon ſymp-toms of great indirect debility, I laid them aſide, and had recourſe to a gentle vomit of ipecacuanha on the firſt day of the fever, and to the uſual re-medies for exciting the action of the ſanguiferous ſyſtem. I gave bark in all its uſual forms of in-fuſion, powder, and tincture. I joined wine, brandy, and aromatics with it. I applied bliſters to the limbs, neck, and head. Finding them all ineffectual, I attempted to rouſe the ſyſtem by wrapping the whole body, agreeably to Dr

O   Hume's

Hume's practice, in blankets dipped in warm vinegar. To thefe remedies I added one more:
I rubbed the right fide with mercurial ointment,
with a view of exciting the action of the veffels in
the whole fyftem, through the medium of the liver, which I then fuppofed to be principally, tho'
fymptomatically, affected by the difeafe. None of
thefe remedies appeared to be of any fervice; for
although three out of thirteen recovered of thofe
to whom they were applied, yet I have reafon to
believe that they would have recovered much
fooner had the cure been trufted to nature. Per-
plexed and diftreffed by my want of fuccefs in
the treatment of this fever, I waited upon Dr
Stephens, an eminent and refpectable phyfician
from St Croix, who happened then to be in our
city, and afked for fuch advice and information
upon the fubject of the difeafe, as his extenfive
practice in the Weft Indies would naturally fuggeft. He politely informed me that he had long
ago laid afide evacuations of all kinds in the yellow fever; that they had been found to be hurtful, and that the difeafe yielded more readily to
bark, wine, and above all, to the ufe of the cold
bath. He advifed the bark to be given in large
quantities by way of glyfter, as well as in the
ufual way; and he informed me of the manner in
which the cold bath fhould be ufed, fo as to de-
rive

rive the greateſt benefit from it. This mode of treating the yellow fever appeared to be reaſonable. I had uſed bark in the manner he recommended it in ſeveral caſes of ſporadic yellow fever with ſuccceſs in former years. I had moreover the authority of ſeveral other phyſicians of reputation in its favour. Dr Cleghorn tells us, that " he ſometimes gave the bark when the bowels were full of vicious humours. Theſe humours (he ſays) are produced by the fault of the circulation. The bark by bracing the ſolids, enables them to throw off the excrementitious fluids, by the proper emunctories *."

I began the uſe of each of Dr Stevens's remedies the next day after my interview with him, with great confidence of their ſucceſs. I preſcribed bark in large quantities ; in one caſe I ordered it to be injected into the bowels every four hours. I directed buckets full of cold water to be thrown frequently upon my patients. The bark was offenſive to the ſtomach, or rejected by it in every caſe in which I preſcribed it. The cold bath was grateful, and produced relief in ſeveral caſes by inducing a moiſture on the ſkin. For a while I had hopes of benefit to my

* Page 223.

· patients

patients from the ufe of thefe remedies, but in a
few days, I was diftreffed to find they were not
more effeftual than thofe I had previoufly ufed.
Three out of four of my patients died to whom
the cold bath was adminiftered in addition to the
tonic remedies before mentioned.

Baffled in every attempt to ftop the ravages of
this fever, I anticipated all the numerous and
complicated diftreffes in our city, which peftilential
difeafes have fo often produced in other countries. The fever had a malignity, and an obftinacy
which I had never before obferved in any difeafe,
and it fpread with a rapidity and mortality, far
beyond what it did in the year 1762. Heaven
alone bore witnefs to the anguifh of my foul in
this awful fituation. But I did not abandon a
hope that the difeafe might yet be cured. I had
long believed that good was commenfurate with
evil, and that there does not exift a difeafe for
which the goodnefs of Providence has not provided a remedy. Under the impreffion of this belief, I applied myfelf with frefh ardour to the inveftigation of the difeafe before me. I ranfacked
my library, and pored over every book that
treated of the yellow fever. The refult of my
refearches for a while was fruitlefs. The accounts
of the fymptoms and cure of the difeafe by the
authors

authors I confulted, were contradictory, and none of them appeared altogether applicable to the prevailing epidemic. Before I defifted from the inquiry to which I had devoted myfelf, I recollected that I had among fome old papers, a manufcript account of the yellow fever as it prevailed in Virginia in the year 1741, which had been put into my hands by Dr Franklin, a fhort time before his death. I had read it formerly, and made extracts from it into my lectures upon that diforder. I now read it a fecond time. I paufed upon every fentence; even words in fome places arrefted and fixed my attention. In reading the hiftory of the method of cure, I was much ftruck with the following paffages.

" It muft be remarked, that this evacuation (meaning by purges) is more neceffary in this, than in moft other fevers. The abdominal vifcera are the parts principally affected in this difeafe, but by this timely evacuation, their feculent corruptible contents are difcharged, before they corrupt and produce any ill effects, and their various emunctories, and fecerning veffels are fet open, fo as to allow a free difcharge of their contents, and confequently a fecurity to the parts themfelves, during the courfe of the difeafe. By this evacuation the very minera of the difeafe, pro-

O 3

ceeding

ceeding from the putrid miafma fermenting with the falivary, bilious, and other inquiline humours of the body, is fometimes eradicated by timely emptying the abdominal vifccra on which it firſt fixes, after which a gentle fweat does as it were nip it in its bud. Where the primæ viæ, but efpecially the ſtomach, is loaded with an offenfive matter, or contracted, and convulfed with the irritation of its ſtimulus, there is no procuring a laudable fweat, till that is removed; after which a neceſſary quantity of fweat breaks *out of its own accord*, thefe parts promoting it when by an abſterging medicine, they are eafed of the burden or ſtimulus which oppreſſes them."

" All thefe acute putrid fevers, ever require fome evacuation to bring them to a perfect crifis, and folution, and that even by ſtools, which muſt be promoted by art, where nature does not do the bufinefs herfelf. On this account an *ill-timed ſcrupuloufnefs about the weaknefs of the body*, is of bad confequence in thefe urging circumftances; for it is that which feems chiefly to make evacuations neceſſary, which nature ever attempts, after the humours are fit to be expelled, but is not able to accomplifh for the moſt part in this difeafe; and I can affirm, that I have given a purge in this cafe, when *the pulfe has been fo low, that it could hardly* be be felt, and the *debility extreme*, yet *both one, and the other* have been *reſtored by it.*"

" This evacuation, muſt be procured by *lenitive chologoque* purges."

Here I pauſed. A new train of ideas ſuddenly broke in upon my mind. I believed the weak and low pulſe which I had obſerved in this fever, to be the effeĉt of debility of the *indireĉt* kind, but the unſuccefsful iſſue of purging, and even of a ſpontaneous diarrhœa, in a patient of Dr Hutchinſon's had led me not only to doubt of, but to dread its effeĉts. My fears from this evacuation were confirmed, by the communications I had received from Dr Stevens. I had been accuſtomed to raiſing a weak and low pulſe in pneumony and apoplexy, by means of blood-letting, but I had attended lefs to the effeĉts of purging in producing this change in the pulſe. Dr Mitchell in a moment diſſipated my ignorance and fears upon this ſubjeĉt. I adopted his theory, and praĉtice, and reſolved to follow them. It remained now only to fix upon a ſuitable purge to anſwer the purpoſe of diſcharging the contents of the bowels. I have before deſcribed the ſtate of the bile in the gall-bladder, and duodenum . in an extraĉt from the hiſtory of a diſſeĉtion made by Dr

O 4 Mitchell.

Mitchell. I fufpected that my want of fuccefs in difcharging this bile, in feveral of the cafes in which I attempted the cure by purging, was owing to the feeblenefs of my purges. I had been in the habit of occafionally purging with calomel in bilious and inflammatory fevers, and had recommended the practice the year before in my lectures, not only from my own experience, but upon the authority of Dr Clark. I had moreover, other precedents for its ufe in the practice of Sir John Pringle, Dr Cleghorn, and Dr Balfour, in difeafes of the fame clafs with the yellow fever. But thefe were not all my vouchers for the fafety, and efficacy of calomel. In my attendance upon the military hofpitals during the late war, I had feen it given combined with jalap in the bilious fever by Dr Thomas Young, a fenior furgeon in the hofpitals. His ufual dofe, was ten grains of each of them. This was given once or twice a day, until it procured large evacuations from the bowels. For a while I remonftrated with the Doctor againft this purge, as being difproportioned to the violence and danger of the fever; but I was foon fatisfied that it was as fafe as cremor tartar, or glauber's falts. It was adopted by feveral of the furgeons of the hofpital, and was univerfally known, and fometimes prefcribed, by the fimple name of *ten* and *ten*. This mode of giving

giving calomel occurred to me in preference to any other. The jalap appeared to be a neceffary addition to it, in order to quicken its paffage through the bowels; for calomel is flow in its operation, more efpecially when it is given in large dofes. I refolved after mature deliberation, to prefcribe this purge. Finding ten grains of jalap infufficient to carry the calomel through the bowels, in the rapid manner I wifhed, I added fifteen grains of the former, to ten of the latter; but even this dofe was flow, and uncertain in its operation. I then iffued three dofes, each confifting of fifteen grains of jalap, and ten of calomel; one to be given every fix hours until they procured four or five large evacuations. The effects of this powder, not only anfwered, but far exceeded my expectations. It perfectly cured four out of the firft five patients to whom I gave it, notwithftanding fome of them were advanced feveral days in the diforder. Mr Richard Spain, a block-maker, in Third-ftreet, took eighty grains of calomel, and rather more of rhubarb and jalap mixed with it, on the two laft days of Auguft, and on the firft day of September. He had paffed twelve hours, before I began to give him this medicine, without a pulfe, and with a cold fweat on all his limbs. His relations had given him over, and one of his neighbours complained to me, of my neglecting

to

to advife them to make immediate preparations
for his funeral. But in this fituation, I did not
defpair of his recovery. Dr Mitchell's account
of the effects of purging in raifing the pulfe, exciting a hope that he might be faved provided his
bowels could be opened. I now committed the
exhibition of the purging medicine to Mr Stall,
one of my pupils, who mixed it, and gave it with
his own hand three or four times a day. At length,
it operated and produced two copious, fœtid
ftools. His pulfe rofe immediately afterwards,
and a univerfal moifture on his fkin, fucceeded
the cold fweat on his limbs. In a few days he
was out of danger, and he now lives in good
health as the firft fruits of the efficacy of mercurial purges in the yellow fever.

After fuch a pledge of the fafety and fuccefs of
my new medicine, I gave it afterwards with confidence. I communicated the prefcription to fuch
of the practitioners as I met in the ftreets. Some
of them I found had been in the ufe of calomel
for feveral days, but as they had given it in fmall
and fingle dofes only, and had followed it by large
dofes of bark, wine, and laudanum, they had
done little or no good with it. I imparted the
prefcription to the College of Phyficians, on the
third of September, and endeavoured to remove
the

the fears of my fellow citizens, by affuring them
that the difeafe was no longer incurable. Mr'
Lewis, the lawyer, Dr M'Ilvaine, Mrs Bethel,
her two fons, and a fervant maid, and Mr Peter
Baynton's whole family, (nine in number) were
fome of the firft trophies of this new remedy.
The credit it acquired, brought me an immenfe
acceffion of bufinefs. It ftill continued to be almoft uniformly effectual in all thofe which I was
able to attend, either in perfon, or by my pupils.
Dr Griffitts, Dr Say, Dr Pennington, and my
former pupils who had fettled in the city, viz.
Dr Leib, Dr Porter, Dr Annan, Dr Woodhoufe,
and Dr Meafe, were among the firft phyficians
who adopted it. I can never forget the tranfport
with which Dr Pennington ran acrofs the ftreet,
to inform me, a few days after he began to give
ftrong purges, that the difeafe, yielded to them in
every cafe. But I did not rely upon purging
alone, to cure the difeafe. The theory of its
proximate caufe, which I had adopted, led me to
ufe other remedies, to abftract excefs of ftimulus
from the fyftem. Thefe were *blood-letting, cool
air, cold drinks, low diet,* and *applications of cold
water* to the body. I had bled Mrs Bradford,
Mrs Leaming, and one of Mrs Palmer's fons with
fuccefs, early in the month of Auguft. But I had
witneffed the bad effects of bleeding in the firft
week

week in September, in two of my patients who
had been bled without my knowledge, and who
appeared to have died in confequence of it. I
had moreover, heard of a man who had been bled
on the firft day of the diforder, who died in twelve
hours afterwards. Thefe cafes produced caution,
but they did not deter me from bleeding as foon
as I found the difeafe to change its type, and inftead of tending to a crifis on the third, to protract
itfelf to a later day. I began by drawing a fmall
quantity at a time. The appearance of the blood,
and its effects upon the fyftem, fatisfied me of its
fafety and efficacy. Never before did I experience fuch fublime joy as I now felt in contemplating the fuccefs of my remedies. It repaid me
for all the toils and ftudies of my life. The con-
queft of this formidable difeafe, was not the effect
of accident, nor of the application of a fingle remedy ; but, it was the triumph of a principle in
medicine. The reader will not wonder at this
joyful ftate of my mind, when I add a fhort extract
from my note book, dated the 10th of September.
" Thank God! Out of one hundred patients,
whom I have vifited, or prefcribed for, this day,
I have loft none."

Being unable to comply with the numerous
demands which were made upon me for the purging

ing powders, notwithftanding I had requefted my fifter, and two other perfons to affift my pupils in putting them up; and finding myfelf unable to attend all the perfons who fent for me, I furnifhed the apothecaries with the recipe for the mercurial purges, together with a copy of the following directions, for giving them, and for the treatment of the diforder.

" As foon as you are affected, (whether by *night* or day) with a pain in the head, or back, ficknefs at ftomach, chills or fever; more efpecially, if thofe fymptoms be accompanied by a rednefs, or faint yellownefs in the eyes, take one of the powders in a little fugar and water, every fix hours, until they produce four or five *large* evacuations from the bowels—drink plentifully of water gruel, or barley water, or chicken water, or any other mild drink that is agreeable, to affift the operation of the phyfic. It will be proper to lie in bed while the medicine is operating; by which means a plentiful fweat will be more eafily brought on. After the bowels are *thoroughly* cleanfed, if the pulfe be *full* or *tenfe*, eight or ten ounces of blood fhould be taken from the arm, and *more*, if the tenfion or fulnefs of the pulfe fhould continue. Balm tea, toaft and water, lemonade, tamarind water, weak camomile tea, or barley water fhould

be

be drank during this state of the disorder—and
the bowels should be kept constantly open, either
by another powder, or by small doses of cremor
tartar, or cooling salts, or by common opening
glysters; but if the pulse should become *weak*
and *low* after the bowels are cleansed, infusions
of camomile and snake-root in water, elixir of vitriol, and laudanum; also wine and water, or
wine, punch, and porter should be given, and the
bark either in infusion in water or in substance,
may be administered in the intermission of the fever. Blisters may likewise be applied to the sides,
neck, or head in this state of the disorder, and
the lower limbs may be wrapped up in flannels
wetted in hot vinegar or water. The food should
consist of gruel, sago, panada, tapioca, tea, coffee,
weak chocolate, wine whey, chicken broth, and
the white meats, according to the weak or active
state of the system. The fruits of the season may
be eaten with advantage at all times. Fresh air
should be admitted into the room in all cases, and
cool air when the pulse is full and tense. The
floor should be sprinkled now and then with vinegar, and the discharges from the body be removed as speedily as possible."

" The best preventives of the disorder, are a
temperate diet, consisting chiefly of vegetables,
great

great moderation in the exercifes of body and mind, warm cloathing, cleanlinefs, and a gently open ftate of the bowels."

Hitherto there had been great harmony among the phyficians of the city, although there was a diverfity of fentiment as to the nature and cure of the prevailing fever. But this diverfity of fentiment and practice, was daily leffening, and would probably have ceafed altogether in a few days, had not the following publication fubfcribed A. K. and faid to be written by Dr Adam Kuhn, made its appearance on the 11th of September, in the General· Advertifer, from which it was copied into all the papers of the city.

" Sir,

PHILADELPHIA, *Sept. 7th,* 1793.

" I RECEIVED your letter to day, and fhall with pleafure give you every information in my power refpecting the malignant fever, which proves fo fatal among us. As I confider debility and putrefaction the alarming circumftances to be attended to, and to be obviated from the earlieft commencement of the difeafe, my method of treatment is inftituted accordingly, and has been generally fuccefsful. I do not adminifter any emetic, neither

do I give a laxative, unlefs indicated by coftivenefs, when I recommend cream of tartar or caftor
oil, but prefer a clyfter to either.   In cafe of naufea I order a few bowls of camomile tea to be
taken ; if the naufea continues, it is to be relieved
with the faline draught in a ftate of effervefcence,
elixir of vitriol, and if neceffary, laudanum.   The
ficknefs of the ftomach may alfo be alleviated by
applying mint, cloves, or any other fpice with
wine or fpirits to the pit of the ftomach.   The
ftomach being compofed, 20 drops of elixir of
vitriol are to be taken every two hours in a tea cup
full of ftrong cold camomile tea, and if bark can
be retained, two drachms of the beft pale bark
in fubftance are to be given every two hours, alternately with the elixir of vitriol.   When an ounce
of bark has been adminiftered in this manner, the
dofe is to be diminifhed to one drachm every two
hours, as the continuance of the large dofes might
diforder the ftomach or bowels.   Should the bark
prove purgative it will be neceffary to give 10 or
15 drops of laudanum after every ftool.   But if
the bark cannot be retained on the ftomach, 20
drops of elixir of vitriol are to be taken every
hour, and recourfe muft be had to bark clyfters.

    " Two ounces of bark are to be put into three
half pints of boiling water, and boiled down to a
                    4   pint ;

pint; the decoction to be strained, and to 4 ounces of the decoction we add from two to four drachms of finely powdered bark and fifty drops of laudanum. This mixture is to be injected every four hours or oftner if the symptoms are violent. One or two glasses of Madeira wine may be added to each injection where the debility is great. Wine is to be given from the beginning; at first the weaker wines such as claret and rhenish; if these. cannot be had, Lisbon or Madeira diluted with rich lemonade. The quantity is to be determined by the effects it produces and by the state of debility which prevails, guarding against its occasioning or encreasing the heat, restlessness and delirium. I prefer pale bark from a conviction that most of the red bark offered for sale, is adulterated. But I place the greated dependance for the cure of the disease, on throwing cool water twice a day over the naked body. The patient is to be placed in a large empty tub, and two ʻbuckets full of water, of the temperature of about 75 or 80 degrees of Fahrenheit's thermometer, according to the state of the atmosphere, are to be thrown over him.

" He is then to be wiped dry and put to bed; it is commonly followed by an easy perspiration and is always attended with great refreshment to the
P   patient.

patient. This remedy however muft be applied from the earlieft attack of the difeafe and continued regularly through the whole courfe of it. Of regimen it is needlefs to fay much to you: ripe fruits, fago with wine, and rich wine-whey are the moft proper. A fpacious chamber with a free circulation of air, and repeatedly changing the bed and body linen are highly neceffary. If the bark clyfters fhould bring on coftivenefs the laudanum may occafionally be omitted; if this is not attended with the defired confequences, we have recourfe to a common injection. Sprinkling the chamber with vinegar, wafhing the face, neck, hands and feet with it, and then wiping them dry, will have their ufe. The fumes of vinegar and of nitre will contribute much to fweeten the air in the chamber.

I am, &c.

A. K.

" N. B. The practice of applying the cold bath in fevers is not new. In a malignant fever which prevailed at Breflau in Silefia and proved extremely fatal, yielded to none of the ufual remedies, Dr De Haehn a phyfician of the place had recourfe to this remedy and found it effectual. It has alfo been ufed with advantage in England in

putrid

putrid fevers. In many of the Weft India iflands it is generally employed in their malignant fevers. Dr Stevens, a gentleman of high character in his profeffion, who is now in this city, affures me that in the ifland of St. Croix where he practifed medicine many years, it has been found more effectual than any method heretofore practifed.

" I am moreover indebted to Dr Stevens for the following obfervations : that laxatives are never employed but when clyfters are not attended with the defired effect of moving the bowels ; that in violent attacks of the difeafe the bark clyfters are repeated every two hours, and the water is applied to the body every 6 or 8 hours and even more frequently ; that when there is a difpofition to diarrhœa, the elixir of vitriol has a tendency to encreafe it, and is therefore laid afide, and that the difeafe which he has feen in this country is of the fame nature with the malignant fever of the Weft Indies."

To obviate the effects of this letter upon the minds of the citizens, I publifhed the next day an account of the ill fuccefs which had attended the ufe of the remedies recommended by Dr Kuhn, in my practice, and of the happy effects of mercurial purges and bleeding. This publication was concluded with the following remarks.

P 2 " The

" The yellow fever now prevailing in our city, differs very materially from that which prevails in the Weft Indies, and in feveral particulars from that of the year 1762. This will eafily be believed, by all thofe who attend to the influence of climate and feafons, upon difeafes. Prefcribing for the *name* of a difeafe, without a due regard to the above circumftances, has flain more than the fword.

" My only defign in withdrawing myfelf for a moment from the folemn duties to my fellow citizens, in which I am now engaged, is to bear a teftimony againft a method of treating the prefent diforder, which if perfifted in, would probably have aided it in defolating three fourths of our city.

" I have had fo many unequivocal proofs of the fuccefs of the fhort and fimple mode which I have adopted, of treating this diforder, that I am now fatisfied, that under more favourable circumftances of attendance upon the fick, the difeafe would yield to the power of medicine with as much certainty as a common intermitting fever.

September 11, }
  1793. }

BENJ. RUSH."

The

The above addrefs to the citizens, produced the following letter from Dr Kuhn to the Mayor of the city.

" Sir,

" I F you are of opinion that the en-clofed ftatement can have the leaft tendency to abate the apprehenfions of the citizens, I beg of you to make any ufe of it you may think proper.

I am, with refpect,

Your moft humble fervant,

September 13, }
1793. }

A. KUHN.

Matthew Clarkfon, Efq. Mayor }
of the city of Philadelphia. }

" FROM the 23d of Auguft, the day on which I faw the firft patient in the yellow fever, to the the third of September, when I was my-felf confined with a remittent fever, I vifited fixty perfons ill of various complaints. The greater part were indifpofed with remittent and inter-mittent fevers, which always prevail among us at this feafon of the year, which all yielded readily to our mode of treating thofe difeafes, except in one gentleman, who had been many years an invalid. Seven only of this num-

P 3

ber

ber had the yellow fever; three of them were patients of other gentlemen of the Faculty. Of thefe feven, I was called to four, in the early ftage of the difeafe. Three of them are now well; the other was in the fourth day of the difeafe, when I became unwell myfelf. He had then no unfavourable fymptoms; but died on the eighth day from the time he was feized."

A day or two afterwards, the following letter appeared in all the newfpapers from Mr Hamilton, the Secretary of the Treafury of United States, to the College of Phyficians.

" GENTLEMEN,

" MOTIVES of humanity and friendfhip to the citizens of Philadelphia, induce me to addrefs to you this letter, in the hope that it may be in fome degree inftrumental in diminifh-ing the prefent prevailing calamity. It is natural to be afflicted not only at the mortality which is faid to obtain, but at the confequences of that undue panic which is faft depopulating the city, and fufpending bufinefs both public and private.

I have myfelf been attacked with the reigning putrid fever, and with violence—but I truft that I am now completely out of danger. This I

am

am to attribute, under God, to the ſkill and care of my friend Doƈtor Stevens, a gentleman lately from the iſland of St. Croix, one to whoſe talents I can atteſt, from an intimate acquaintance began in early youth, whoſe medical opportunities have been of the beſt, and who has had the advantage of much experience both in Europe (having been in Edinburgh ſome years ſince, when the ſame fever raged there) and in the Weſt Indies, where it is frequent. His mode of treating the diſorder varies eſſentially from that which has been generally practiſed—And I am perſuaded, where purſued, reduces it to one of little more than ordinary hazard.

I know him ſo well, that I entertain no doubt, that he will freely impart his ideas to you, collectively or individually; and being in my own perſon a witneſs to the efficacy of his plan, I venture to believe, that if adopted, and if the courage of the citizens can be rouſed, many lives will be ſaved, and much ill prevented. I may add, that as far as can be yet pronounced, its efficacy has been alike proved on Mrs Hamilton, who is now in the diſorder, contracted from me, with every favourable appearance.

In

In giving you this information, Gentlemen, I have done what I thought difcharging a duty. I qnly add, that if any conference with Dr Stevens, is defired, that he is going to-morrow to New-York, from which journey he has been detained feveral days on my account.

I am, Gentlemen, with refpeƈt,

your obedient fervant,

September, 11.

A. HAMILTON.

" He lodges at Mrs Williams's, corner of Spruce and Third ftreets.

" *College of Phyficians.*"

This letter was followed by a letter from Dr Stephens to Dr Redman, the prefident of the College of Phyficians, which was publifhed in the Federal Gazette of the 16th of September,

" Sir,

" In compliance with the requeft of the learned body over whom you prefide, I now chearfully tranfmit them a few brief and detached obfervations on the nature and treatment of the prefent

prefent malignant and fatal diforder which prevails in this city. Their humane anxiety to afcertain the real character of the complaint, and
to eftablifh fome fixed and fteady mode of cure
for it, are frefh proofs of their benevolence, and
clearly evinces that difinterefted liberality for
which they are fo eminently diftinguifhed. I
only regret that their application to me has approached fo near the moment of my departure,
that I have not fufficient leifure to elucidate the
fubject fo amply and fo fatisfactorily as the importance of it deferves. Imperfect, however, as the
enclofed fketch may be, I can with truth affure
them, that it is the refult of extenfive experience
and accurate obfervation ; and that it is dictated
folely by a philanthropic defire of checking the
ravages of difeafe, and of reftoring tranquillity to
the dejected minds of the public.

" This diforder arifes from contagion. Its approaches are flow and infiduous at the commencement. It is ufhered in with a flight degree of languor and laffitude, lofs of appetite, reftleffnefs and
difturbed dreams, depreffion of fpirits, and a want
of inclination to perform the ordinary occupations
of life. The patient does not confider himfelf fufficiently fick to complain or call in the affiftance
of a phyfician. His feelings are rather unplea-
fant

fant than alarming. This train of fymptoms continue for two or three days, and if not removed
by timely aid, is fucceeded by a fharp pain in the
head, anxiety, and fuppreffion about the præcordia, a feeble pulfe, great proftration of ftrength,
and a variety of other morbid phenomena, which
are too well known to the faculty to need defcription. In the firft ftage of the diforder, a little attention, and the well directed efforts of a fkilful
practitioner, may generally prove fuccefsful in mitigating the violence of future fymptoms, and preventing either much danger or long confinement.

" At the firft appearance of languor, laffitude,
&c. efpecially if the patient has been near the
fource of contagion, he fhould carefully avoid all
fatigue of body and application of mind. Every
thing that can tend to debilitate fhould be carefully guarded againft. He fhould remain at perfect reft. His diet fhould be fuller and more cordial than ufual, and a few extraordinary glaffes of
old Madeira may be allowed. He fhould take
the cold bath every morning; and if his fleep is
difturbed, a gentle opiate combined with a few
grains of the volatile falts and fome grateful aromatic may be adminiftered at night. A few dofes
of good genuine bark may be taken in powder
during the day; and if the ftomach fhould be affected

fected with naufea, a ftrong decoction of the fame may be fubftituted. Great care fhould be taken to keep the mind of the patient calm and ferene, —neither to terrify it with needlefs apprehenfion, nor alarm it by the melancholy relation of the fpreading mortality which furrounds him. It is at this ftage of the complaint, that the phyfician may lay the foundation of future fuccefs. But unfortunately, it is alfo the period of the difeafe which is commonly too much neglected by the patient. Gentlemen of the faculty are rarely called in until the fymptoms are more alarming and dangerous. But it is a matter of material confequence to the patient to know that by a little attention at the commencement, and by carefully watching the approaches of the difeafe even tho' it fhould be contracted, it may be rendered mild, and may terminate favourably. It is alfo of equal confequence for practitioners to attend to thefe particulars in laying down the prophylaxis to their patients.

" When the diforder has gained ground and become violent and when the danger is imminent, the moft unremitted exertions fhould be made by the phyfician to mitigate the fymptoms. The naufea and vomiting may be relieved by an infufion of camomile flowers, given frequently until the ftomach

is

is fufficiently emptied of all crude matter. Small
dofes of a cordial mixture compofed of the oil of
peppermint and compound fpirits of lavender, may
then be taken until the fever abates. If, notwithftanding, the irritability of the ftomach fhould ftill
continue, recourfe muft be inftantly had to the
cold bath, which muft be ufed every two hours
or oftener if the urgency of the fymptoms fhould
require it. After each immerfion a glafs of old
Madeira, or a little brandy burnt with cinnamon,
may be adminiftered. Flannel cloths wrung out
of fpirits of wine, impregnated with fpices, may
be applied to the pit of the ftomach, and changed
frequently.

" An injeftion containing an ounce of powdered bark, mixed with thin falap or fago, to which
a tea-fpoon full of laudanum has been added,
fhould be adminiftered. Thefe injeftions may be
continued every two or three hours, omitting the
laudanum after the firft. As foon as the ftomach
can bear the medicines and nourifhment, the bark
may be adminiftered in fmall dofes ; as much Madeira wine may be given as the patient can bear
without affecting his head, or heating him too
much. All emetics and violent cathartics fhould
· be avoided. If the bowels fhould not be fufficiently open, a laxative clyfter may be neceffary,

or

or a few grains of powdered rhubarb added to each dose of bark until the defired effect is produced. If diarrhœa fhould prevail, it muft be checked by ftarch injections blended with laudanum by the tinctura E. kino japonica, or a decoction of carcarilla. All draftic cathartics do injury when the difeafe is in its advanced ftage. If ftupor, coma, or delirium fhould come on, a large blifter fhould be applied between the fhoulders, and fmall ones to the thighs; ftimulant cataplafms fhould alfo be applied to to the foles of the feet: when hemorrhagies appear, the elixir of vitriol may be adminiftered in conjunction with the bark, but great care fhould be taken to prevent it from affecting the bowels.

" If the pulfe fhould be much funk, the proftration of ftrength great, and fubfultus tendinum take place, fmall dofes of the liquor mineralis Hoffmanni, or even vitriolic æther diluted with water may be given. Mufk and camphor in this ftage of the difeafe have likewife proved effectual. Upon the whole, fir, I may fum up this hafty outline, by inculcating the ufe of the tonic plan in its fulleft extent, and by warning againft the ill confequences of debilitating applications, or profufe evacuations in every period of the difeafe: the cold bath, bark and wine, a fpacious well ventilated

ted room, frequent change of bed and body linen, and attention to reft and quiet, if properly perfevered in, will in moft cafes prove fuccefsful, and ftrip this formidable difeafe of its malignity, its terror, and its danger.

" The defcription I have given of this diforder, and the utility of the plan of cure I have laid down, are confirmed by experience and coincides with our reafon and the foundeft theory; the caufe producing the effeft is a ftrong debilitating power; the fymptoms occafioned by its application, indicate extreme debility in the animal functions, and great derangement of the nervous fyftem: ought not therefore the remedies adapted to this complaint to be cordial, ftimulating, and tonic? Should not violent evacuations, which evidently weaken and relax, be avoided? Thefe are hints which it would be prefumptuous and affuming in me to extend or dwell upon: to gentlemen of fuch eminence as your colleagues, it is fufficient to point out what reafon and experience conjointly fuggeft to me. Their fuperior judgment will, I am convinced, fupply every deficiency, and enable them to purfue that plan which is beft adapted to public utility, and the effeftual removal of the prefent dreadful malady. If the few obfervations I have fuggefted be ferviceable to

the

the inhabitants of this city, my intentions will be fully anfwered, and my feelings completely gratified.

I have the honour to be, Sir,

Sept. 16*th*,}
1793. }   Your moft obedient fervant,

EDWARD STEVENS.

John Redman, M. D. prefident}
of the College of Phyficians. }

An effay upon the theory of this difeafe at this juncture, would have been as ill-timed as a difcourfe upon tactics would be to an army in the height of a battle; but Dr Stevens's publication made it neceffary for me to appeal to the *reafon* of my brethren upon the theory of the difeafe. I did it in a few words in the following addrefs to the College of Phyficians.

" Gentlemen,

" It is with extreme regret that I have read Dr Stevens's letter to the prefident of our College in one of the news-papers. It will,

4   I fear,

I fear, co-operate with Dr Kuhn's plan of treating the diforder, and Mr Hamilton's well-meant
letter, in adding to the mortality of the diforder.
If I fhould furvive my prefent labours, I hope to
prove that Dr Stevens's theory of the difeafe in
the Weft Indies, is as erroneous, as the practice
he has recommended has been fatal, in Philadelphia.   It is a moft inflammatory diforder in its
firft ftage.   The contagion, it is true, in its firft
action upon the fyftem, frequently produces debility ; but the debility here is of the *indirect* kind,
and arifes wholly from an excefs of the ftimulus of
contagion upon the fyftem.   This indirect debility,
as in many other difeafes, yields only to the abftraction of other ftimuli, and to none fo fpeedily
as to large evacuations from the bowels and the
blood-veffels.

" I have fo high an opinion of Dr Stevens's
candor and liberality as a gentleman and a phyfician, that I fhall make no apology for thus publicly diffenting from his opinions and practice.

" Could patients be vifited by phyficians as often, and attended by nurfes as carefully, as in
other acute difeafes, I am fatisfied that the mode
of treating it which I have adopted and recommended,

mended, would foon reduce it in point of danger and mortality, to a level with a common cold.

From, Gentlemen,

Sept. 17*th*, }
1793. }

Your fincere friend and brother,

B. RUSH."

During this controverfy with the opinions and practice of Dr Kuhn and Dr Stevens, I publifhed in the Federal Gazette, the following letter to the College of Phyficians; alfo fome additions to the directions I had publifhed with the mercurial purges.

" GENTLEMEN,

" As the weekly meetings of our College have become no longer practicable, I have taken the liberty of communicating to you, the refult of further obfervations upon the prevailing epidemic.

" I have found bleeding to be ufeful, not only in cafes where the pulfe was full and quick, but where it was *flow* and *tenfe*. I have bled in one cafe, where the pulfe beat only 48 ftrokes in a minute, and recovered my patient by it. The pulfe became more full and more frequent after it.

Q

it. This ſtate of the pulſe ſeems to ariſe from an inflamed ſtate of the brain, which ſhows itſelf in a preternatural dilatation of the pupils of the eyes. It is always unſafe to truſt to the moſt perfect re-miſſions of fever and pain in this ſtate of the pulſe. It indicates the neceſſity of more bleeding and purging. I have found it to occur moſt fre-quently in children.

" I have bled twice in many, and in one acute caſe, four times, with the happieſt effects. I con-ſider intrepidity in the uſe of the lancet at preſent to be as neceſſary, as it is in the uſe of mercury and jalap, in this inſidious and ferocious diſeaſe.

" I lament the contrariety of opinion among the members of our College, upon the remedies proper in this diſeaſe. This contrariety ſeems to ariſe from the yellow fever being confounded with the jail or hoſpital fever. The fevers of Breſlau, Vienna, and Edinburgh, mentioned in ſome late publications, in which the cold bath was uſed with ſo much ſucceſs, were of the latter kind. The two diſeaſes are totally different from each other in their cauſe, ſeaſons of prevailing, ſymptoms, danger, and method of cure.

From, Gentlemen,

" *Sept.* 12*th*,⎱
   1793. ⎰

Your friend and brother,

BENJ. RUSH."

FEDERAL GAZETTE.

" Dr Ruſh regrets, that he is unable to com‑
ply with all the calls of his fellow citizens, who
are indiſpoſed with the prevailing fever. He begs
leave to recommend to ſuch of them as cannot
have the benefit of medical aid, to take the mercurial purges, which may now be had with ſuitable directions at moſt of the apothecaries, and to
loſe ten or twelve ounces of blood as ſoon as is
convenient after taking the purges, if the head‑
ach and fever continue. Where the purges cannot be obtained, or do not operate ſpeedily,
bleeding may *now* be uſed before they are taken.
The almoſt univerſal ſucceſs with which it hath
pleaſed God to bleſs the remedies of ſtrong mercurial purges and bleeding in this diſorder, enables Dr Ruſh to aſſure his fellow citizens, that
there is no more danger to be apprehended from
it, when thoſe remedies are uſed in its early ſtage,
than there is from the meaſles or the influenza.

" Dr Ruſh aſſures his fellow citizens further,
that the riſk from viſiting and attending the ſick,
in common caſes, at preſent, is not greater than
from walking the ſtreets. He hopes this information will be attended to, as many of the ſick ſuffer
greatly from the want of the aſſiſtance of bleeders,
and of the attendance of nurſes and friends.

" While

" While the difeafe was fo generally mortal, or
the fuccefsful mode of treating it only partially
adopted, Dr Rufh advifed his friends to leave
the city : at prefent he conceives this advice to
be unneceffary ; not only becaufe the difeafe is
now under the power of medicine, but becaufe
the citizens who now wifh to fly into the country,
cannot avoid carrying the infection with them.
They had better remain near to medical aid, and
avoid exciting the infection into action, which is
now in their bodies, by a ftrict attention to former
directions.

" Dr R. does not believe it will be prudent for
thofe perfons who are in the country to return to
town, until after *froft* or *heavy rains* have taken
place ; both of which alike weaken or deftroy the
contagion of the yellow fever.

" *September* 12*th*, 1793."

Having mentioned the conditional ufe of bark,
wine, and laudanum, in my firft publication, and
finding them not only ufelefs, but hurtful, I publifhed the following addrefs to the citizens of Philadelphia, on the 16th of September. In this
addrefs I repeated my advice to live upon a milk
and vegetable diet.

" Dr

" Dr Rush recommends to all such of his fellow citizens as are expofed to the contagion of the prevailing fever, to live upon a milk and vegetable diet, and take cooling purges once or twice a week. The effects of this regimen in rendering the difeafe mild (where it is taken) are nearly the fame as in preparing the body for the fmall-pox.

" Dr R. advifes thofe perfons who cannot obtain the attendance of a phyfician, by no means to take vomits, bark, wine, or laudanum, during the firft three or four days of the diforder. As the difeafe is highly inflammatory at prefent in its firft ftages, the only proper remedies for it are, ftrong purges, copious bleeding, if the pulfe be *full* or *tenfe*, or if it be *flower* than natural, and at the fame time fubject to paufes in its pulfation.

" During this inflammatory ftate of the difeafe, the drinks fhould be fimple and cold. No animal food fhould be tafted ; cool air fhould be admitted into the room, and napkins dipped in pump water, fhould be applied frequently to the forehead,

Q 3

" Dr

" Dr R. recommends further, that the beds and clothes of perfons who have had the difeafe, fhould, *upon no account*, be expofed to the heat of the fun, but be wafhed in warm, or foaked in cold water.

" It would be an act of great humanity to the city, to provide all the phyficians and bleeders, with horfes and chairs, as it will be impoffible for them long to efcape the difeafe, while they are fo much pre-difpofed to it by conftant fatigue."

" *September* 16*th*, 1793."

I fhall mention hereafter the fubftitutes I ufed for the tonic remedies which I had thus publicly decried.

On the 20th of September the following pub-lication appeared in the Federal Gazette, fub-fcribed by Dr Currie.

" Mr BROWN,

" IT affords me particular fatisfac-tion, that I now have it in my power to inform my fellow citizens, that the progrefs of the infec-tious fever has greatly abated, and that with a
little

little longer perfeverance in avoiding intercourfe with the infeſted, as far as humanity will permit, paying at the fame time, proper attention to fumigating and ventilating the houfes, clothing, and utenfils from whence the fick have been removed, or where they have been confined, the infeſtion which has proved fo mortal, will moſt certainly, be entirely eradicated in a few days. The beſt method for effeſting this, is contained in a late publication by the learned Dr Ruſſel.

" I have made the ſtriſteſt enquiry refpeſting the number at prefent confined by the genuine yellow fever, and am convinced that it does not exceed 40 or 50 in the whole city.

" There is, however, another formidable difeafe prevalent, by which, I have reafon to believe, there are above a thoufand ill at this time.

" The difeafe I mean, is the common remittent or fall fever. This fever, however, is not infeſtious.

" When the remitting fever attacks perfons not fully recovered from the effeſts of the influenza, (which is alfo ſtill prevalent here) it occafions a violent determination of the blood to the head,

Q 4   accompanied

accompanied with acute pain, a rednefs of the eyes, with a faint tinge of yellow—the pulfe is quick and the fkin hot. This is the difeafe which is fo much under the power of blood-letting and purging ; and is as different from the infectious, or genuine yellow fever, as the fun is from the moon, or light from darknefs.

" In the fall fever, which fucceeds the influenza, the eye is fprightly, though red, the face turgid and flufhed :—Whereas, in the genuine yellow fever, the eye is dull and inanimate, and fuffufed with a dufky brown, the face pale, fhrunk, and cadaverous, almoft from the firft attack. It is in the remitting fever, with the violent affection of the head, that the mode of treatment advifed by Dr Rufh, can only be proper ; and not in the in-fectious or yellow fever. On the contrary, in the yellow fever, it cannot fail of being certain death. In the yellow fever, the means recom-mended by Dr Kuhn and Dr Stevens, are the moft effectual, and the only ones that can be relied on, with fuch a variation as circumftances, and the period of the difeafe may indicate.

" It is in the fall fever, circumftanced as already defcribed, that there is fafety in vifiting and at-tending the fick, becaufe this fever is not conta-ragious.

gious. Can there be the fame fafety in vifiting patients confined with the genuine yellow fever, which made its appearance in Water-ftreet, the third of Auguft laft? Let thofe judge who have had opportunities of feeing its ravages! Is that fever, in which the bond of union is immediately diffolved between the folids and fluids, and where the purple current iffues from every pore, the fame as that, for which Dr Rufh directs bleeding and purging? and can there be fafety in vifiting perfons fo affected? Have we all got the contagion of the yellow fever in our bodies, only waiting for fome exciting caufe to put it into action? By no means. The difeafe, which Dr Rufh calls the yellow fever, and of which Dr P. fays he has cured fuch numbers by the *new method*, is only the fall fever, operating on perfons who have been previoufly affected by the influenza.

" It is time the veil fhould be withdrawn from your eyes, my fellow citizens!

Wm. CURRIE."

" *Sept.* 17*th*, 1793."

To this, I publifhed the following anfwer the next day.

" Dr

" Dr Rufh is extremely forry to differ from
his friend Dr Currie, in his opinion refpecting the
prevailing epidemic, publifhed in the Federal Gazette of laft evening.   Dr R. afferts, from the authority of Dr Sydenham, as well as from the
obfervations of three and thirty years upon epidemic difeafes, that no two epidemics of *unequal*
force can exift long together in the fame place ;
and he is fure, from what he has feen of the prefent difeafe, that all the fevers now in the city, •
are from *one* caufe, and that they all require different portions of the fame remedies.   Dr R. has
no other motives for wifhing to be believed by
his fellow citizens in thefe affertions, than to beget
a confidence in them, in remedies, which he conceives to be as rational, as he knows them to be
fuccefsful in the prevailing diforder.   If Dr Currie will confult Blane, Hume, Lining, and Hillary,
upon the fubject of the yellow fever, he will find
that they all defcribe it as making its firft attack
with the fymptoms of a bilious remittent.   Dr
R. perfectly recollects its appearing not only in
this form, but in that of an intermittent, in the
year 1762.

" Among many arguments which might be adduced to prove that all our prefent fevers arife
from one fource, and require the fame treatment,
(varied

(varied according to their degrees of violence) Dr R. will mention only one, and that is, he has cured many perfons by plentiful purging and bleeding, of the prefent epidemic, who have lived in families, in which perfons had died with a black vomiting, and a yellow ſkin.

" No one can fuppofe that Dr. R's late indif-poſition (after having been conſtantly expofed for three weeks, to the contagion of the yellow fever in all its degrees of malignity) was not occaſioned by an attack of that diforder, and yet he owes his perfeſt recovery through divine goodnefs, fim-ply to two copious bleedings, and two dofes of the mercurial medicine, and that too, in the ſhort term of only *two* days.

" *September* 18*th*, 1793."

Befides the publications I have mentioned, Dr Wiſtar addreſſed a hiſtory of an attack he had of the fever, to the phyſicians of Philadelphia, in the General Advertifer of the 26th of September. He began it by obferving, that " he be-lieved many perfons had been fuppofed to have been cured of the difeafe, who had never had it," and he concluded without deciding upon any of the remedies which were the fubjeſts of con-troverfy. He added a ſtrong teſtimony from his

own

own experience of the efficacy of cool air in abating the exceffive action of the arterial fyftem.

I pafs over many anonymous effays upon the fever, which appeared in the newfpapers; alfo feveral, from medical gentlemen who beheld the difeafe at a diftance. They all tended more or lefs to diftract the public mind, and to leffen the confidence of the citizens in the fimple, and powerful remedies which I had recommended.

In fupport of the efficacy of thefe remedies, Dr Porter, Dr Annan, and Dr Meafe, gave very decided teftimonies in the public papers. I fhall infert as an epitome of them all, the following letter from Dr Porter.

" DEAR SIR,

" A S I know it will afford you much pleafure, I fend you the following ftatement of cafes. Within three days paft I have been called to thirty feven perfons labouring under the prevailing epidemic. I have treated them all in the new method, with the greateft fuccefs; nearly half of them are fo far recovered as to require no farther affiftance from me. I cannot avoid mentioning one cafe of a man in whom the advantages

of

of bleeding were remarkable.—The pain in his head was fo violent as to lead me to order bleeding, previous to purging—from fome inaccuracy in the operation, he loft a greater quantity than I directed, his attendants fuppofe fixteen ounces; the confequence however was, that at my next vifit found that my patient had walked out perf fully recovered. This cafe was clearly marked with all the fymptoms attendant on the difeafe in it's firft ftages, particularly pain in the head and rednefs in the eyes.

With great regard,

I am your

Obedient fervant,

September 17.

JOHN PORTER."

" *Dr Rufh.*"

The *fafety* of the new remedies (as they were fometimes called) was finally admitted by their greateft enemies, but their *efficacy* was fuppofed to be confined only to common remittents, to the influenza, or to pleurifies, and other inflammatory fevers; for thofe difeafes were believed to be conftantly prefent in the city; and the certificates which were publifhed of large families having been cured of the yellow fever by the new remedies,

dies, were difcredited, or treated with contempt, becaufe the patients had recovered without a *yellow colour* in their faces.

To refute this error, as well as to fhew that I was not fingular in my opinions refpecting bloodletting, purges, and opium, I publifhed the following extracts from Dr Mofely, in the Federal Gazette of the 11th of October.

" MR BROWN,

        " A NUMBER of the phyficians of this city, who fuppofe that we have two fevers now prevailing among us, have afferted that a yellow colour is effential to what is called the yellow fever. The following extract from Dr Mofely will fhew how much they have been miftaken. This judicious phyfician practifed phyfic many years in Jamaica, and faw the fever which he defcribes, in all its different forms.

        " I have ufed (fays the Doctor) the word *yellow* in compliance with cuftom; but I even diftruft that name, as the *inexperienced* may be looking out for that appearance, and not find, until it is *too late*, the difeafe he has to contend with. And indeed, the yellownefs of the fkin, like the black vomiting,

vomiting, is not an invariable fymptom of this fever. Thofe who are *fortunate enough* to recover, feldom have it; and many die without its appearance. Befides, the yellownefs alone, leads to nothing certain; it may arife from an inoffenfive fuffufion of bile." p. 411—fecond edition.

The prefent epidemic has likewife been called a putrid fever and the remedies for the cure of that fpecies of fever have been very generally prefcribed. The following extract from the fame author will fhow the error and mifchief of that opinion and practice:

" This difeafe is in the higheft degree poffible, an inflammatory one, accompanied with fuch fymptoms, in a greater extent as attend all inflammatory fevers, and moft ftrikingly the reverfe of any difeafe that is putrid, or of one *continued exacerbation*. It attacks all fuch people and under fuch circumftances as are feldom the objects of putrid difeafes." p. 412.

" In another place he fays, " Bleeding muft be performed, and repeated every fix or eight hours, or whenever the exacerbations come on, while the heat, fullnefs of pulfe, and pains continue;

tinue; and if thefe fymptoms be violent and obftinate, and do not abate during the firft 36 or 48
hours of the fever, bleeding fhould be executed
even to fainting. Taking away only fix or eight
ounces of blood becaufe the patient may be faint,
which is a fymptom of the difeafe, is doing nothing towards the cure. Where bleeding is improper, no blood fhould be taken away; where
it is proper that quantity will not relieve, and it is
lofing that time, which can never be regained."
p. 427—428.

" On PURGES, the doƈtor makes the following
remarks.,

" When a fufficient quantity of blood has been
taken away, (which is *never* done) let the patient's
habit be what it may, while the heat, reiterated
exacerbations, flufhings in the face, thirft, pains
in the head, and burning in the eyes remain, the
next ftep is to evacuate the contents of the bowels, and turn the humours downwards." p. 435.

" Speaking of opium, the Doƈtor fays, " In a
fever fo highly inflammatory, where the contents
of the whole alimentary canal are fo hot and acrid,
opium muft be a fatal medicine." p. 459.

" To

" To thefe quotations I fhall only add, that the difeafe, from the influence of the cool weather is probably more univerfally, and more highly inflammatory, in our city, and requires more copious evacuations than in the Ifland of Jamaica. It certainly requires more fpeedy and more plentiful bleeding than a common pleurify, inafmuch as the blood-veffels, rendered weak by the previous hot fummer, are in more danger of being ruptured both externally and internally, from the violent ftimulus of the contagion, than in an inflammatory fever, which fucceeds cold weather.

" *October* 9, 1793."   BENJ. RUSH."

In juftice to Dr Currie, I take great pleafure in inferting the following fhort addrefs to the citizens, in which he retracts the opinion he had given to the public in the Federal Gazette of the the 20th of September.

" *October* 2d, 1793.

" A L L the phyficians engaged in practice at prefent in the city, agree with Dr Rufh that blood-letting and copious purging are requifite in the cure of the prevailing epidemic, in every

R   cafe

cafe, where inflammatory fymptoms are evident, and that the difpute hitherto has been about the name of the difeafe, rather than the proper mode of treatment.

W. CURRIE."

The conclufion of the above addrefs was unfortunately erroneous. The difpute between the phyficians turned upon more interefting points than the name of the difeafe, as muft be very obvious from the perufal of the preceding pages.

I have fupprefled a letter to Dr John Rodgers of New York, dated the third of October, containing a fhort hiftory of the treatment of the difeafe, only becaufe it will be detailed more fully in this work. That publication was intended as an anfwer to many letters which I received from practitioners in the country, requefting an account of my mode of treating the diforder. I have likewife fupprefled a fecond letter to Dr Rodgers, containing fome extracts from Dr Sydenham, which were intended to eftablifh the exclufive influence of powerful epidemics over inferior febrile difeafes. This fubject has been difcufled in a more ample manner in the hiftory of the fever.

From

From the different publications which I have inferted, it appears that there were two modes of practice purfued; the one dictated by an opinion that the difeafe was highly putrid, and the other, that it was of a highly inflammatory nature. But befides thefe there were two other modes of treating the difeafe, the one by *moderate* purging with calomel only, and moderate bleeding, on the firft or fecond day of the fever, and afterwards by the copious ufe of bark, wine, laudanum, and aromatic tonics. This practice was fupported by an opinion, that the fever was inflammatory in its firft, and putrid in its fecond ftage; the other mode referred to, was peculiar to the French phyficians, feveral of whom had arrived in the city from the Weft Indies juft before the diforder made its appearance. Their remedies were various. Some of them prefcribed nitre, cremor tartar, camphor, centaury tea, the warm bath, glyfters, and moderate bleeding, while a few, ufed lenient purges, and large quantities of tamarind water, and other diluting drinks. The diffentions of the American phyficians threw a great number of patients into the hands of thefe French phyficians. They were moreover fuppofed to be better acquainted with the difeafe than the phyficians of the city, moft of whom it was well known had never feen it before.

R 2   I fhall

I fhall hereafter inquire into the relative fuccefs of each of the four modes of practice which have been mentioned.

Having delivered a general account of the remedies which I ufed in this diforder, I fhall now proceed to make a few remarks upon each of them. I fhall afterwards mention the effects of the remedies ufed by other phyficians.

OF PURGING.

I HAVE already mentioned my reafons for promoting this evacuation, and the medicine I preferred for that purpofe. It had many advantages over any other purge. It was detergent to the bile and mucus which lined the bowels. It probably acted in a peculiar manner upon the biliary ducts, and it was rapid in its operation. One dofe was fometimes fufficient to open the bowels; but from two to fix dofes were often neceffary for that purpofe; more efpecially as part of them was frequently rejected by the ftomach. I did not obferve any inconvenience from the vomiting which was excited by the jalap.

It

It was always without that ftraining which is produced by emetics ; and it ferved to difcharge bile
when it was lodged in the ftomach. I did not
reft the difcharge of the contents of the bowels on
the iffue of one cleanfing on the firft day, There
is in all bilious fevers, a reproduction of morbid
bile as faft as it is difcharged. I therefore gave a
purge every day while the fever continued. I
ufed caftor oil, falts, cremor tartar, and rhubarb
(after the mercurial purges had performed their
office) according to the inclinations of my patients, in all thofe cafes where the bowels were eafily moved ; but where this was not the cafe, I
gave a fingle dofe of calomel and jalap every day.
Strong as this purge may be fuppofed to be, it
was often ineffectual ; more efpecially after the
20th of September, when the bowels became
more obftinately conftipated. To fupply the place
of the jalap, I now added gamboge to the calomel. Two grains and an half of each made into
a pill, were given to an adult every fix hours until
they procured four or five ftools. I had other de-
figns in giving a purge every day befides difcharging
the re-accumulated bile. I had obferved the fever
to fall with its principal force upon fuch parts of
the body as had been previoufly weakened by any
former difeafe. By creating an artificial weak
part in the bowels, I diverted the force of the fe-

ver

ver to them, and thereby faved the liver and brain
from fatal or dangerous congeftions. The practice was further juftified by the beneficial effects
of a plentiful fpontaneous diarrhœa in the beginning of the diforder*; by hemorrhagies from the
bowels, when they occurred from no other parts
of the body, and by the difficulty or impracticability of reducing the fyftem by means of plentiful fweats. The purges feldom anfwered the intentions for which they were given, unlefs they
produced four or five ftools a day. As the fever
fhewed no regard to day or night in the hours of
its exacerbations, it became neceffary to obferve
the fame difregard to time in the exhibition of
▴ purges ; I therefore prefcribed them in the evening at all times when the patient had paffed a day
without two or three plentiful ftools. When
purges were rejected, or flow in their operation,
I always directed opening glyfters to be given

* In fome fhort manufcript notes upon Dr Mitchell's
account of the yellow fever in Virginia, in the year 1741,
made by the late Dr Kearíley, Sen. of this city, he remarks,
that in the yellow fever which prevailed in the fame year in
Philadelphia "fome recovered by an *early* difcharge of *black*
matter by ftool." This gentleman, Dr Redman informed
me, introduced purging with Glauber falts in the yellow
fever in our city. He was preceptor to Dr Redman in
medicine.

every

every two hours. The effects of purging were as follow:

1. It raifed'the pulfe when low, and reduced it when it was preternaturally tenfe or full.

2. It revived and ftrengthened the patient. This was evident in many cafes, in the facility with which patients who had ftaggered to a clofe-ftool, walked back again to their beds, after a co-pious evacuation. Dr Sydenham takes notice of a fimilar encreafe of ftrength after a plentiful fweat in the plague. They both acted by ab-ftracting excefs of ftimulus, and thereby removing indirect debility.

3. It abated the paroxifm of the fever. Hence arofe the advantage of giving a purge in fome cafes in the evening, when an attack of the fever was expected in the courfe of the night.

4. It frequently produced fweats when given on the firft or fecond day of the fever, after the moft powerful fudorifics had been taken to no purpofe.

5. It fometimes checked that vomiting which oc-curs in the beginning of the diforder; and it al-ways affifted in preventing the more alarming occur-rence of that fymptom, about the 4th or 5th day.

R 4 6. It

6. It removed obftrutions in the lymphatic fyftem. I afcribe it wholly to the action of mercury, that in no inftance did any of the glandular
fwellings, which I formerly mentioned, terminate
in a fuppuration.

7. By difcharging the bile through the bowels
as foon and as faft as it was fecreted, it prevented
in moft cafes a yellownefs of the fkin.

However falutary the mercurial purge was, objections were made to it by many of our phyficians; and prejudices, equally weak and ill-found-
ed, were excited againft it.   I fhall enumerate
and anfwer thofe objections.

1. It was faid to be of too draftic a nature.   It
was compared to arfenic; and it was called a dofe
for a horfe. This objection was without foundation.   Hundreds who took it declared they had
never taken fo mild a purge.   I met with but one
cafe in which it produced bloody ftools; but I
faw the fame effect from a dofe of falts.   It fometimes, it is true, operated from twenty to thirty
times in the courfe of twenty-four hours; but I
heard of an equal number of ftools in two cafes
from falts and cremor tartar.   It is not an eafy
thing to affect life, or even fubfequent health, by
                                                    copious

copious or frequent purging. Dr Kirkland mentions a remarkable cafe of a gentleman who was cured of a rheumatifm by a purge, which gave him between 40 and 50 ftools. This patient had been previoufly affected by his diforder 16 or 18 weeks *. Dr Mofely not only proves the fafety, but eftablifhes the efficacy of numerous and copious ftools in the yellow fever. Dr Say probably owes his life to three-and-twenty ftools procured by a dofe of calomel and gamboge, taken by my advice. Dr Redman was purged until he fainted, by a dofe of the fame medicine. This venerable gentleman, in whom 70 years had not abated the ardour of humanity, nor produced obftinacy of opinion, came forward from his retirement, and boldly adopted the remedies of purging and bleeding, with fuccefs in feveral families, before he was attacked by the difeafe. His recovery was as rapid, as the medicine he had ufed was active in its operation. Befides taking the above purge, he loft twenty ounces of blood by two bleedings †.

* Treatife on the Inflammatory Rheumatifm, vol. i. p. 407.

† Dr Redman was not the only inftance furnifhed by the diforder, in which *reafon* got the better of the habits of old age, and of the formalities of medicine. About the time the fever declined, I received a letter from Dr Shippen, Sen. (then above 82 years of age) dated Oxford Furnace, New

But who can fuppofe that a dozen or twenty
ftools in a day could endanger life, that has feen
a diarrhœa continue for feveral months, attended
with fifteen or twenty ftools every day, without
making even a material breach in the conftitution?
Hence Dr Hillary has juftly remarked, that " it
rarely or never happens that the purging in this
difeafe, though violent, takes the patient off, but
the fever and inflammation of the bowels *. Dr
Clark in like manner remarks, that evacuations do
not deftroy life in the dyfentery, but the fever with
the emaciation or mortification which attend and
follow the difeafe †.

New Jerfey, October 13th, 1793, in which, after approving
in polite terms of my mode of practice, he adds " Defperate
difeafes require defperate remedies. I would only propofe
fome fmall addition to your prefent method. Suppofe you
fhould fubftitute, in the room of the jalap, *fix* grains of
gamboge, to be mixed with 10 or 15 grains of calomel;
and after a dofe or two as occafion may require, you fhould
bleed your patients *almoft* to death, at leaft to *fainting*; and
then direct a plentiful fupply of mallows tea, with frefh lemon juice, and fugar and barley water, together with the
moft fimple, *mild*, and nutritious food." The Doctor concludes his letter by recommending to my perufal Dr Dover's account of nearly a whole fhip's crew having been
cured of a yellow fever, on the coaft of South America, by
being bled until they fainted.

  * Difeafes of Barbadoes, p. 212.
  † Difeafes in Voyages to Hot Climates, vol. ii. p. 322.

2. A

2. A fecond objection to this mercurial purge was, that it excited a falivation, and fometimes loofened the teeth. I met with but two cafes in which there was a lofs of teeth from the ufe of this medicine, and in both, the teeth were previoufly loofe or decayed. The falivation was a trifling evil, compared with the benefit which was derived from it. I loft only one patient in whom it occurred. I was taught by this accidental effect of mercury, to adminifter it with other views, than merely to cleanfe the bowels, and with a fuccefs which added much to my confidence in the power of medicine over this difeafe. I fhall mention thofe views under another head.

3. It was faid that the mercurial purge, excoriated the rectum, and produced the fymptoms of pain and inflammation in that part, which were formerly mentioned.

To refute this charge, it will be fufficient to remark that the bile produces the fame excoriation and pain in the rectum in the bilious and yellow fever, where no mercury has been given to difcharge it. In the bilious remitting fever which prevailed in Philadelphia in 1780, we find the bile which was difcharged by " gentle dofes of falts, and cream of tartar, or the butternut pill, was fo

acrid

acrid as to excoriate the rectum, and so offensive
as to occasion in some cases, sicknefs and faintnefs
both in the patients, and in their attendants*."

Dr Hume fays further upon this subject, that
the rectum was so much excoriated by the natural
difcharge of bile in the yellow fever, as to render
it impoffible to introduce a glyfter pipe into it.

4. It was objected to this purge, that it inflamed, and lacerated the ftomach and bowels. In
fupport of this calumny, the inflamed and mortified appearances which thofe vifcera exhibited
upon diffection in a patient who died at the hofpital at Bufh-hill, were fpoken of with horror in
fome parts of the city. To refute this objection,
it will only be neceffary to review the account
formerly given of the ftate of the ftomach and
bowels after death from the yellow fever, in
cafes in which no mercury had been given. I
have before taken notice that Sir John Pringle,
and Dr Cleghorn, had prefcribed mercurial purges
with fuccefs in the dyfentery, a difeafe in which
the bowels are affected with more irritation and
inflammation than in the yellow fever. Dr Clark

* Medical Inquiries and Obfervations, London edition,
vol. i. p. 112.

informs

informs us that he had adopted this practice. I
shall infert the eulogium of this excellent phyfician, upon the ufe of mercury in the dyfentery in
his own words. " For feveral years paft, when
the dyfentery has refifted the common mode of
practice, I have adminiftered mercury with the
greateft fuccefs ; and am thoroughly perfuaded
that it is poffeffed of powers to *remove inflamma-*
tion, and *ulceration* of the inteftines, which are
the chief caufes of death, in this diftemper *."

5. It was urged againft this powerful and effi-
cacious medicine, that it was prefcribed indifcriminately in all cafes ; and that it did harm in all
weak habits. To this I anfwer, that there was
no perfon fo weak by conftitution, or a previous
difeafe, as to be injured by a fingle dofe of this
medicine. Mrs Meredith the wife of the Trea-
furer of the United States, a lady of uncommon
delicacy of conftitution, took two dofes. of the
powder in the courfe of twelve hours, not only
without any inconvenience, but with an evident
increafe of ftrength foon afterwards. Many fimilar cafes might be mentioned. Even children
took two or three dofes of it with perfect fafety.
This will not furprife thofe phyficians who have

* Vol. ii. p. 342.

been

been in the practice of giving from ten to twenty grains of mercury, with an equal quantity of jalap, as a worm purge, and from fifty to an hundred grains of calomel in the courfe of four or five days, in the internal dropfy of the brain. But I am happy in being able to add further, that many women took it in every ftage of pregnancy without fuffering the leaft inconvenience from it. Out of a great number of pregnant women whom I attended in this fever, I did not lofe one to whom I gave this medicine, nor did any of them fuffer an abortion. One of them had twice mifcarried in the courfe of the two or three laft years of her life. She bore a healthy child three months after her recovery from the yellow fever.

No one has ever objected to the *indifcriminate* mode of preparing the body for the fmall-pox by purging medicines. The *uniform* inflammatory diathefis of that difeafe, juftifies the practice, in a certain degree in all habits. The yellow fever admits of a famenefs of cure much more than the fmall-pox, for it is *more* uniformly and more highly inflammatory. An obfervation of Dr Sydenham, upon epidemics applies in its utmoft extent to our late fever. " Now it muft be obferved (fays this moft acute Phyfician) that fome epidemic difeafes, in fome years are uniformly and conftantly the fame."

fame*." However diverfified our fever was in fome of its fymptoms, it was in all cafes accompa- nied by more or lefs inflammatory diathefis, and by a morbid ftate of the alimentary canal.

Much has been faid of the bad effects of this purge from its having been put up carelefsly by the apothecaries, or from its having been taken contrary to the printed directions, by many peo- ple. If it did harm in any one cafe (which I do not believe) from the former of the above caufes, the fault is not mine. Twenty men employed con- ftantly in putting up this medicine, would not have been fufficient to have complied with all the de- mands which were made of me for it. Hundreds who were in health, called or fent for it as well as the fick, in order to have it in readinefs in cafe they fhould be furprifed by the diforder in the night, or at a diftance from a phyfician.

In all the cafes, in which this purge was fup- pofed to have been hurtful, when given on the firft or fecond day of the diforder, I believe it was becaufe it was not followed by repeated dofes of the fame, or of fome other purge ; or becaufe it was not aided by blood-letting. I am led to make

* Vol. i. p. 9.

this

this affertion, not only from the authority of Dr
Sydenham, who often mentions the good effects
of bleeding in moderating or checking a diarrhœa,
but by having heard no complaints of patients
being purged to death by this medicine, after
blood-letting was univerfally adopted by all the
phyficians in the city.

It was remarkable that the demand for this
purging powder continued to encreafe under all
oppofition, and that the fale of it by the apothecaries was greateft towards the clofe of the difeafe.
I fhall hereafter fay, that this was not the cafe
with the Weft India remedies.

It is poffible that this purge fometimes proved
hurtful when it was given after the 5th day of the
diforder, but it was feldom given for the *firft*
time after the third day, and when it was, the patient was generally in fuch a fituation that nothing
did him either good or harm.

I derived great pleafure from hearing after the
fever had left the city, that calomel had been
given with fuccefs as a purge in bilious fevers in
other parts of the Union befides Philadelphia. Dr
Lawrence informed me that he had cured many
patients by it, of the yellow fever which prevailed

in

in New York in the year 1791, and the New York papers have told us that several practitioners had been in the habit of giving it in the autumnal fevers, with great success in the Western parts of that state. They had probably learned the use of it from Dr Young, who formerly practised in that part of the United States, and who lost no opportunity of making its praises public, wherever he went.

My pupil Mr Potter gave calomel and jalap in large doses, with great success in the bilious fever of Caroline county in Maryland, before he knew that I had adopted that purge in the cure of our epidemic. He had heard the history of its origin and use from me, some months before, in a conversation upon bilious fevers in my shop.

I have only to add to my account of that purging medicine, that under an expectation, that the yellow fever would mingle some of its bilious symptoms, with the common inflammatory fevers of the winter, and first spring months, I gave that purge in the form of pills in every case of inflammatory fever to which I was called. The fatal issue of several fevers in the city, during the winter, in which this precaution had been neglected, satisfied me that my practice was proper and useful.

S   It

It is to be lamented that all new remedies are forced to pafs through a fiery ordeal. Opium and bark were long the objects of terror and invective in the fchools of medicine. They were adminiftered only by phyficians for many years, and that too with all the folemnity of a religious ceremony. This fuperftition with refpect to thofe medicines, has at laft paffed away. It will I hope foon be fucceeded by á time, when the prejudices againft *ten* and *ten*, or *ten* and *fifteen*, will fleep with the vulgar fears which were formerly entertained of the bark producing difeafes and death, years after it had been taken, by " lying in the bones."

OF BLOOD-LETTING.

THE theory of this fever which led me to adminifter purges, determined me to ufe blood-letting, as foon as it fhould be indicated. I am difpofed to believe, that I was tardy in the ufe of this remedy, and I fhall long regret the lofs of three patients, who might probably have been faved by it. I cannot blame myfelf for not having ufed it earlier, for the immenfe number of patients which poured in upon me, in the firft week of September,

tember, prevented my attending so much to each of them, as was neceffary to determine upon the propriety of this evacuation. I was in the fituation of a furgeon in a battle, who runs to every call, and only ftays long enough with each foldier, to ftop the bleeding of his wound, while the encreafe of the wounded, and the unexpected length of the battle, leave his original patients to fuffer from the want of more fuitable dreffings. The reafons which determined me to bleed were,

1. The ftate of the pulfe, which became more tenfe, in proportion as the weather became cool.

2. The appearance of a moift, and *white* tongue on the firft day of the diforder; a certain fign of an inflammatory fever!

3. The frequency of hemorrhagies from every part of the body, and the perfect relief given in fome cafes, by them.

4. The fymptoms of congeftion in the brain refembling thofe which occur in the firft ftage of hydrocephalus internus, a difeafe in which I had lately ufed bleeding with fuccefs.

S 2   5. The

5. The character of the difeafes which had preceded the yellow fever. They were all more or
lefs inflammatory. Even the fcarlatina anginofa
had partaken fo much of that diathefis, as to require one bleeding to fubdue it.

6. The warm and dry weather which had likewife preceded the fever. Dr Sydenham attributes
a highly inflammatory ftate of the fmall-pox, to a
previoufly hot and dry fummer; and I have fince
obferved that Dr Hillary, takes notice of inflammatory fevers having frequently fucceeded hot and
dry weather in Barbadoes *. He informs us further, that the yellow fever is always moft acute
and inflammatory, after a very hot feafon †.

7. The authority of Dr Mofely had great weight
with me in advifing the lofs of blood, more efpecially as his ideas of the highly inflammatory nature
of the fever, accorded fo perfectly with my own.

8. I was induced to prefcribe blood-letting by
recollecting its good effects in Mrs Plalmer's fon,
whom I bled on the 20th of Auguft; and who appeared to have been recovered by it.

* Difeafes of Barbadoes, p. 16, 43, 46, 48, 52. 122.
† P. 147.

Having

Having begun to bleed, I was encouraged to continue it by the appearance of the blood, and by the obvious and very great relief my patients derived from it.

The following is a fhort account of the appearances of the blood drawn from a vein in this diforder.

1. It was in the greateft number of cafes, denfe, and of a fcarlet colour, without any feparation into craffamentum and ferum.

2. There was in many cafes a feparation of the blood into craffamentum and *yellow* ferum.

3. There were a few cafes in which this feparation took place, and the ferum was of a *natural* colour.

4. There were many cafes in which the blood was as fizy as in pneumony and rheumatifm.

5. The blood was in fome inftances covered above with a blue pellicle of fizy lymph, while the part which lay in the bottom of the bowl was diffolved. The lymph was in two cafes mixed with green ftreaks.

6. It

6. It was in a few inftances of a dark colour, and as fluid as molaffes. I faw this kind of blood in a man who walked about·his houfe during the whole of his ficknefs, and who finally recovered. Both this, and the 5th kind of blood which has been mentioned, occurred chiefly where bleeding had been omitted altogether, or ufed too fparingly in the beginning of the diforder.

7. In fome patients, the blood, in the courfe of the difeafe, exhibited nearly *all* the appearances which have been mentioned. They were varied by the time in which the blood was drawn, and by the nature and force of the remedies which had been ufed in the diforder.

The effects of blood-letting upon the fyftem were as follow :

1. It raifed the pulfe when depreffed, and quick-ened it, when it was preternaturally flow, or fubject to intermiffions.

2. It reduced its force and frequency.

3. It checked in many cafes, the vomiting which-occurred in the beginning of the diforder, and thereby enabled the ftomach to retain the purging medicine.

medicine. It likewife affifted the purge in preventing the dangerous or fatal vomiting which
came on about the 5th day.

4. It leffened the difficulty of opening the
bowels. Upon this account, in my publication
of the 12th of September, I advifed bleeding to
be ufed *before*, as well as after taking the mercurial purge. Dr Woodhoufe informed me that he
had feveral times feen patients call for the clofe
ftool while the blood was flowing from the vein.

5. It removed delirium, coma, and obftinate
wakefulnefs. It alfo prevented or chccked hemorrhagies; hence perhaps another reafon why
not a fingle inftance of abortion occurred in fuch
of my female patients as were pregnant.

6. It difpofed in fome cafes to a gentle perfpi-
ration.

7. It leffened the fenfible debility of the fyftem,
hence patients frequently rofe from their beds,
and walked acrofs their rooms in a few hours after
the operation had been performed.

8. The rednefs of the eyes frequently difappeared in a few hours after bleeding. Mr Coxe

obferved

obferved a dilated pupil to contract to its natural
fize, within a few minutes after he had bound up
the arm of his patient. I remarked in the former
part of this work, that blindnefs in many inftances
attended or followed this fever. Only two fuch
cafes occurred among my patients. In one of
them it was of fhort continuance, and in the other
it was probably occafioned by the want of fufficient bleeding. In every cafe of blindnefs that
came to my knowledge, bleeding had been omitted, or ufed only in a very moderate degree.

- 9. It eafed *pain*. Thoufands can teftify this
effect of blood-letting. Many of my patients'
whom I bled with my own hand, acknowledged
to me while the blood was flowing, that they were
better; and fome of them declared, that all their
pains had left them, before I had completely
bound up their arms.

10. But blood letting had in many cafes an
effect, the oppofite of *eafing* pain. It frequently
encreafed it in every part of the body, more efpecially in the head. It appeared to be the effect of
the fyftem rifing fuddenly from a ftate of indirect
debility, and of an encreafed action of the blood-
veffels which took place in confequence of it. I
have frequently feen complaints of the breaft, and
of

of the head, made worfe by a fingle bleeding, and from the fame caufe. It was in fome cafes an unfortunate event in the yellow fever, for it prevented the blood-letting being repeated, by exciting, or ftrengthening the prejudices of patients and phyficians againft it. In fome inftances, the patients grew worfe after a fecond, and in one, after a third bleeding. This was the cafe in Mifs Redman. Her pains encreafed after three bleedings, but yielded to the fourth. Her father Dr. Redman concurred in this feemingly abfurd practice. It was at this time, my old mafter reminded me of Dr Sydenham's remark, that moderate bleeding did harm in the plague, where copious bleeding was indicated, and that in the cure of that diforder, we fhould leave nature wholly to herfelf, or take the cure altogether out of her hands. The truth of this obfervation was very obvious. By taking away as much blood as reftored the blood-veffels to a morbid degree of action, without reducing this action afterwards, pain, congeftion, and inflammation, were frequently encreafed, all of which were prevented, or occurred in a lefs degree, when the fyftem rofe gradually from the ftate of depreffion which had been induced by indirect debility. Under the influence of the facts and reafonings which have been mentioned, I bore the fame teftimony in

acute

acute cafes, againſt whſt was called *moderate*
bleeding, that I did againſt bark, wine and laudanum in this fever.

11. Blood-letting when uſed *early* on the firſt
day, frequently ſtrangled the diſeaſe in its birth,
and generally rendered it more light, and the convaleſcence more ſpeedy and perfect. I am not ſure
that it ever ſhortened the duration of the fever
where it was not uſed within a few hours of the time
of its attack. Under every mode of treatment, it
ſeemed diſpoſed after it was completely formed to
run its courſe. I was ſo ſatisfied of this peculiarity in the fever, that I ventured in ſome cafes to
predict the day on which it would terminate, notwithſtanding I took the cure entirely out of the
hands of nature. 1 did not loſe a patient on the
third, whom I bled on the firſt, or ſecond day of
the diſorder.

12. In thoſe cafes which ended fatally, blood-
letting reſtored, or preſerved the uſe of reaſon,
rendered death eaſy, and retarded the putrefaction of the body after death.

I ſhall now mention ſome of the circumſtances
which directed and regulated the uſe of this
remedy.

1. Where

1. Where bleeding had been omitted, for three days, in acute cafes it was feldom ufeful. Where purging had been ufed, it was fometimes fuccefsful. I recovered two patients who had taken the mercurial purges, whom I bled for the firft time on the 7th day. One of them was the daughter of Mr James Creffon, the other was a journeyman fhip-carpenter at Kenfington. In thofe cafes where bleeding had been ufed on the firft day, it was both fafe and ufeful to repeat it every day afterwards, during the continuance of the fever.

2. I preferred bleeding in the exacerbation of the fever. The remedy here was applied when the dif-eafe was in its greateft force. A fingle paroxifm, was like a fudden fquall to the fyftem, and unlefs abated by bleeding, or purging, produced univer-fal diforganization. I preferred the former to the latter remedy in cafes of great danger, be-caufe it was more fpeedy, and more certain in its operation.

3. I bled in feveral inftances in the remif-fion of the fever, where the pulfe was tenfe or chorded. It leffened the violence of the fucceed-ing paroxifm.

4. I

4. I bled in all thofe cafes in which the pulfe was
preternaturally flow, provided it was tenfe.   Mr
Benj. W. Morris, Mr Thomas Wharton Jun.
and Mr Wm. Sanfom, all owe their lives probably
to their having been bled in the above ftate of the
pulfe.   I was led to ufe bleeding in this ftate of
the pulfe, not only by the theory of the difeafe
which I had adopted, but by the fuccefs which had
often attended this remedy, in a flow and depreffed ftate of the pulfe in apoplexy and pneumony.   I
had, moreover, the authority of Dr Mofely in its
favour, in the yellow fever, and of Dr Sydenham,
in his account of a new fever, which appeared in
the year 1685.   The words of the latter phyfician
are fo appofite to the cafes which have been mentioned, that I hope I fhall be excufed for inferting them in this place.   " All the fymptoms of
weaknefs (fays our author) proceed from nature's
being in a manner oppreffed, and overcome by the
firft attack of the difeafe, fo as not to be able to
raife regular fymptoms adequate to the violence of
the fever. I remember to have met with a remarkable inftance of this feveral years ago, in a young
man I then attended ; for though he feemed in a
manner expiring, yet the outward parts felt fo cool,
that I could not perfuade the attendants he had a
fever, which could not difengage, and fhew itfelf
clearly, becaufe the veffels were fo full as to ob-
ftruct

ftruct the motion of the blood. However, I faid, that they would foon find the fever rife high enough upon bleeding him. Accordingly after taking away a large quantity of blood, as violent a fever appeared as ever I met with, and did not go off till bleeding had been ufed three or four times *."

5. I bled in thofe cafes in which the fever appeared in a tertian form, provided the pulfe was full and tenfe. I well recollect the furprife with which Mr Van Berkel heard this prefcription from me, at a time when he was able to walk and ride out on the intermediate days of a tertian fever. The event which followed this prefcription, fhewed that it was not difproportioned to the violence of his difeafe, for it foon put on fuch acute and inflammatory fymptoms as to require fix fubfequent bleedings to fubdue it.

6. I bled in thofe cafes where patients were able to walk about, provided the pulfe was the fame as has been mentioned under the 4th head. I was determined as to the propriety of bleeding in thefe two fuppofed mild forms of the fever, by having obferved each of them when left to themfelves frequently to terminate in death.

* Vol. ii p. 351.

6. I

7. I paid no regard to the diffolved ftate of the blood, when it appeared on the firft or fecond day of the diforder, but repeated the bleedings afterwards in every cafe, where the pulfe continued to indicate it. It was common to fee fizy blood fucceed that which was diffolved. This occurred in Mr Jofiah Coates, and Mr Samuel Powel. Had I believed that this diffolved ftate of the blood arofe from its putrefaction, I fhould have laid afide my lancet as foon as I faw it; but I had long ago parted with all ideas of putrefaction in bilious fevers. The refutation of this doctrine, was the object of one of my papers in the Medical Society of Edinburgh, in the year 1767. The diffolved appearance of the blood, I fuppofe to be the effect of a certain action of the blood-veffels upon it. It occurs in fevers in which no putrid, or foreign matter has been introduced into the fyftem. The typhoid pneumony defcribed by Dr Huxham in his epidemics, and well known in the fouthern ftates of America, in the fpring of the year, has never been afcribed to any other remote caufe, than the fenfible qualities of the air.

8. The prefence of petechiæ did not deter me from repeating blood-letting, where the pulfe retained its fulnefs or tenfion. I prefcribed it with fuccefs in the cafes of Dr Meafe, and of Mrs Gebler,

ler, in Dock-ftreet, in each of whom petechiæ
had appeared. Bleeding was equally effe&ual in
the cafe of the Rev. Mr Keating at a time when his
arms were fpotted with that fpecies of eruptions
which I have compared to mofcheto-bites. I had
precedents in Dr De Haen *, and Dr Sydenham †
in favour of this practice. So far from viewing
thefe eruptions as figns of putrefaction, I confidered them as marks of the higheft poffible inflammatory diathefis. They difappeared in each of the
above cafes after bleeding.

9. In determining the quantity of blood to be
drawn, I was governed by the ftate of the pulfe,
and by the temperature of the weather. In the
beginning of September, I found one or two moderate bleedings fufficient to fubdue the fever;
but in proportion as the fyftem rofe by the diminution of the ftimulus of heat, and the fever put
on more *vifible* figns of inflammatory diathefis,
more frequent bleedings became neceffary. I
bled many patients twice, and a few three times
a day. I preferred frequent and fmall, to large
bleedings, in the beginning of September; but
towards the height and clofe of the epidemic, I

* Ratio medendi, Vol. ii. p. 162. Vol. iv. p. 172.
† Vol. 1. p. 210, and 264.

faw

faw no inconvenience from the lofs of a pint, and even twenty ounces of blood at a time. I drew from many perfons feventy and eighty ounces in five days ; and from a few, a much larger quantity. Mr Gribble, cedar-cooper, in Front-ftreet, loft by ten bleedings an hundred ounces of blood ; Mr George, a carter in Ninth-ftreet, loft about the fame quantity by five bleedings ; and Mr Peter Mierken, one hundred and fourteen ounces in five days. In the laft of the above perfons the quantity taken was determined by weight. Mr Toy, blackfmith near Dock-ftreet, was eight times bled in the courfe of feven days. The quantity taken from him was about an hundred ounces. The blood in all thefe cafes was denfe, and in the laft very fizy. They were all attended in the month of October, and chiefly by my pupil Mr Fifher ; and they are all this day living and healthy inftances of the efficacy of copious blood-letting, and of the intrepidity and judgment of their young phyfician. Children, and even old people, bore the lofs of much more blood in this fever, than in common inflammatory fevers. I took above thirty ounces, in five bleedings, from a daughter of Mr Robert Bridges, who was then in the 9th year of her age. Even great debility, whether natural or brought on by previous difeafes, did not in thofe few cafes in which it yielded to the fever, deprive

4   it

it of the uniformity of its inflammatory character. The following letter from my friend Dr Griffitts, written foon after his recovery from a third attack of the fever, and juft before he went into the country for the re-eftablifhment of his health, will furnifh a ftriking illuftration of the truth of the above obfervation.

"I CANNOT leave town without a parting adieu to my kind friend, and fincere prayers for his prefervation.

"I am forry to find that the ufe of the lancet is ftill fo much dreaded by too many of our phyficians; and while lamenting the death of a valuable friend this morning, I was told that he was bled but *once* during his diforder. Now if my poor frame, reduced by previous ficknefs, great anxiety, and fatigue, and a very low diet, could bear *feven* bleedings in five days, befides purging, and no diet but toaft and water, what fhall we fay of phyficians who bleed but once?"

"*October* 19*th*, 1793."

'I have compared a paroxifm of this fever to a fudden fquall; but the difeafe in its whole courfe was like a tedious equinoctial gale, acting upon a fhip at fea; its deftructive force was only to be op-

T   pofed

poſed by handing every ſail, and leaving the ſyſtem to float, as it were, under bare poles.   Such
was the fragility (if I may be allowed the expreſ-
ſion) of the blood-veſſels, that it was neceſſary to
unload them of their contents, in order to prevent
the ſyſtem ſinking, from hemorrhagies, or from
effuſions in the viſcera, particularly the brain.

9. Such was the indomitable nature of the pulſe
in ſome patients, that it did not loſe its force after
numerous and copious bleedings.   In all ſuch
caſes, I conſidered the diminution of its frequency,
and the abſence of a vomiting, as ſignals to lay
aſide the lancet.   The continuance of this preternatural force in the pulſe, appeared to be owing
to the contagion which was univerſally diffuſed
in the air, acting upon the arterial ſyſtem in the
ſame manner that it did in perſons who were in
apparent good health.

Thus have I mentioned the principal circumſtances which were connected with blood-letting,
in the cure of the yellow fever.   I ſhall now con-
ſider the objections that were made to it at the
time, and ſince the prevalence of the fever.

It was ſaid that the bleeding was unneceſſarily
copious ; and that many had been deſtroyed by it.
To

To this I anfwer, that I did not lofe a fingle patient whom I bled feven times, or more, in this fever. As a further proof that I did not draw an
ounce of blood too much, it will only be neceffary
to add, that hemorrhagies frequently occurred after a third, a fourth, and in one inftance (in the
only fon of Mr William Hall) after a fixth bleeding had been ufed ; and further, that not a fingle
death occurred from natural hemorrhagies in the
firft ftage of the diforder. A woman who had
been bled by my advice, awoke the night following in a bath of her blood, which had flowed
from the orifice in her arm. The next day fhe
was free from pain and fever. There were many
recoveries in the city from fimilar accidents. There
were likewife fome recoveries from copious natural hemorrhagies in the more advanced ftages of
the diforder, particularly when they occurred from
the ftomach and bowels. I left a fervant maid of
Mrs Morris's, in Walnut-ftreet, who had difcharged at leaft four pounds of blood from her
ftomach, without a pulfe, and with fcarcely a
fymptom that encouraged a hope of her life ; but
the next day I had the pleafure of finding her out
of danger.

It is remarkable that fainting was much lefs
common after bleeding in this fever, than in com-

mon

mon inflammatory fevers. This circumſtance was obſerved by Dr Griffitts, as well as myſelf. It has ſince been confirmed to me by three of the principal bleeders in the city, who performed the operation upwards of four thouſand times. It occurred chiefly in thoſe caſes where it was uſed for the firſt time on the third or fourth day of the diſeaſe. A ſwelling of the legs, moreover, ſo common after plentiful bleeding in pneumony and rheumatiſm, rarely ſucceeded the uſe of this remedy in the yellow fever.

2. Many of the indiſpoſitions, and much of the ſubſequent weakneſs of perſons who had been cured by copious blood-letting, have been aſcribed to it. This is ſo far from being true, that the reverſe of it has occurred in many caſes. Mr Mierken worked in his ſugar-houſe in good health, nine days after his laſt bleeding ; and Mr Gribble, and Mr George ſeem by their appearance to have derived freſh vigour from their evacuations. I could mention the names of many people who think their conſtitutions have been improved by the uſe of thoſe remedies ; and I know ſeveral perſons in whom they have carried off habitual complaints. Mr Richard Wells attributes his relief from a chronic rheumatiſm to the copious bleeding and purging which were uſed to cure him of

the

the yellow fever ; and Mr William Young, the bookfeller, was relieved of a chronic pain in his fide, by means of the fame remedies.

3. It was faid, that blood-letting was prefcribed indifcriminately in all cafes, without any regard to age, conftitution, or the force of the difeafe. This is not true as far as it relates to my practice. In my prefcriptions for patients whom I was unable to vifit, I advifed them, when they were incapable of judging of the ftate of the pulfe, to be guided in the ufe of bleeding, by the degrees of pain they felt, particularly in the head ; and I feldom advifed it for the *firft* time, after the fecond, or third day of the diforder.

In pneumonies which affect whole neighbourhoods in the fpring of the year, bleeding is the univerfal remedy. Why fhould it not be equally fo, in a fever which is of a more uniform inflammatory nature, and which tends more rapidly to effufions, in parts of the body, much more vital than the lungs ?

I have before remarked, that the debility which occurs in the yellow fever, is of the indirect kind. The debility in the plague is of the fame nature. It has long been known that direct debility is to

T 3   be

be removed by the *gradual* application of ſtimuli, but it has been leſs obſerved, that the exceſs of ſtimulus in the ſyſtem is beſt removed in a *gradual* manner, and that too, in proportion to the degrees of indirect debility, which exiſt in the ſyſtem.

This principle in the animal economy has been acknowledged by the practice of occaſionally ſtopping the diſcharge of water from a canula in tapping, and of blood from a vein, in order to prevent fainting.

Child-birth, induces fainting, and ſometimes death, only by the *ſudden* abſtraction of the ſtimulus of diſtention and pain.

In all thoſe caſes where purging or bleeding have produced death in the yellow fever or plague, when they have been uſed on the firſt or ſecond day of thoſe diſorders, I ſuſpect that it was occaſioned by the quantity of the ſtimulus abſtracted, being diſproportioned to the degrees of indirect debility. The following facts will I hope throw light upon this ſubject.

1. Dr Hodges informs us, that " although blood could not be drawn in the plague, even in

the

the fmalleft quantity without danger, yet an *hundred* times the quantity of fluids, was difcharged in pus from buboes without inconvenience*."

2. Pareus, after condemning bleeding in the plague, immediately adds an account of a patient, who was faved by an hemorrhage from the nofe which continued *two* days†."

3. I have before remarked that bleeding proved fatal in three cafes in the yellow fever in the month of Auguft; but at that time, I faw one, and heard of another cafe, in which death feemed to have been prevented by a bleeding at the nofe. Perhaps the uniform good effects which were obferved to follow a fpontaneous hemorrhage from an orifice in the arm, arofe wholly from the *gradual* manner in which the ftimulus of the blood was in this way abftracted from the body. Dr Williams relates a cafe of the recovery of a gentleman from the yellow fever by means of fmall hemorrhagies which continued three days from wounds in his fhoulders made by being cupped. He likewife mentions feveral other recoveries by hemorrhagies from the nofe, after " a vomit-

* Page 114.
† Skenkius, Lib. vi. p. 881.

ing

ing of black humours, and a hiccup had taken place*."

4. There is a difeafe in North Carolina known among the common people by the name of the " pleurify in the head." It occurs in the winter after a fickly autumn, and feems to be an evane-fcent fymptcm of a bilicus remitting fever. The cure of it has been attempted by bleeding, in the common way, but generally without fuccefs. It has however, yielded to this remedy in another form, that is, to the difcharge of a few ounces of blood obtained by thrufting a piece of quill up the nofe.

5. Riverius defcribes a peftilential fever which prevailed at Montpelier in the year 1623, which carried off one half of all who were affected by it†. After many unfuccefsful attempts to cure it, this judicious phyfician prefcribed the lofs of *two* or *three* ounces of blood. The pulfe rofe with this fmall evacuation. Three or four hours after-wards, he drew fix ounces of blood from his pa-tients, and with the fame good effect. The next

* Effay on the Bilious or Yellow Fever of Jamaica, p. 40.
† De Febre Peftilenti, vol. ii. p. 145; 146, and 147.

day,

day, he gave a purge, which he fays refcued his patients from the grave. All whom he treated in this manner recovered. The whole hiftory of this epidemic is highly interefting, from its agreeing with our late epidemic in fo many of its fymptoms, more efpecially as they appeared in the different ftates of the pulfe.

An old and intelligent citizen of Philadelphia, who remembers the yellow fever of 1741, fays that when it firft made its appearance, bleeding was attended with fatal confequences. It was laid afide afterwards, and the difeafe prevailed with great mortality, until it was checked by the cold weather. Had blood been drawn in the manner mentioned by Riverius, or had it been drawn in the ufual way, after the abftraction of the ftimulus of heat by the cool weather, the difeafe might probably have been fubdued, and the remedy of blood-letting, thereby have recovered its character.

Dr Hodges has another remark in his account of the plague in London in the year 1665, which is ftill more to our purpofe than the one which I have quoted from it upon this fubject. He fays that " bleeding as a preventive of the plague was only fafe and ufeful, when the blood was drawn

by

by a *fmall* orifice, and a *fmall* quantity taken at *different* times*."

I have remarked in the hiftory of the yellow fever of laft autumn, that it was often cured on the firft or fecond day by a copious fweat. The Rev. Mr Uftick was one among many whom I could mention, who were faved from a violent attack of the fever, by this evacuation. It would be abfurd to fuppofe that the contagion which produced the difeafe, was difcharged in this manner from the body. The fweat feemed to cure the fever, only by leffening the quantity of the fluids, and thus *gradually* removing the indirect debility of the fyftem. The profufe fweats which fometimes cure the plague, as well as the difeafe which is brought on by the bite of poifonous fnakes, feem to act in the fame way.

The fyftem under the impreffion of the contagion of a malignant fever, refembles a man ftruggling beneath a load of two hundred weight, who is able to lift only one hundred and feventy-five. In order to affift him it will be to no purpofe to attempt to infufe additional vigour into his mufcles by the ufe of a whip or of ftrong

* Page 209.

drink.

drink. Every exertion will ferve only to wafte his ftrength. In this fituation (fuppofing it impof-fi'le to divide the weight which confines him to the ground) let the pockets of this man be emp-.... of their contents, and let him be ftripped of uch of his clothing, as to reduce his weight and twenty or thirty pounds. In this fitua-... he will rife from the ground; but if the ...hts be abftracted fuddenly, while he is in an ... of exertion, he will rife with a fpring that will endanger a fecond fall, and probably produce a temporary convulfion in his fyftem. By abftract-ing the weights from his body more gradually, he will rife by degrees from the ground, and the fyf-tem will accommodate itfelf in fuch a manner to the diminution of its preffure, as to refume its erect form, without the leaft deviation from the natural order of its appearance and motions.

It has been faid that the ftimulating remedies of bark, wine, and the cold bath, were proper in our late epidemic in Auguft, and in the beginning of September, but that they were improper after-wards. If my theory be juft, they were more improper in Auguft and the beginning of Septem-ber, than they were after the difeafe put on the outward and common figns of inflammatory dia-thefis. The reafon why a few ftrong purges cured
the

the difeafe at its firft appearance was, becaufe
they abftracted in a *gradual* manner fome of the
immenfe portion of ftimulus under which the arterial fyftem laboured, and thus gradually relieved
it from its low degrees of indirect debility. Bleeding was fatal in thefe cafes, only becaufe it removed this indirect debility in too fudden a manner.

The principle of the gradual abftraction, as well
as of the gradual application of ftimuli to the body, in all the difeafes of indirect debility on the one
hand, and of direct, on the other, opens a wide
field for the improvement of medicine. Perhaps
all the difcoveries of future ages will confift more
in a new application of eftablifhed principles, and
in new modes of exhibiting old medicines, than
in the difcovery of new theories, or of new articles of the Materia Medica.

The reafons which induced me to prefcribe
purging and bleeding, in fo liberal a manner, naturally led me to recommend COOL and FRESH AIR
to my patients. The good effects of it were obvious in almoft every cafe in which it was applied.
It was equally proper whether the arterial fyftem
was depreffed, or whether it difcovered in the
pulfe, a high degree of morbid excitement. Dr
Griffitts

Griffiths furnifhed a remarkable inftance of the influence of cool air upon the fever. Upon my vifiting him on the morning of the eighth of October, I found his pulfe fo full and tenfe, as to indicate bleeding, but after fitting a few minutes by his bed-fide, I perceived that the windows of his room had been fhut in the night by his nurfe, on account of the coldnefs of the night air. I defired that they might be opened. In ten minutes afterwards, the Doctor's pulfe became fo much flower and weaker, that I advifed the poftponement of the bleeding, and recommended a purge inftead of it. The bleeding notwithftanding became neceffary, and was ufed with great advantage in the afternoon of the fame day.

The cool air was improper only in thofe cafes where a chillinefs attended the difeafe.

For the fame reafon that I advifed cool air, I directed my patients to ufe cold DRINKS. They confifted of lemonade, tamarind, jelly, and raw apple water, toaft and water, and of weak balm, and camomile tea. The fubacid drinks were preferred in moft cafes, as being not only moft agreeable to the tafte, but becaufe they tended to correct by mixture, the acrid quality of the bile. All thefe drinks were taken in the early ftage of the diforder.

diforder. Towards the clofe of it, I permitted
the ufe of porter and water, weak punch, and
when 'the ftomach would bear it, weak v˙ ˙ ˙˙
whey.

I forbad all cordial and ftimulating food in the
active ftate of the arterial fyftem. The lefs ny
patients ate, of even the mildeft vegetable food,
the fooner they recovered. Weak coffee, which
(as I have formerly remarked) was almoft univerfally agreeable, and weak tea were always inoffenfive. As the action of the pulfe diminifhed, I in-
dulged my patients with weak chocolate; alfo
with milk, to which roafted apples, or minced
peaches, and (where they were not to be had,)
bread, or Indian mufh were added.

Towards the crifis, I advifed the drinking of
weak chicken, veal, or mutton broth, and after
the crifis had taken place, I permitted mild animal
food to be eaten in a fmall quantity, and to be
increafed according to the wafte of the excitability of the fyftem. This ftrict abftinence which
I impofed upon my patients did not efcape obloquy, but the benefits they derived from it, and
the ill effects which arofe in many cafes from a
contrary regimen, fatisfied me that it was proper
in every cafe in which it was prefcribed.

COLD

COLD WATER was a moft agreeable and powerful remedy in this diforder. I directed it to be
applied by means of napkins to the head, and to
be injected into the bowels by way of glyfter. It
gave the fame eafe to both, when in pain, which
opium gives to pain from other caufes. I likewife advifed the wafhing of the face and hands,
and fometimes the feet with cold water, and always
with advantage. It was by fuffering the body to
lie for fome time in a bed of cold water, that the
inhabitants of the ifland of Maffuah cured the moft
violent bilious fevers*. When applied in this
way, it *gradually* abftracts the heat from the body,
and thereby leffens the action of the fyftem. It
differs as much in its effects upon the body from
the cold bath, as reft in a cold room, differs from
exercife in the cold and open air.

I was firft led to the practice of the partial application of cold water to the body, in fevers of
too much force in the arterial fyftem, by obferving its good effects in active hemorrhagies, and by
recollecting the effects of a partial application of
warm water to the feet, in fevers of an oppofite
character. Cold water when applied to the feet
as certainly reduces the pulfe in force and fre-

* Bruce's Travels.

quency, as warm water applied in the fame way, produces contrary effects upon it. In an experiment which was made at my requeſt by one of my pupils, by placing his feet in cold pump water for a few minutes, the pulſe was reduced 24 ſtrokes in a minute, and became ſo weak as hardly to be perceptible.

In the uſe of the remedies which were neceſſary to overcome the inflammatory action of the ſyſtem, I was obliged to reduce it below its natural point of excitement. In the preſent imperfect ſtate of our knowledge in medicine, perhaps no diſeaſe of too much action, can be cured without it.

I have ſaid in another place, that I was early obliged to defiſt from the uſe of wine, bark, and laudanum in the firſt ſtage of this diforder. I found them as offenſive to the ſtomach, and nearly as hurtful in its ſecond ſtage, as I had found them in its firſt. In this fituation new reſources in the materia medica were opened to me. I had obſerved a favourable iſſue of the fever in 'every caſe, in which a ſpontaneous diſcharge took place from the ſalivary glands. I had obſerved further, that all ſuch of my patients (one excepted) as were ſalivated by the mercurial purges recovered in a few days.

days. This, early fuggefted an idea to me that
the calomel might be applied to other purpofes,
than the difcharging of bile from the bowels. I
afcribed its falutary effects when it falivated in the
firft ftage of the diforder, to the excitement of inflammation and effufion in the throat, diverting
them from more vital parts of the body. In the
the fecond ftage of the diforder, I was led to prefcribe it as a ftimulant, and with a view of obtaining this operation from it, I aimed at exciting a
falivation as fpeedily as poffible in all cafes. Two
precedents encouraged me to make trial of this
remedy.

In the month of October 1789, I attended a gentleman in a bilious fever, which ended in many of
the fymptoms of a typhus mitior. In the loweft
ftate of his fever, he complained of a pain his right
fide, for which I ordered half an ounce of mercurial ointment to be rubbed on the part affected.
The next day, he complained of a fore mouth, and
in the courfe of four and twenty hours, he was in
a moderate falivation. From this time his pulfe
became full and flow, and his fkin moift. His fleep
and appetite fuddenly returned, and in a day or
two he was out of danger. The fecond precedent
for a falivation in a fever; which occurred to me
was in Dr Haller's fhort account of the works of

U Dr

Dr Cramer *, and which I had a year before copied into ·my note book. The practice was moreover, juftified in point of fafety, as well.as the probability of fuccefs, by the accounts which Dr Clark has lately given of the effects of a faliva-tion in the dyfentery †. I began by prefcribing the the calomel in fmall dofes, at fhort intervals, and afterwards I directed large quantities of the oint-ment to be rubbed upon the limbs. The effects of it in every cafe in which it affected the mouth, were falutary. Dr Woodhoufe improved upon my me-thod of exciting the falivation, by rubbing the gums with calomel, in the manner directed by Mr Clare. It was more fpeedy in its operation in this way than in any other, and equally effectual. Several per-fons appeared to be benefited by the mercury in-troduced into the fyftem in the form of an ointment, where it did *not* produce a falivation. Among thefe, were the Rev. Dr Blackwell, and Mr John Davis.

Since the above account was written of the good effects of a mercurial falivation in this fever, I have had great fatisfaction in difcovering that it was pre-fcribed with equal, and even greater fucccefs, by Dr Wade in Bengal, in the year 1791, and by Mr Chifholm in the ifland of Granada, in the cure of

* Bibliotheca Medicinæ Practicæ, vol. iii. p. 491.
† Difeafes of long voyages to Hot Climates, vol. ii. p. 334.

bilious

bilious yellow fevers *. Dr Wade did not lofe one, and Mr Chifholm loft only one, out of forty eight prtients in whom the mercury affected the falivary glands. The latter gave 150 grains of colomel, and applied the ftrongeft mercurial ointment below the groin of each fide, in fome cafes. He adds further, that not a fingle inftance.of a relapfe occurred, where the difeafe was cured by falivation.

After the reduction of the fyftem, *blifters* were applied with great advantage to every part of the body. They did moft fervice when they were applied to the crown of the head. I did not fee a fingle cafe, in which a mortification followed the fore, which was created by a blifter.

Brandy and water, or porter and water, when agreeable to the ftomach, with now and then a cup of chicken broth, were the drinks I prefcribed to affift in reftoring the tone of the fyftem.

In fome cafes I directed the limbs to be wrapped in flannels dipped in warm fpirits, and cataplafms of bruifed garlic to be applied to the feet. But my principal dependence, next to the ufe of mercurial medicines, for exciting a healthy action in the arterial fyftem, was upon mild and gently fti-

* Medical Commentaries, vol. xviii. p. 209. 288.

U 2   mulating

mulating food. This confifted of rich broths, the
flefh of poultry, oyfters, thick gruel, mufh and
milk, and chocolate. I directed my patients to
eat or drink a portion of fome of the above articles of diet every hour or two during the day,
and in cafes of great debility, I advifed their being
waked for the fame purpofe two or three times
in the night. The appetite frequently craved
more favoury articles of food, fuch as beef-ftakes,
and faufages ; but they were permitted with great
caution, and never 'till the fyftem had been prepared for them by a lefs ftimulating diet.

There were feveral *fymptoms* which were very
diftreffing in this diforder, and which required a
fpecific treatment.

For the vomiting, with a burning fenfation in
the ftomach, which came on about the 5th day,
I found no remedy equal to a table fpoonful of
fweet milk taken every hour, or to fmall draughts
of milk and water. I was led to prefcribe this
fimple medicine, from having heard from a Weft
India practitioner, and afterwards read in Dr
Hume's account of the yellow fever, encomiums
upon the milk of the cocoa-nut for this troublefome fymptom. Where fweet milk failed of giving
relief, I prefcribed fmall dofes of fweet oil, and in
fome cafes a mixture of equal parts of milk, fweet

oil

oil and molaſſes. They were all intended to dilute, or blunt the acrimony of the humors which were either effuſed, or generated in the ſtomach. Where they all failed of checking the vomiting, I preſcribed weak camomile tea, or porter, or cyder and water, with advantage. In ſome of my patients, the ſtomach rejected all the mixtures, and liquors which have been mentioned. In ſuch caſes, I directed the ſtomach to be left to itſelf for a few hours, after which it ſometimes received and retained the drinks that it had before rejected, provided they were adminiſtered in a ſmall quantity at a time.

The vomiting was ſometimes ſtopped by a bliſter applied to the external region of the ſtomach.

A mixture of liquid laudanum and ſweet oil, applied to the ſame place, gave relief where the ſtomach, was affected by pain only, without a vomiting.

I have formerly mentioned that a diſtreſſing *pain* often ſeized the lower part of the *bowels*. I was early taught that laudanum was not a proper remedy for it. It yielded in almoſt every caſe, to two or three emolient glyſters, or to the loſs of a few ounces of blood.

The

The convalefcence from this fever was in general rapid, but in fome cafes it was very flow.
I was more than ufually ftruck by the great refemblance which the fyftem in the convalefcence
from this fever, bore to the ftate of the body and
mind in old age. It appeared, 1. in the great
weaknefs of the body, more efpecially of the
limbs. 2. In uncommon depreffion of mind,
and in a great aptitude to fhed tears. 3. In the abfence or fhort continuance of fleep. 4. In the
frequent occurrence of appetite, and in fome cafes
in its inordinate degrees. And 5. In the lofs of
the hair of the head, or in its being fuddenly
changed in fome cafes to a grey colour.

Pure air, gentle exercife, and agreeable fociety, removed the debility both of body and mind
of this premature, and temporary old age. I met
with a few cafes, in which the yellow colour
continued for feveral weeks after the patient's recovery from all the other fymptoms of the fever.
It was removed moft fpeedily and effeftually by
two or three moderate dofes of calomel and rhubarb.

A feeble and irregular intermittent, was very
troublefome in fome people, after an acute attack
of the fever. It yielded gradually to camomile or
fnake-root tea, and country air,

In

In a publication dated the 16th of September, I recommended a diet of milk and vegetables, and cooling purges to be taken once or twice a week, to the citizens of Philadelphia. This advice was the refult of the theory of the difeafe I had adopted, and of the fuccefsful practice which had arifen from it. In my intercourfe with my fellow citizens, I advifed this regimen to be regulated by the degrees of fatigue and contagion to which they were expofed. I likewife advifed moderate blood-letting to all fuch perfons as were of a plethoric habit. To men whofe minds were influenced by the publications in favour of bark and wine, and who were unable at that time to grafp the extent and force of the contagion of this terrible fever, the idea of dieting, purging, or bleeding the inhabitants of a whole village or city, appeared to be extravagant and abfurd : but I had many precedents, befides the authority of reafon, in favour of the advice. Dr Mitchell recommended moderate bleeding with fuccefs, as a preventive of the yellow fever in Virginia, in the year 1741. A military furgeon belonging to the French troops at Hifpaniola, affured Dr Foulke that he had for many years bled the recruits from France, as foon as they arrived, and thereby fecured them from a feafoning by the yellow fever. The lefs mortality of this diforder in the French and Spa-

U 4 . nifh,

nifh, than in the Englifh Iflands, has been juftly
attributed to the natives of France and Spain carrying with them to the Weft Indies more temperate habits, in the ufe of wine and animal food,
than the natives of Great Britain. I had moreover, the analogy of the regimen made ufe of to
prepare the body for the fmall-pox and plague,
in favour of this advice. Dr Haller has given
extracts from the hiftories of two plagues, in
which the action of the contagion was prevented,
or mitigated, by bleeding *. Dr Hodges confirms the utility of the fame practice. The benefits of low diet, as a preventive of the plague,
were eftablifhed by many authors, long before
they received the teftimony of the benevolent Mr
Howard in their favour. Socrates in Athens,
and Juftinian in Conftantinople, were preferved by
means of their abftemious modes of living, from
the plagues which occafionally ravaged thofe cities. By means of the low diet, gentle phyfic, and
occafional bleedings, which I thus publicly recommended, the difeafe was prevented in many inftances, or rendered mild where it was taken.
But my efforts to prevent the difeafe in my fellow-citizens, did not end here. I advifed them,
not only in the public papers, but in my inter-

* Bibliotheca Medicinæ Practicæ, vol. ii. p. 93, and 387.

courfe

courfe with them, to avoid heat, cold, labour,
and every thing elfe that could excite the contagion (which I knew to be prefent in all their bodies) into action. I forgot upon this occafion the
ufual laws which regulate the interrourfe of man
with man in the ftreets, and upon the public
roads, in my excurfions into the neighbourhood
of the city. I cautioned many perfons whom I
faw walking or riding in an unfafe manner, of the
danger to which they expofed themfelves ; and
thereby I hope prevented an attack of the diforder in many people. If in a fingle inftance I unhappily excited an emotion of terror in a fellow-
citizen, by this conduct, I thus publicly afk his
pardon. There fhould be no ceremony in calling to a man to avoid a precipice ; or in pulling
him out of a fire.

It was from a conviction of the utility of low
diet, gentle evacuations, and of carefully fhunning
all the exciting caufes which I have mentioned,
that I concealed in no inftance from my patients,
the name of their diforder. This plainnefs, which
was blamed by weak people, produced ftrict obe-
dience to my directions, and thereby limited the
propagation of the fever, in many families, or
rendered it when taken, as mild as inoculation
does the fmall-pox. The oppofite conduct of feveral

veral phyficians, by preventing the above precautions, encreafed the mortality of the difeafe ; and
in fome inftances contributed to the extinction of
whole families. Such have been, and ever will
be, the effects of ignorance and fraud in the profeffion of medicine.

I proceed now to make a few remarks upon
the remedies recommended by Doctors Kuhn and
Stevens, and by the French phyficians.

Had the whole materia medica been ranfacked,
there could not have been found any three medicines more oppofite to the diforder than bark,
wine, and laudanum. In every cafe in which I prefcribed bark, it was offenfive to the ftomach. In
feveral tertians which attended the convalefcence
from a common attack of the fever, I found it always unfuccefsful, and once hurtful. Mr Willing took it for feveral weeks without effect.
About half a pint of a weak decoction of the
bark produced in Mr Samuel Meredith, a paroxifm of the fever, fo violent as to require the lofs
of ten ounces of blood to moderate it. Dr Annan informed me that he was forced to bleed one
of his patients twice, after having given him a
fmall quantity of bark, to haften his convalefcence.
If in any cafe it was inoffenfive, or did fervice, I
                                                    fufpect

fufpect it muft have acted upon the bowels as a purge. Dr Sydenham fays the bark cured intermittents by this evacuation * ; and Mr Bruce fays it operated in the fame way, when it cured the bilious fevers at Maffuah.

Wine was nearly as difagreeable as the bark to the ftomach, and equally hurtful. I tried it in every form, and of every quality, but without fuccefs. It was either rejected by the ftomach, or produced in it a burning fenfation. I fhould fufpect that I had been miftaken in my complaints againft wine, had I not fince met with an account in Skenkius of its having deftroyed all who took it in the famous Hungarian fever, which prevailed with great mortality over nearly every country in Europe, about the middle of the 16th century †. Dr Wade declares wine to be " ill adapted to the fevers of Bengal, where the treatment has been proper in other refpects."

Laudanum has been called by Dr Mofely "a fatal medicine" in the yellow fever. In one of

* Vol. i. p. 440.

† Omnes qui vini potione non abftinuerunt, interiere, adeo ut fumma fpes falvationis in vini abftinentia collocata videreter. Lib. vi. p. 847.

my

my patients who took only fifteen drops of it,
without my advice, to eafe a pain in his bowels,
it produced a delirium, and death in a few hours.
I was much gratified in difcovering that my practice, with refpect to the ufe of opium in this fever, accorded with Dr Wade's in the fever of
Bengal. He tells us that " it was mifchievous in
almoſt every inſtance, even in combination with
antimonials."

The *fpices* were hurtful in the firſt ſtage of the
fever, and when fufficient evacuations had been
ufed, they were feldom neceffary in its fecond.

The *elixir of vitriol* was in general, offenfive to
the ſtomach.

The *cold bath* was ufeful in thofe cafes where
its fedative prevailed over its ſtimulating effects.
But this could not often happen, from the fud-
dennefs and force with which the water was
thrown upon the body. In two cafes in which I
prefcribed it, it produced a gentle fweat, but it
did not fave life. In a third it removed a delirium, and reduced the pulfe for a few minutes, in
frequency and force, but this patient died. The
recommendation of it indifcriminately in all cafes,
was extremely improper. In that chillinefs and
                                          tendency

tendency to fainting upon the leaft motion, which attended the diforder in fome patients, it was an unfafe remedy. I heard of a woman who was feized with delirium immediately after ufing it, from which fhe never recovered ; and of a man who died a few minutes after he came out of a bathing tub. Had this remedy been the exclufive antidote to the yellow fever, the mortality of the difeafe would have been but little checked by it. Thoufands muft have perifhed from the want of means to procure tubs, and of a fuitable number of attendants to apply the water, and to lift the patient in and out of bed. The reafon of our citizens ran before the learning of the friends of this remedy, and long before it was abandoned by the phyficians ; it was rejected as ufelefs, or not attempted, becaufe impracticable, by the good fenfe of the city. It is to be lamented that the remedy of cold water has fuffered in its character by the manner in which it was advifed. In fevers of too much action, it reduces the morbid excitement of the blood-veffels, provided it be *applied without force,* and for a confiderable time to the body. It is in the jail fever, and in the fecond ftage of the yellow fever only, in which its ftimulant and tonic powers are proper. Dr Jackfon eftablifhes this mode of ufing it, by in-

forming

forming us, that when it did fervice, it " gave vigour and tone" to the fyftem*.

The *third* mode of practice which I mentioned
in this fever confifted of a union of the evacuating,
and tonic remedies. The phyficians who adopted
this mode, gave calomel by itfelf in fmall def·s on
the firft, or fecond day of the fever, bled once or
twice in a fparing manner, and gave the bark,
wine, and laudanum in large quantities upon the
firft appearance of a remiffion. After they began
the ufe of thefe remedies, purging was omitted,
or if the bowels were moved, it was only by
means of gentle glyfters. This practice I fhall
fay hereafter was not much more fuccefsful than
that which was recommended by Dr Kuhn and
Dr Stevens. It refembled throwing water and
oil at the fame time upon a fire, in order to ex-
tinguifh it.

The *French* remedies were nitre, and cremor
tartar in fmall dofes, centaury tea, camphor, and
feveral other warm medicines; fubacid drinks
taken in large quantities, the warm bath, and
moderate bleeding.

* Fevers of Jamaica.

                                        After

After what has been faid, it muft be obvious to the reader, that the nitre and cremor tartar in fmal dofes, could do no good, and that camphor and all cordial medicines muft have done harm. The diluting fubacid drinks which the French phyficians gave in large quantities were ufeful in diluting and blunting the acrimony of the bile, and to this remedy affifted by occafional bleeding, I afcribe moft of the cures which were performed by thofe phyficians.

Thofe few perfons in whom the *warm bath* produced oppious and univerfal fweats recovered, but in nearly all the cafes which came under my notice, it did harm.

I come now to inquire into the comparative fuccefs of the *four* different modes of practice which have been mentioned.

I have already faid that ten out of thirteen patients whom I treated with bark, wine, and laudanum, and that three out of four, in whom I added the cold bath to thofe remedies, died. Dr Pennington informed me, that he had loft all the patients, (fix in number) to whom he had given the above medicines. Dr Johnfon affured me with great concern, about two weeks before he died, that

that he had not recovered a fingle patient by them.
Whole families were fwept off, where thefe medicines were ufed. But further, moft of thofe
perfons who caught the fever in the city, and fickened in the country, or in the neighbouring towns,
and who were treated with tonic remedies, died.
There was not a fingle cure performed by them
in New York, where they were ufed with every
poffible advantage. But why do I multiply proofs
of their deadly effects ? The clamours of hundreds
whofe relations had perifhed by them, and the
fears of others, compelled thofe phyficians who
had been moft attached to them, to lay them afide,
or to prepare the way for them (as it was called)
by purging and bleeding. The bathing tub foon
fhared a worfe fate than bark, wine, and laudanum, and long before the difeafe difappeared, it
was difcarded by all the phyficians in the city.

In anfwer to thefe facts, we have been told that
Mr Hamilton, and his family recovered by the ufe
of Dr Stevens's remedies. I fhall not fay of thofe
cures, what fome gentlemen of the faculty who
had feen but little of the difeafe, and who had forgotten that a powerful epidemic banifhes, or unites
with all other difeafes, have faid of my cures, viz.
that they were not of the yellow fever. It was
impoffible for Mr Hamilton to have had a fever
at

at that time of-any other kind. The neighbourhood in which he lived, was healthy, and he had
been daily expofed at his office in Chefnut-ftreet,
to the contagion of the prevailing epidemic. The
difeafe in this cafe was either very light, or Mr
Hamilton owes more to the ftrength of his conftitution, and the goodnefs of heaven, than moft of
the people who recovered from the diforder. That
it was light in all the branches of Mr Hamilton's
family who were infected by him, I infer from this
being the cafe in every fimilar inftance in which
the difeafe fpread in the country.

" Succefs (fays Dr Sydenham) is not a fufficient
proof of the excellency of a method of cure in
acute difeafes, fince fome are recovered by the im-
prudent procedure of old women ; but it is further required, that the diftemper fhould be *eafily
cured*, and yield conformably to its *own* nature*,"
and again, fpeaking of the cure of the new fever
of 1685, this incomparable phyfician obferves,
" If it be objected, that this fever frequently yields
to a quite contrary method to that which I have
laid down, I anfwer, that the cure of a difeafe by
a method which is attended with fuccefs only *now*
and *then* in a *few* inftances, differs extremely from

* Vol. ii. p. 254.

X   that

that practical method, the efficacy whereof appears both from its recovering *greater numbers*, and all the practical phenomena happening in the cure*."

After what has been faid of Mr Hamilton's cure, it will not be expected that I fhould fay any thing of the three patients mentioned in Dr Kuhn's letter to the mayor who recovered under the ufe of Dr Stevens's remedies. The fourth patient mentioned by Dr Kuhn, whom he left on the 4th day of the difeafe with " no unfavourable fymp-toms" was Dr Hutchinfon. I vifited him the day after Dr Kuhn left him, and found him fitting in a chair near the head of his bed, with all his clothes on, as if he had been in his ufual health. A fhort examination of his cafe, fatisfied me that he was in extreme danger. His face was fuffufed with blood. He had a full pulfe, and an hemor-fhage from his gums, which laft fymptom I was told came on the day before. I preffed him to take a ftrong mercurial purge, but he refufed it. From that moment I defpaired of his recovery. He died three days afterwards.

The reader will naturally paufe after reviewing thefe remarks upon the above cures, and afk,

* Vol. ii. p. 354.

whether

whether it was confiftent with the rules of juft and fafe reafoning in medicine, to deduce a general and uniform method of treating this diforder, from the favourable iffue of only four or five cafes, and whether it was candid, to condemn in the moft unqualified manner, a contrary mode of practice, after repeated public, and private declarations, that it had at that time, cured feveral hundred people.

Far be it from me to deny that indirect debility may not be overcome by fuch ftimuli as are more powerful than thofe which occafion it. This has fometimes been demonftrated by the efficacy of bark, wine, and laudanum, in the confluent and petechial fmall-pox; but even this ftate of that diforder, yields more eafily to blood-letting, or to plentiful evacuations from the ftomach and bowels on the firft or fecond day of the eruptive fever. This I have often proved, by giving a large dofe of tartar emetic, and calomel, as foon as I was fatisfied from circumftances, that my patient was infected with the fmall-pox. But the indirect debility of the yellow fever appears to be much greater than that which occurs in the fmall-pox, and hence it more uniformly refifted the moft powerful tonic remedies.

I have

I have publicly afferted, that the remedies which
I adopted, and of which I have given a hiftory,
cured a greater proportion than ninety-nine out
of an hundred of all who applied to me on the
firft day of the diforder before the 15th day of
September. I regret that it is not in my power
to furnifh a lift of them, for a majority of them
were poor people, whofe names are ftill unknown
to me. I was not fingular in this fuccefsful practice in the firft appearance of the diforder. Dr
Penington affured me on his death bed, that he
had not loft one, out of forty-eight patients whom
he had treated agreeably to the principles and
practice I had recommended. Dr Griffitts triumphed over the difeafe in every part of the city,
by the ufe of what were called the new remedies.
My former pupils fpread by their fuccefs, the reputation of purging, and bleeding, wherever they
were called. Unhappily the pleafure we derived
from this fuccefs in the treatment of the diforder,
was of fhort duration. Many circumftances contributed to leffen it, and to revive the mortality
of the fever. I fhall briefly enumerate them.

1. The diftraction produced in the public mind,
by the recommendation of remedies, the oppofites
in every refpect of purging and bleeding.

2. The opinion which had been publifhed by feveral phyficians, and inculcated by others, that we had other fevers in the city befides the yellow fever. This produced a delay in many people in fending for a phyfician, or in taking medicines for two or three days, from a belief that they had nothing but a cold, or a common fever. Some people were fo much deceived by this opinion, that they refufed to fend for phyficians left they fhould be infected by them, with the yellow fever. In moft of the cafes in which thefe delays took place, the difeafe proved mortal.

To obviate a fufpicion, that I have lave laid more ftrefs upon the fatal influence of this error than is juft, I fhall here infert an extract of a letter I have lately been favoured with from Mr John Connelly one of the city committee, who frequently left his brethren in the City Hall, and fpent many hours in vifiting and prefcribing for the fick. " The publications (fays he) of fome phyficians that there were but few perfons infected with the yellow fever, and that many were ill with colds and common remitting and fall fevers, proved fatal to almoft every family which was credulous enough to believe them. That opinion flew its hundreds, if not its thoufands, many of whom did not fend for a phyfician until they were in the laft

ftage

ftage of the diforder, and beyond the power of medicine."

3. The interference of the friends of the ftimulating fyftem, in diffuading patients from fubmitting to fufficient evacuations.

4. The deceptions which were practifed by fome patients upon their phyficians in their reports of the quantity of blood they had loft, or of the quality, and number of their evacuations by ftool.

5. The impracticability of procuring bleeders as foon as bleeding was prefcribed. Life in this difeafe, as in the apoplexy, frequent'y turned upon that operation being performed within an *hour*. It was often delayed from the want of a bleeder, one or two days.

6. The inability of phyficians, from the number of their patients, and from frequent indifpofition, to vifit the fick, at fuch times, as was neceffary to watch the changes in their diforder.

7. The great accumulation, and concentration of the contagion in fick rooms from the continuance of the difeafe in the city, whereby the fyftem

was

was expofed to a conftant ftimulus, and the effect of evacuations was thus defeated.

8. The want of fkill or fidelity in nurfes to ad-minifter the medicines properly, to perfuade pa-tients to drink frequently; alfo to fupply them with food or cordial drinks when required in the night.

9. The great degrees of indirect debility in-duced in the fyftems of many of the people who were affected by the diforder, from fatigue in at-tending their relations or friends.

10. The univerfal depreffion of mind, amounting in fome inftances to defpair, which affected many people. What medicine could act upon a patient who awoke in the night, and faw through the broken and faint light of a candle, no human creature, but a black nurfe, perhaps afleep in a diftant corner of the room; and who heard no noife, but that of a herfe conveying, perhaps a neighbour or a friend, to the grave? The ftate of mind under which many were affected by the dif-eafe, is fo well defcribed by the Rev. Dr Smith in the cafe of his wife, in a letter I received from him in my fick room, two days after her death, that I hope I fhall be execufed for inferting an

X 4   extract

extract from it. It forms a part of the hiftory of the difeafe. The letter was written in anfwer to a fhort note of condolence which I fent to the Doctor immediately after hearing of Mrs Smith's death. After fome pathetic expreffions of grief, he adds, " The fcene of her funeral, and fome preceding circumftances, can never depart from my mind. On our return from a vifit to our daughter, whom we had been ftriving to confole on the death of Mrs Keppele, who was long familiar, and dear to both, my dear wife paffing the burying ground gate, led me into the ground, viewed the graves of her two children, called the old grave digger, marked a fpot for herfelf as clofe as poffible to them and the grave of Dr Phineas Bond, whofe memory fhe adored. Then by the fide of the fpot fhe had chofen, we found room and chofe *mine*, pledging ourfelves to each other, and directing the grave digger that this fhould be the order of our interment. We returned to our houfe. Night approached. I hoped my dear wife had gone to reft as fhe had chofen fince her return from nurfing her daughter, to fleep in a chamber by herfelf, through fear of infecting her grand-child and me. But it feems fhe clofed not her eyes; fitting with them fixed through her chamber window on Mrs Keppele's houfe, 'till about midnight fhe faw her herfe, and followed it

with

with her eyes as far as it could be feen. Two days afterwards Mrs Rodgers, her next only furviving intimate friend, was carried paft her window, and by no perfuafion could I draw her from thence, nor ftop her fympathetic foreboding tears, fo long as her eyes could follow the funeral, which was through two fquares, from Fourth to Second ftreet, where the herfe difappeared." The Doctor proceeds in defcribing the diftrefs of his wife. But pointed as his expreffions are, they do not convey the gloomy ftate of her mind with fo much force as fhe has done it herfelf in two letters to her niece Mrs Cadwallader, who was then in the country. The one was dated the 9th, the other the 11th of October. I fhall infert a few extracts from each of them. " October 9th; It is not poffible for me to pafs the ftreets without walking in a line with the dead. Paffing infected houfes, and looking into open graves. This has been the cafe for many weeks. " I don't know what to write, my head is gone, and my heart is torn to pieces." " I intreat you to have no fears on my account. I am in the hands of a juft and merciful God, and his will be done."

October 11th: " Don't wonder that I am fo low to day. My heart is funk down within me."

The

The next day this excellent woman sickened, and died on the 19th of the fame month.

If in a perfon poffeffed naturally of uncommon equanimity, and fortitude, the diftreffes of our city, produced fuch dejection of fpirits, what muft have been their effect upon hundreds, who were not endowed with thofe rare and extraordinary qualities of mind? Death in this, as well as in many other cafes in which medicine had done its duty, appeared to be the inevitable confequence of the total abftraction of the energy of the mind in reftoring the natural motions of life.

Under all the circumftances which have been mentioned, which oppofed the fyftem of depletion in the cure of this fever, it was ftill far more fuccefsful than any other mode of cure that had been purfued before in the United States or in the Weft Indies.

Three out of four died of the diforder in Jamaica, under the care of Dr Hume.

Dr Blane confiders it as one of the " moft mortal" of difeafes, and Dr Jackfon places a more fuccefsful mode of treating it, among the
subjects

fubjects which will admit of " innovation" in
medicine.

After the 15th of September my fuccefs was
much limited, compared with what it had been
before that time. But at no period of the dif afe
did I lofe more than one in twenty of thofe whom
I faw on the firft day, and attended regularly
through every ftage of the fever; provided they
had not been previoufly worn down by attending
the fick.

The following ftatement which will admit of
being corrected, if it be inaccurate, will I hope,
eftablifh the truth of the above affertions.

About one half of the families whom I have attended for many years, left the city. Of thofe
who remained, many were affected by the diforder. Out of the whole of them, after I had
adopted my fecond mode of practice, I loft only
five heads of families, and about a dozen fervants
and children. In no inftance did I lofe both heads
of the fame family. My fuccefs in thefe cafes was
owing to two caufes; 1ft, To the credit my former patients gave to my public declaration, that
we had only *one* fever in the city; hence they applied

plied on the *firſt* day, and fometimes on the *firſt*
hour of their indifpofition ; and 2dly, To the numerous pledges many of them had feen of the
fafety and efficacy of copious blood-letting by my
advice, in other difeafes : hence my prefcription
of that neceffary remedy, was always obeyed in
its utmoſt extent.   Of the few adults whom I loſt,
among my former patients, two of them were old
people ; two took laudanum without my knowledge ; and one refufed to take medicine of any
kind ; all the reſt had been worn down by previous fatigue.

I have before faid that a great number of the
blacks were my patients.   Of thefe not one died
under my care.   This uniform fuccefs among
thofe people, was not owing altogether to the
mildnefs of the difeafe, for I fhall fay prefently,
that a great proportion of a given number died
under other modes of practice.

In fpeaking of the comparative effects of purging and bleeding, it may not be amifs to repeat,
that not one pregnant woman to whom I prefcribed them died, or fuffered abortion.   Where
the tonic remedies were ufed, abortion or death,
and in many inſtances both, were nearly univerfal.
                                                    Many

Many whole families, confifting of five, fix, and in three inftances, of nine members, were recovered by plentiful purging and bleeding. I could fwell this work by publifhing a lift of thofe families; but I take more pleafure in adding, that I was not fingular in my fuccefs in the ufe of the above remedies. They were prefcribed with great advantage by many of the phyficians of the city, who had for a while given tonic medicines without effect. I fhall not mention the names of any of the phyficians who *totally* renounced thofe medicines, left I fhould give offence by not mentioning them all. Many large families were cured by fome of them, after they adopted and prefcribed copious purging and blood-letting. One of them cured ten in the family of Mr Robert Haydock, by means of thofe remedies. In one of that family the difeafe came on with a vomiting of black bile.

But the ufe of the new remedies was not directed finally by the phyficians alone. The clergy, the apothecaries, many private citizens, feveral intelligent women, and two black men, prefcribed them with great fuccefs. Nay more, many perfons prefcribed them to themfelves; and as I fhall fay hereafter, with a fuccefs that was unequalled by any of the regular or irregular practitioners in the city.

It

It was owing to the almoſt univerſal uſe of
purging and bleeding, that the mortality of the
diſeaſe diminiſhed in proportion as the number of
perſons who were affected by it, encreaſed about the
middle of October. It was ſcarcely double of what
it was in the middle of September, and yet ſix
times the number of perſons were probably at
that time confined by it.

The ſuccefs of copious purging and bleeding
was not confined to the city of Philadelphia. Several perſons who caught the diſeaſe in town, and
ſickened in the country, were cured by them.

Could a compariſon be made of the number of
patients who died of our late fever, after having
been plentifully bled and purged, with thoſe who
died of the yellow fever in the years 1699, 1741,
1747, and 1762, I am perſuaded that the proportion would be very ſmall in the year 1793, compared with the former years *. Including all who
died under every mode of treatment, I ſuſpect the

* It appears from one of Mr Norris's letters, dated the
9th of November, O. S. that there died 220 perſons in the
year 1699, with the yellow fever. Between 80 and 90 of
them he ſays belonged to the ſociety of Friends. The city
at this time probably did not contain more than 2 or 3000
people, many of whom it is probable fled from the diſorder.

mortality.

mortality to be lefs in proportion to the population of the city, and the number of perfons who were affected, than it was in any of the other years that have been mentioned.

Not lefs than 6000 of the inhabitants of Philadelphia probably owe their lives to purging and bleeding, during the late autumn.

I proceed with reluctance to inquire into the comparative fuccefs of the French practice. It would not be difficult to decide upon it from many facts that came under my notice in the city; but I fhall reft its merit wholly upon the returns of the number of deaths at Bufh-hill. This hofpital, after the 22d of September, was put under the care of a French phyfician, who was affifted by one of the phyficians of the city. The hofpital was in a pleafant and airy fituation; it was provided with all the neceffaries and comforts for fick people that humanity could invent, or liberality fupply. The attendants were devoted to their duty; and cleanlinefs and order pervaded every room in the houfe. The reputation of this hofpital, and of the French phyfician, drew patients to it in the early ftage of the diforder. Of this I have been affured in a letter from Dr Annan, who was appointed to examine and give orders of admiffion

into

into the hofpital, to fuch of the poor of the di-
ftrict of Southwark, as could not be taken care of
in their own houfes.   Mr Olden has likewife informed me, that moft of the patients who were
fent to the hofpital by the city committee (of
which he was a member) were in the firft ftage of
the fever.   With all thefe advantages, the deaths
between the 22d of September and the 6th of
November, amounted to 448 out of 807 patients who were admitted into the hofpital within
that time.   Three fourths of all the blacks (nearly 20) who were patients in this hofpital died.
A lift of the medicines prefcribed there may be
feen in the minutes of the proceedings of the city
committee.   Calomel and jalap are not among
them.   *Moderate* bleeding and purging with
Glauber falts, I have been informed, were ufed
in fome cafes by the phyficians of this hofpital.
The proportion of deaths to the recoveries, as it
appears in the minutes of the committee from
whence the above report is taken, is truly melancholy! I hurry from it therefore to a part of this
work, to which I have looked with pleafure, ever
fince I fat down to compofe it.

    I have faid that the clergy, the apothecaries,
and many other perfons who were uninftructed in
the principles of medicine, prefcribed purging, and
                                          bleeding

bleeding with great fuccefs in this diforder. Neceffity gave rife to this undifciplined fect of practitioners, for they came forward to fupply the places
of the regular bred phyficians who were fick or
dead. I fhall mention the names of a few of thofe
perfons who diftinguifhed themfelves as volunteers
in this new work of humanity. The late Rev.
Mr Fleming one of the minifters of the Catholic
church, carried the purging powders in his pocket,
and gave them to his poor parifhioners with great
fuccefs. He even became the advocate of the new
remedies. In a converfation I had with him on
the 22d of September, he informed me, that he
had advifed four of our phyficians whom he met
a day or two before, " to renounce the pride of
fcience, and to adopt the new mode of practice,
for that he had witneffed its good effects in many
cafes." Mr John Keihmle, a German apothecary,
has affured me that out of 314 patients whom he
vifited, and 187 for whom he prefcribed from the
reports of their friends, he loft only 47 (which is
nearly but one in eleven) and that he treated them
all agreeably to the method which I had recommended. The Rev. Mr Schmidt one of the minifters of the Lutheran church, was cured by him.
I have before mentioned an inftance of the judgment of Mr Connelly, and of his zeal in vifiting
and prefcribing for the fick. His remedies were

Y

bleeding

bleeding and purging. He moreover, bore a conftant and ufeful teftimony againft bark, wine, laudanum, and the warm bath*. Mrs Paxton in
Carter's alley, and Mrs Evans the wife of Mr
John Evans in Second-ftreet, were indefatigable;
the one in diftributing mercurial purges compofed
by herfelf, and the other in urging the neceffity
of *copious* bleeding and purging among her friends
and neighbours, as the only fafe remedies for the
fever. Thefe worthy women were the means of
faving many lives†. Abfalom Jones, and Richard
Allen, two black men, fpent all the intervals of

---

* In the letter before quoted, from Mr Connelly he ex-
preffes his opinion of thofe four medicines in the following
words. " Laudanum, bark, and wine, have put a period
to the exiftence of fome, where the fever has been apparently broken, and the patients in a fair way of recovery;
a fingle dofe of laudanum has hurried them fuddenly into eternity. I have vifited a few patients, where the hot
bath was ufed, and am convinced that it only tended to
weaken, and relax the fyftem, without producing any good
effect."

† The yellow fever prevailed at the Caraccos in South
America in October 1793, with great mortality, more efpecially among the Spanifh troops. Nearly all died who
were attended by Phyficians. Recourfe was finally had to
the old women, who were fuccefsful in almoft every cafe to
which they were called. Their remedies were a liquor called
narencado (a fpecies of lemonade) and a tea made of a root
called

time, in which they were not employed in burying the dead, in vifiting the poor who were fick, and in bleeding and purging them, agreeably to the directions which had been printed in all the news papers. Their fuccefs was unparalleled by what is called regular practice. This encomium upon the practice of the blacks, will not furprife the reader when I add, that they had no fear of putrefaction in the fluids, nor of the calumnies of a body of fellow citizens in the republic of medicine, to deter them from plentiful purging and bleeding. They had befides no more patients, than they were able to vifit two or three times a day. But great as their fuccefs was, it was exceeded by thofe perfons who in defpair of procuring medical aid of any kind, purged and bled themfelves. This palm of fuperior fuccefs, will not be withheld from thofe people, when I explain the caufes of it. It was owing to their *early* ufe of the proper remedies, and to their being guided in the repetition of them, by the continuance of a tenfe pulfe, or of pain and fever. A day, an af-

called *fiftula*. With thefe drinks, they drenched their patients for the firft two or three days. They induced plentiful fweats, and probably, after blunting, difcharged the bile from the bowels. I received this information from an American gentleman who had been cured by one of thofe amazons in medicine, in the above way.

ternoon,

ternoon, and even an hour, were not loft by thefe
people in waiting for the vifit of a Phyfician who
was often detained from them, by ficknefs, or by
new and·unexpected engagements, by which means
the precious moment for ufing the remedies, with
effect, paffed irrevocably away.   I have ftated
thefe facts from faithful inquiries, and numerous
obfervations.   I could mention the names, and
families of many perfons who thus cured themfelves.   One perfon only fhall be mentioned, who
has fhewn by her conduct what reafon is capable
of doing when it is forced to act for itfelf.   Mrs
Long, a widow, after having been twice unfuccefsful in her attempts to procure a phyfician, undertook at laft to cure herfelf.   She took feveral
of the mercurial purges, agreeably to the printed
directions, and had herfelf bled *feven* times in the
courfe of five or fix days.   The indication for repeating the bleeding, was the continuance of the
pain in her head.   Her recovery was rapid, and
complete.   The hiftory of it was communicated
to me by herfelf, with great gratitude, in my own
houfe, during my fecond confinement with the
fever.   To thefe accounts of perfons who cured
themfelves in the city, I could add many others,
of citizens who fickened in the country, and who
cured themfelves by plentiful bleeding and purging, without the attendance of a phyfician.

From

From a fhort review of thefe facts, reafon, and humanity awake from their long repofe in medicine, and unite in proclaiming, that it is time to take the cure of peftilential fevers out of the hands of phyficians, and to place it in the hands of the people. Let not the reader ftartle at this propofition. I fhall give the following reafons for it.

1. In confequence of thefe peftilential fevers affecting a great number of people at one time, it has always been, and always will be impoffible, for them *all* to have the benefit of medical aid, more efpecially as the proportion of phyficians to the number of fick, is generally diminifhed upon thefe occafions, by defertion, ficknefs and death.

2. The fafety of committing to the people the cure of peftilential fevers, particularly the yellow fever and the plague, is eftablifhed by the fimplicity and uniformity of their proximate caufe, and of their remedies. However diverfified they may be in their fymptoms, the fyftem in both difeafes is always under a ftate of indirect debility, and in all cafes requires the abftraction of ftimulus in a greater or lefs degree, or in a fudden or gradual manner. There can never be any danger of the people injuring themfelves by miftaking any other difeafe for a yellow fever, or a plague,

for

for no other febrile diforder can prevail with them. It was probably to prevent this miftake, that the Benevolent Father of mankind, who has permitted no evil to exift which does not carry its antidote along with it, originally impofed that law upon all great and mortal epidemics.

3. The hiftory of the yellow fever in the Weft Indies, proves the advantage of trufting patients to their own judgment. Dr Lind has remarked, that a greater proportion of failors who had no phyficians, recovered from that fever, than of thofe who had the beft medical affiftance. The frefh air of the deck of a fhip, a purge of falt water, and the free ufe of cold water, probably triumphed here over the cordial juleps of phy-ficians.

4. By committing the cure of this and other peftilential difeafes to the people, all thofe cir-cumftances which prevented the univerfal fuccefs of purging, and bleeding in our late epidemic, will have no operation. The fever will be mild in moft cafes, for all will prepare themfelves to receive it by a vegetable diet, and by moderate evacuations. The remedies will be ufed the *mo-ment* the difeafe is felt, or even feen, and the con-tagion generated by it, will be feeble and propa-gated

-gated only to a fmall diftance from fuch patients. There will then be no difputes among phyficians about the nature of the difeafe to diftract the public mind, for they will feldom be confulted in it. None will fuffer from chronic debility induced by previous fatigue, in attending the fick, nor from the want of nurfes, for few will be fo ill as to require them, and there will be no " foreboding" fears of death or defpair of recovery, to invite an attack of the difeafe, or to enfure its mortality.

The fmall-pox was once as fatal as the yellow fever and the plague. At prefent, it yields as univerfally to a vegetable diet, and evacuations, in the hands of apothecaries, the clergy, and even of the good women, as it does in the hands of Doctors of phyfic.

They have narrow conceptions, not only of the divine goodnefs, but of the gradual progrefs of human knowledge, who fuppofe that all peftilential difeafes fhall not, like the fmall-pox, fooner or later ceafe to be the fcourge and terror of mankind.

For a long while air, water and even the light of the fun, were dealt out by phyficians to their patients with a fparing hand. They poffeffed for feveral centuries the fame monopoly of many artificial
Y 4   remedies.

remedies. But a new order of things is rifing in medicine as well as in government. Air, water, and light are taken without the advice of a phyfi-cian, and bark and laudanum are now prefcribed every where by nurfes, and miftreffes of families, with fafety and advantage. Human reafon cannot be ftationary upon thefe fubjeɛts. The time muft, and will come, when in addition to the above reme-dies, the general ufe of calomel, jalap, and the lancet, fhall be confidered among the moft effen-tial articles of the knowledge, and rights of man.

It is no more neceffary, that a patient fhould be ignorant of the medicine he takes to be cured by it, than that the bufinefs of government fhould be conducted with fecrecy in order to enfure obedi-ence to juft laws. Much lefs is it neceffary that the means of life 'fhould be prefcribed in a dead language, or dictated with the folemn pomp of a necromancer. The effeɛts of impofture in every' thing are like the artificial health produced by the ufe of ardent fpirits. Its vigour is temporary, and is always followed by mifery and death.

The belief that the yellow fever and the plague are neceffarily mortal, is as much the effeɛt of a fuperftitious torpor in the underftanding, as the ancient belief, that the epilepfy was a fupernatural difeafe, and that it was an offence againft heaven

to

to attempt to cure it. It is partly from the influence of this torpor in the minds of fome people,
that the numerous cures of the yellow fever performed by a few fimple remedies, were faid to be
of *other* difeafes. It is neceffary, for the conviction of fuch perfons, that patients fhould always
die of that, and other dangerous diforders, to prove
that they have been affected by them.

The repairs which our world is undergoing, as
far as they relate to the melioration of the condition of man, will be incomplete, until peftilential
fevers ceafe to be numbered among the wideft
outlets of human life.

There are many things which are now familiar
to women and children which were known a century ago only to a few men who lived in clofets,
and were diftinguifhed by the name of philofo-
phers.

We teach an hundred things in our fchools lefs
ufeful, and many things more difficult, than the
knowledge that would be neceffary to cure a yellow fever or the plague.

In my attempts to teach the citizens of Philadelphia by my different publications, the method
of

.of curing themselves of our late fever, I observed
. no difficulty in their apprehending every thing
that was addressed to them, except what related
· to the different states of the pulse. All the knowledge that is necessary to discover when blood-
letting is proper, might be taught to a boy or
.girl of twelve years old in a few hours. I taught
it in less time to several persons during the prevalence of our late epidemic.

I would as soon believe that ratafia was intended by the Author of Nature, to be the only
drink of man, instead of water, as believe that
the knowledge of what relates to the health and
lives of a *whole* city, or nation, should be confined to one, and that a small or a privileged order
of men.—But what have physicians, what have
unversities, or medical societies done after the
labours, and studies of many centuries towards
lessening the mortality of pestilential fevers?
They have either copied, or contradicted each
other in all their publications. Plagues and malignant fevers, are still leagued with war and famine, in their ravages upon human life.

Botallus in France, and Dr Sydenham in England, it is true, long ago used the proper remedies
for those diforders with universal succefs; but
they

they were unable to introduce them into general practice. The reafon is obvious: They recommended them in their writings only to phyficians. At the expence of an immenfe load of obloquy, I have addreffed my publications to the people. The appeal though hazardous, in the prefent ftate of general knowledge in medicine, has fucceeded. The citizens of Philadelphia are delivered from their fears of copious evacuations, of cold air, and cold water, and above all, of a fore mouth from mercury, in the cure of the yellow fever; and the pride and formalities of medicine, as far as they relate to this difeafe, are now as completely difcarded in our city, as the deceptions of witchcraft were, above a century ago.

To prevent the propagation and mortality of this fever, it will be neceffary when it makes its appearance in a city or country, to publifh an account of thofe fymptoms which I have called the *precurfors* of the difeafe, and to exhort the people as foon they feel thofe fymptoms, to have immediate recourfe to the remedies of purging or bleeding. The danger of delay in ufing one, or both thofe remedies, fhould be inculcated in the ftrongeft terms, for the difeafe, like Time, has a lock on its forehead, but is bald behind. The bite of a rattle-fnake is feldom fatal, becaufe the

medicines

medicines which cure it, are applied, or taken, as foon as the poifon comes in contact with the blood. There is lefs danger to be apprehended from the contagion of the yellow fever in the fyftem than from the poifon of the fnake, provided the remedies for it, are adminiftered within a few hours after it is excited into action.

Let perfons who are fubject to chronic pains, or difeafes of any kind, be advifed not to be deceived by them. Every pain at fuch a time, is the beginning of the difeafe; for the contagion I have faid, always acts firft on debilitated parts of the body. From an ignorance of this law of epidemics many perfons by delaying their applications for help, perifhed with our late fever.

Let nature be trufted in no cafe whatever, to cure this difeafe; and let no attack of it, however light, be treated with 'neglect. Death as certainly performs his work, when he fteals on the fyftem in the form of a mild intermittent, as he does, when he comes on with the fymptoms of apoplexy, or a black vomiting.

Cleanlinefs in houfes and drefs, cannot be too often inculcated during the prevalence of a yellow fever.

Laftly,

Laftly, Let thofe who are in health be directed to prepare their bodies by means of a low diet, for the reception of the difeafe in the manner that has been formerly mentioned ; and let pleafure, and even labour, where it expofes men to the heat of the fun, or of a culinary fire, be every where fufpended. Thus, while the fyftem is prepared to bend like the willow, the contagion of the fever will pafs over it, without doing any harm.

Let it not be fuppofed, that I mean, that the hiftory which I have given of the method of cure of our late epidemic, fhould be applied in all its parts, to the yellow fevers which may appear hereafter in the United States, or which exift at all times in the Weft India iflands. Seafon and climate vary this, as well as all other difeafes. Bark and wine, fo fatal in our late, may be proper in a future yellow fever. But without the fear of being refuted, I will notwithftanding affert, that the proper remedies for this fever at all times, and in all places in its *firft* ftage, *muft be* evacuations. The only inquiry, when the difeafe makes its appearance, fhould be, from what part of the body thefe evacuations fhould be procured ; the order which fhould be purfued in obtaining them, and the quantity of each of the matters to

-be

be difcharged, which fhould be withdrawn at a time.

Thus far did I venture from my theory of the difeafe, and from the authorities of Dr Hillary and and Dr Mofely, to decide in favour of evacuations in the yellow fever in hot climates ; but Dr Wade, and Mr Chifholm again fupport me by their practice in the fevers of the Eaft and Weft Indies. They both gave ftrong mercurial purges, and bled in fome cafes. Dr Wade confirmed by his practice, the advantage, of *gradually* abftracting ftimulus from the fyftem. He never drew blood even in the moft inflammatory cafes, until he had firft difcharged the contents of the bowels. The Doctor has further eftablifhed the efficacy of a vegetable diet, and of water as a drink, as the beft means of preventing the difor-der in a hot climate.

The manner in which the contagion of the plague acts upon the fyftem, is fo much like that which has been defcribed in the yellow fever, and the accounts of the efficacy of low diet in pre-paring the body for its reception, and of copious bleeding, cold air and cold water, in curing it, are fo fimilar, that all the directions which relate

to

to preventing, mitigating, or curing the yellow
fever, may be applied to it. The fluids in the
plague fhew a greater tendency to the fkin,
than they do, in the yellow fever. Perhaps
upon this account, the early ufe of powerful
fudorifics may be more proper in the former,
than in the latter diforder. From the influence of early purging, and bleeding in promoting fweat in the yellow fever; there can be
little doubt, but the efforts of nature to unload
the fyftem in the plague through the channel of
the pores, might be accelerated by the early ufe
of the fame remedies. One thing with refpeft
to the plague is certain; that its cure depends
upon the abftraction of ftimulus, either by means
of plentiful fweats, or of purulent matter from external fores. Perhaps the efficacy of thefe remedies depends wholly upon their diminifhing
the indirect debility of the fyftem in a *gradual*
manner. If this be the cafe, thofe natural difcharges might be eafily and effectually imitated
by fmall and repeated bleedings.

To correfpond in quantity with the difcharge
from the fkin, blood-letting in the plague fhould
be copious. A profufe fweat continued for twenty four hours, cannot fail of wafting many pounds
of the fluids of the body. This was the duration
of

4

of the critical fweats in the famous plague which
was known by the name of the Englifh fweating
ficknefs, and which made its appearance in the
army of Henry VII. in Milford-Haven in Wales,
and fpread from thence through every part of the
kingdom.

The principles which lead to the prevention and
cure of the yellow fever and the plague, apply
with equal force to the mitigation of the meafles,
and to the prevention or mitigation of the fcarlatina
anginofa, the dyfentery, and the jail or hofpital fever. I have remarked in a former publication *, that
a previous vegetable diet leffened the violence and
danger of the meafles.   Dr Sims taught me feveral years ago, to prevent or mitigate the fcarlatina
anginofa, by means of gentle purges after children
are infected by it †.   Purges of falts have in many
inftances preferved whole families and neighbourhoods from the dyfentery where they have been
expofed to the contagion.   During the late American war, an emetic feldom failed of preventing
an attack of the hofpital fever, when given in its
forming ftate ‡.   I have had no experience of the

* Medical Inquiries and Obfervations, vol. ii. page 244.
† Medical Memoirs, vol. i.
‡ Medical Inquiries and Obfervations. London Edition,
vol. i. page 211.

effects

effects of previous evacuations in abating the violence, or preventing the mortality of the malignant fore throat, but I can have no doubt of their efficacy from the famenefs of the ftate of the fyftem in that diforder, as in other malignant fevers. The debility induced in it, is of the indirect kind, and the fuppofed fymptoms of putrefaction, are nothing but the difguifed effects of a fudden and violent preffure of an inflammatory ftimulus upon the arterial fyftem.

With thefe obfervations I clofe the hiftory of the rife, progrefs, fymptoms, and treatment of the bilious remitting yellow fever which lately appeared in Philadelphia. My principal aim has been to revive, and apply to it, the principles, and practice of Dr. Sydenham, and however coldly thofe principles, and that practice may be received by fome phyficians of the prefent day, I am fatiffied that experience in all ages, and in all coun-tries will vouch for their truth and utility.

Z

NARRATIVES of efcapes from great dangers of fhipwreck, war, captivity, and famine, have always formed an interefting part of the hiftory of the body, and mind of man. But there are deliverances from equal dangers, which have hitherto paffed unnoticed; I mean, from peftilential fevers. I fhall briefly defcribe the ftate of my body and mind, during my intercourfe with the fick in our late epidemic. The account will throw additional light upon the diforder, and probably illuftrate fome of the laws of the animal economy. It will moreover ferve to furnifh a leffon to all who may be placed in fimilar circumftances, to commit their lives without fear, to the protection of that BEING who is able to fave to the uttermoft, not only from future, but from prefent evil.

Some time before the fever made its appearance, my wife and children went into the ftate of New-Jerfey where they had long been in the habit of fpending the fummer months. My family about

Z 2   the

the 25th of Auguft, confifted of my mother, a fifter who was on a vifit to me, a black fervant man,
and a mulatto boy. I had five pupils, viz. Warner
Wafhington, and Edward Fifher, of Virginia,
John Alfton of South Carolina, and John Redman Coxe (grandfon to Dr Redman) and John
Stall both of this city. They all crouded around
me upon the fudden encreafe of bufinefs, and with
one heart devoted themfelves to my fervice, and
to the caufe of humanity.

The credit which the new mode of treating the
difeafe acquired in all parts of the city, produced
an immenfe influx of patients to me from all quar-
ters. My pupils were conftantly employed; at
firft in putting up purging powders, but after a
while only in bleeding and vifiting the fick.

Between the eighth and the 15th of September
I vifited and prefcribed for, between an hundred
and an hundred and twenty patients a day. Several
of my pupils vifited a fourth or fifth part of that
number. For a while we refufed no calls. In
the fhort intervals of bufinefs which I fpent at my
meals, my houfe was filled with patients, chiefly
the poor, waiting for advice. For many weeks I
feldom ate without prefcribing for numbers as I
fat at my table. To affift me at thefe hours, as
well

well as in the night, Mr Stall, Mr Fisher and Mr Coxe accepted of rooms in my houfe, and became members of my family. Their labours now had no remiffion.

Immediately after I adopted the antiphlogiftic mode of treating the diforder, I altered my manner of living. I left off drinking wine and malt liquors. The good effects of the difufe of thefe liquors, helped to confirm me in the theory I had adopted of the difeafe. A troublefome head-ach, which I had occafionally felt, and which excited a conftant apprehenfion that I was taking the fever, now fuddenly left me. I likewife at this time left off eating folid animal food, and lived wholly, but fparingly, upon weak broth, potatoes, raifins, coffee, and bread and butter.

From my great intercourfe with the fick, my body became highly impregnated with the contagion. My eyes were yellow, and fometimes a yellownefs was perceptible in my face. My pulfe was preternaturally quick, and I had profufe fweats every night. Thefe fweats were fo offenfive as to oblige me to draw the bed-cloths clofe to my neck to defend myfelf from their fmell. They loft their factor entirely upon my leaving

Z 3 off

off the ufe of broth, and living intirely upon
milk and vegetables. But my nights were rendered difagreeable, not only by thefe fweats, but
by the want of my ufual fleep, produced in part
by the frequent knocking at my door, and in part
by anxiety of mind, and the ftimulus of the contagion upon my fyftem. I lay down in conformi-
ty to habit only, for my bed ceafed to afford me
reft or refrefhment. When it was evening, I
wifhed for morning; and when it was morning,
the profpect of the labours of the day, caufed me
to wifh for the return of evening. The degrees
of my anxiety may be eafily conceived, when I
add, that I had at one time upwards of thirty
heads of families under my care: among thefe
were Mr Jofiah Coates, the father of eight, and
Mr Benjamin Scull, and Mr John Morrell, each
fathers of ten children. They were all in imminent danger; but it pleafed God to make me the
inftrument of faving each of their lives. I rofe
at 6 o'clock, and generally found a number of
perfons waiting for advice in my fhop or parlour.
Hitherto the fuccefs of my practice gave a tone
to my mind, which imparted preternatural vigour
to my body. It was meat and drink to me to ful-
fil the duties I owed to my fellow citizens in this
time of great and univerfal diftrefs. From a hope

that

that I might efcape the difeafe, by avoiding every
thing that could excite the contagion in my body
into action, I carefully avoided the heat of the
fun, and the coldnefs of the evening air. I likewife avoided yielding to every thing that fhould
raife or deprefs my paffions. But at fuch a time,
the events which influence the ftate of the body
and mind are no more under our command, than
the winds or weather. On the evening of the
14th of September, after eight o'clock, I vifited
the fon of Mrs Berriman, near the Swedes'
church, who had fent for me early in the morning. I found him very ill. He had been bled in
the forenoon by my advice, but his pulfe indicated a fecond bleeding. It would have been difficult to procure a bleeder at that late hour. I
therefore bled him myfelf. From hanging over
his breath and blood for ten minutes, and afterwards riding home in the night air, debilitated as
I was by the labours of the day, I found myfelf
much indifpofed the enfuing night. I rofe not-
withflanding at my ufual hour. At 8 o'clock I
loft ten ounces of blood, and immediately afterwards got into my chair, and vifited between forty and fifty patients before dinner. At the houfe
of one of them, I was forced to lie down a few
minutes. In the courfe of this morning's labours,
my mind was fuddenly thrown off its pivots, by

the

the laft look, and the pathetic cries of a friend
for *help*, who was dying under the care of a
French phyfician. I came home about two o'clock,
and was feized immediately afterwards with a
chilly fit and a high fever. I took a dofe of the
mercurial medicine, and went to bed. In the
eveaing I took a fecond purging powder, and loft
ten ounces more of blood. The next morning I
bathed my face, hands, and feet in cold water for
fome time. I drank plentifully during the day and
night of weak hyfon tea, and of water, in which
currant jelly had been diffolved. At eight o'clock
I was fo well as to admit perfons who came for advice into my room, and to receive reports from
my pupils of the ftate of as many of my patients
as they were able to vifit; for unfortunately they
were not able to vifit them all (with their own)
in due time; by which means feveral died. The
next day I came down ftairs, and prefcribed in my
parlour for not lefs than an hundred people. Oni
the 19th of the fame month, I refumed my labours, but in great weaknefs. It was with difficulty that I afcended a pair of ftairs, by the help
of a banifter. A flow fever, attended with irregular chills, and a troublefome cough, hung conftantly upon me. The fever difcovered itfelf in
the heat of my hands, which my patients often
told me were warmer than their own. The contagion

tagion now began to affect me in fmall and infected rooms, in the moft fenfible manner. On the
morning of the 4th of October I fuddenly funk
down in a fick room upon a bed, with a giddinefs
in my head. It continued for a few minutes, and
was fucceeded by a fever which confined me to
my houfe the remaining part of the day.

Every moment in the intervals of my vifits to
the fick, was employed in prefcribing in my own
houfe for the poor, or in fending anfwers to mef-
fages from my patients ; time was now too precious to be fpent in counting the number of perfons who called upon me for advice. From circumftances, I believe it was frequently 150, and
feldom lefs than 50 in a day, for five or fix weeks.
The evening did not bring with it the leaft relaxation from my labours. I received letters every
day from the country, and from diftant parts of
the Union, containing inquiries into the mode of
treating the diforder, and after the health and
lives of perfons who had remained in the city.
The bufinefs of every evening was to anfwer thefe
letters, alfo to write to my family. Thefe employments by affording a frefh current to my
thoughts, kept me from dwelling on the gloomy
fcenes of the day. After thefe duties were performed, I copied into my note book all the obfervations

vations I had collected during the day, and which I had marked with a pencil in my pocket book in fick rooms, or in my carriage. To thefe conftant labours of body and mind were added diftreffes, from a variety of caufes. Having found myfelf unable to comply with the numerous applications that were made to me, I was obliged to refufe many, every day. ˙ My fifter counted forty feven in one forenoon before 11 o'clock. Many of them left my door with tears, but they did not feel more diftrefs than I did, from refufing to follow them. Sympathy when it vents itfelf in acts of humanity, affords pleafure, and contributes to health, but the reflux of pity, like anger, gives pain, and diforders the body. In riding through the ftreets, I was often forced to refift the entreaties of parents imploring a vifit to their children, or of children to their parents. I recollect, and even yet, I recollect with pain, that I tore myfelf at one time from five perfons in Moravian-alley who attempted to ftop me ; by fuddenly whipping my horfe, and driving my chair as fpeedily as poffible beyond the reach of their cries.

The folicitude of the friends of the fick for help, may further be conceived of, when I add, that the moft extravagant compenfations were fometimes offered for medical fervices, and in one

inftance,

inftance, for only a fingle vifit. I had no merit in refuling thefe offers, and I have introduced an account of them, only to inform fuch phyficians as may hereafter be thrown into a fimilar fituation, that I was favoured with an exemption from the fear of death, in proportion as I fubdued every felfifh feeling, and laboured exclufively for the benefit of others. In every inftance in which I was forced to refufe thefe pathetic and earneft applications, my diftrefs was heightened. by the fear, that the perfons whom I was unable to vifit, would fall into improper hands, and perifh by the ufe of bark, wine, and laudanum.

But I had other afflictions befides the diftrefs which arofe from the abortive fympathy which I have defcribed. On the 11th of September, my ingenious pupil Mr Wafhington, fell a victim to his humanity. He had taken lodgings in the country, where he fickened with the diforder. Having been almoft uniformly fuccefsful in curing others, he made light of his fever, and concealed the knowledge of his danger from me, until the day before he died. On the 18th of September Mr Stall fickened in my houfe. A delirium attended his fever from the firft hour it affected him. He refufed, and even refifted force when ufed to compel him to take medicine. He died on the 23d

of

of September*. Scarcely had I recovered from the shock of the death of this amiable youth, when I was called to weep for a third pupil, Mr Alfton, who died in my neighbourhood, the next day. He had worn himfelf down before his ficknefs, by uncommon exertions in vifiting, bleeding, and even fitting up with fick people. At this time Mr Fifher was ill in my houfe. On the 26th of the month at 12 o'clock Mr Coxe my only affiftant was feized with the fever, and went to his grand father's.

---

* This accomplifhed youth had made great attainments in his profeffion. He poffeffed with an uncommon genius for fcience, talents for mufic, painting and poetry. The following copy of an unfinifhed letter to his father (who had left the city) was found among his papers, after his death. It fhews that the qualities of his heart, were equal to thofe of his head.

Philadelphia, September 15, 1793.

" My DEAR FATHER,

" I TAKE every moment I have to fpare to write to you, which is not many, but you muft excufe me as I am doing good to my fellow creatures. At this time every moment I fpend in idlenefs, might probably coft a life. The ficknefs encreafes every day, but moft of thofe who die, die for want of good attendance. We cure all we are called to on the firft day, who are well attended, but fo many Doctors are fick, the poor creatures are glad to get a Doctor's fervant."

I fol-

I followed him with a look, which I feared would be the laft, in my houfe. At two o'clock my fifter who had complained for feveral days, yielded to the diforder, and retired to her bed. My mother followed her, much indifpofed, early in the evening. My black fervant man had been confined with the fever for feveral days, and had on that day for the firft time quitted his bed. My little mulatto boy of eleven years old, was the only perfon in my family who was able to afford me the leaft affiftance. At 8 o'clock in the evening, I finifhed the bufinefs of the day. A folemn ftillnefs at that time pervaded the ftreets. In vain did I ftrive to forget my melancholy fituation by anfwering letters, and by putting up medicines to be diftributed next day among my patients. My faithful black man crept to my door, and at my requeft fat down by the fire, but he added by his filence and dullnefs, to the gloom which fuddenly overpowered every faculty of my mind.

On the firft day of October at two o'clock in the afternoon, my fifter died. I got into my carriage within an hour after fhe expired, and fpent the afternoon in vifiting patients. According as a fenfe of duty, or as grief has predominated in my mind, I have approved, and difapproved of this act, ever fince. She had borne a fhare in my labours. She

had

had been my nurfe in ficknefs, and my cafuift in my choice of duties. My whole heart repofed itfelf in her friendfhip. Upon being invited to a friend's houfe in the country, when the difeafe made its appearance in the city, fhe declined accepting the invitation, and gave as a reafon for fo doing, that I might probably require her fervices in cafe of my taking the diforder, and that if fhe were fure of dying, fhe would remain with me, provided that by her death, fhe could fave my life. From this time I declined in health and ftrength. All motion became painful to me. My appetite began to fail. My night fweats continued. My fhort and imperfect fleep, was difturbed by diftreffing, or frightful dreams. The fcenes of them were derived altogether from fick rooms, and grave yards. I concealed my forrows as much as poffible from my patients, but when alone, the retrofpect of what was paft, and the profpect of what was before me, the termination of which was invifible, often filled my foul with the moft poignant anguifh. I wept frequently when retired from the public eye, but I did not weep over the loft members of my family alone. I beheld or heard every day of the deaths of citizens ufeful in public, or amiable in private life. It was my misfortune to lofe as patients, the Rev. Mr Fleming and Mr Graefel, both exhaufted by their

labours

labours of piety and love among the poor, before they fickened with the diforder. I faw the laft ftruggles of departing life in Mr Powel, and de-plored in his death, an upright and faithful fervant of the public, as well as a fincere and affectionate friend. Often did I mourn over perfons who had by the moft unparalleled exertions, faved their friends and families from the grave, at the expence of their own lives. Many of thefe martyrs to humanity, were in humble ftations. Among the members of my profeffion with whom I had been moft intimately connected, I had daily caufe of grief and diftrefs. I faw the great and expanded mind of Dr Penington, fhattered by delirium, juft before he died. He was to me dear and beloved, like a younger brother. He was moreover a Joab in the conteft with the difeafe. Philadelphia muft long deplore the premature death of this ex-cellent phyfician. Had he lived a few years lon-ger, he would have filled an immenfe fpace in the republic of medicine*. It was my affliction to fee my friend Dr John Morris breathe his laft, and

* Before he finifhed his ftudies in medicine, he publifhed a volume of ingenious and patriotic " Chemical and Œco-nomical Effays, defigned to illuftrate the connection between the theory and practice of chemiftry, and the application of that fcience to fome of the arts and manufactures of the United States of America."

to hear the firſt effuſions of the moſt pathetic grief from his mother, as ſhe burſted from the room in which he died. But I had diſtreſs from the ſickneſs, as well as the deaths of my brethren in phyſic. My worthy friends Dr Griffitts, Dr Say, and Dr Meaſe, were ſuſpended by a thread over the grave, nearly at the ſame time. Heaven in mercy to me, as well as in kindneſs to the public, and their friends, preſerved their lives. Had they died, the meaſure of my ſorrows would have been complete.

I have ſaid before, that I early left off drinking wine; but I uſed it in another way. I carried a little wine in a vial in my pocket, and when I felt myſelf fainty, after coming out of a ſick room, or after a long ride, I kept about a ſpoonful of it in my mouth for half a minute, or longer, without ſwallowing it. So weak and excitable was my ſyſtem, that this ſmall quantity of wine refreſhed and invigorated me as much as half a pint would have done at any other time. The only difference was, that the vigour I derived from the wine in the former, was of ſhorter duration than when taken in the latter way.

For the firſt two weeks after I viſited patients in the yellow fever, I carried a rag wetted with

I   vinegar,

vinegar, and fmelled it occafionally in fick rooms :
but after I faw and felt the figns of the univerfal
prefence of the contagion in my fyftem, I laid
afide this, and all other precautions. I refted myfelf on the bed-fide of my patients, and I drank
milk, or eat fruit in their fick rooms.   Befides being faturated with the contagion, I had another
fecurity againft being infected by my patients,
and that was, I went into fcarcely a houfe which
was more infected than my own.   Moft of the
people who called upon me for advice, left a portion of contagion behind them.   Four perfons
died next door to me on the eaft ; three a few
doors above me on the weft ; and five in a fmall
frame houfe on the oppofite fide of the ftreet, towards the fouth.   On the north fide, and about
150 feet from my houfe, the fever prevailed with
great malignity in the family of Mr James Creffon.   But this was not all.   Many of the poor
people who called upon me for advice, were bled
by my pupils in my fhop, and in the yard, which
was between it, and the ftreet.   From the want
of a fufficient number of bowls to receive their
blood, it was fometimes fuffered to flow and pu-
trify upon the ground.   From all thefe fources,
ftreams of contagion were conftantly poured into
my houfe, and conveyed into my body by the air,
and in my aliment.   Thus charged with the fuel

of

of death, I was frequently difpofed to fay with Job, and almoft without a figure, to " corruption, thou art my father; and to the worm, thou art my mother and my fifter."

The deaths of my pupils and fifter have often been urged as objections to my mode of treating the fever. Had the fame degrees of labour and fatigue which preceded the attack of the yellow fever in each of them, preceded an attack of a common pleurify, I think it probable that fome, or perhaps all of them, would have died with it. But when the influence of the concentrated contagion which filled my houfe, was added to that of conftant fatigue upon their bodies, what remedies could be expected to fave their lives? Under the above circumftances, I confider the recovery of the other branches of my family from the fever (and none of them efcaped it) with emotions, fuch as I fhould feel, had we all been revived from apparent death, by the exertions of a humane fociety.

In getting haftily out of my carriage about the 22d of September, I wounded one of my fingers with a fmall nail. As my hands were conftantly expofed to the contagion of the fever in feeling pulfes, I had this wound carefully wrapped up,

from

from an apprehenfion that the contagion when received directly into the blood, might more certainly excite the fever, than when received in the ordinary way. In the hurry of bufinefs, the rag dropped off my finger without my noticing it. The wound inflamed, but healed notwithftanding in a few days, and I found no inconvenience from it.

The iffue of this accident was highly fatisfactory to me, as it eftablifhed the analogy between the fmall-pox and yellow fever, and confirmed me in the propriety of preparing the body for the reception of the latter, by the fame regimen, as for the former diforder.

For upwards of fix weeks I did not tafte animal food, nor fermented liquors of any kind. The quantity of aliment which I took inclufive of drinks, during this time, was frequently not more than one or two pounds in a day. Yet upon this diet, I poffeffed for a while uncommon activity of body. This influence of abftinence upon bodily exertion, has been happily illuftrated by Dr Jackfon in his directions for preferving the the health of foldiers in hot climates. He tells us, that he walked an hundred miles in three days in Jamaica, during which time he breakfafted on tea, fupped on bread and fallad, and drank nothing

A a 2   but

but lemonade or water. He adds further, that he walked from Edinburgh to London in eleven days and an half, and that he travelled with the moſt eaſe when he only breakfaſted and ſupped, and drank nothing but water. The fatigue of riding on horſeback, is prevented or leſſened by abſtinence from ſolid food. Even the horſe ſuffers leaſt from a quick and and long journey, when he is fed ſparingly with hay. Theſe facts add weight to the arguments formerly adduced, in favour of a vegetable diet in preventing or mitigating the action of the contagion of malignant fevers upon the ſyſtem. In both caſes the abſtraction of ſtimulus, removes the body further from the reach of indirect debility.

Food ſupports life as much by its ſtimulus, as by affording nouriſhment to the body. Where an artificial ſtimulus acts upon the ſyſtem, the natural ſtimulus of food ceaſes to be neceſſary. Under the influence of this principle, I encreaſed, or diminiſhed my food with the ſigns I diſcovered of the encreaſe, or diminution of the contagion in my body. Until the 15th of September I drank weak coffee, but after that time, I drank nothing but milk, or milk and water in the intervals of my meals. I was ſo ſatisfied of the efficacy of this mode of living, that I believed life
might

might have been preferved, and a fever prevented, for many days with a much greater accumulation of the contagion in my fyftem, by means of a total abftinence from food. Poifon is a relative term, and an excefs in quantity, or a derangement in place, is neceffary to its producing deleterious effects. The contagion of the yellow fever produced ficknefs and death, only from the excefs of its quantity, or from its force being encreafed by the addition of thofe other ftimuli which I have elfewhere called exciting caufes.

In addition to low diet, as a preventive of the diforder, I obviated coftivenefs by taking occafionally a calomel pill, or by chewing rhubarb.

I had read, and taught in my lectures, that fafting encreafes acutenefs in the fenfe of touch. My low living had that effect in a certain degree upon my fingers. I had a quicknefs in my perception, of the ftate of the pulfe in the yellow fever, that I had never experienced before in any other diforder. My abftemious diet, affifted perhaps by the ftate of my feelings, had likewife an influence upon my mind. Its operations were performed with an eafe, and a celerity, which rendered my numerous, and complicated duties, much lefs burdenfome, than they would

A a 3   probably

probably have been under other circumftances of diet, or a lefs agitated ftate of my paffions.

My perception of the lapfe of time was new to me. It was uncommonly flow. The ordinary bufinefs and purfuits of men appeared to me in a light that was equally new. The herfe and the grave mingled themfelves with every view I took of human affairs. Under thefe impreffions I re-collect being as much ftruck with obferving a number of men employed in digging the of cellar a large houfe, as I fhould have been at any other time, in feeing preparations for building a palace upon a cake of ice. I recollect further, being ftruck with furprife about the 1ft of October, in feeing a man bufily employed in laying in wood for the approaching winter. I fhould as foon have thought of making provifion for a dinner on the firft day of the year 1800.

In the account of my diftreffes, I have paffed over the flanders which were propagated againft me by fome of my brethren. I have mentioned them only for the fake of declaring in this public manner, that I moft heartily forgive them ; and that if I difcovered at any time, an undue fenfe of the unkindnefs and cruelty of thofe flanders, it was not becaufe I felt myfelf injured by them, but

becaufe

becaufe I was fure they would irreparably injure
my fellow citizens, by leffening their confidence
in the only remedies that I believed to be effectual
in the reigning epidemic. One thing in my conduct towards thefe gentlemen may require juftifi-
cation ; and that is, my refufing to confult with
them. A Mahometan and a Jew might as well
attempt to worfhip the Supreme Being in the
fame temple, and through the medium of the
fame ceremonies, as two phyficians of oppofite
principles and practice, attempt to confer about
the life of the fame patient. What is done in
cenfequence of fuch negociations (for they are.
not confultations) is the ineffectual refult of neu-
tralifed opinions ; and wherever they take place,
would be confidered as the effect of a criminal
compact between phyficians, to affefs the property
of their patients, by a fhameful proftitution of the
dictates of their confciences. Befides, I early difcovered that it was impoffible for me by any reafonings, to change the practice of fome of my brethren. Humanity was therefore on the fide of
leaving them to themfelves ; for the extremity of
wrong in medicine, as in morals and government,
is often a lefs mifchief, than that mixture of *right*
and *wrong* which ferves by palliating, to perpetu-
ate evil.

After

After the lofs of my health, I received letters
from my friends in the country, preffing me in the
ftrongeft terms to leave the city. Such a ftep had
become impracticable. My aged mother was too
infirm to be removed, and I could not leave her.
I was moreover, part of a little circle of phyficians, who had affociated themfelves in fupport of
the new remedies. This circle would have been
broken by my quitting the city. The weather
varied the difeafe, and in the weakeft ftate of my
body, I expected to be able from the reports of
my pupils, to affift my affociates in detecting its
changes, and in accommodating our remedies to
them. Under thefe circumftances, it pleafed
God to enable me to reply to one of the letters
that urged my retreat from the city, that " I had
refolved to ftick to my principles, my practice,
and my patients, to the laft extremity."

On the ninth of October, I vifited a confiderable number of patients, and as the day was warm,
I leffened the quantity of my clothing. Towards
evening I was feized with a pain in the back,
which obliged me to go to bed at eight o'clock.
About twelve I awoke with a chilly fit. A violent
fever with acute pains in different parts of my body, followed it. At one o'clock I called for Mr
Fifher who flept in the next room. He came inftantly

ſtantly, with my affectionate black man to my relief. I ſaw my danger painted in Mr Fiſher's
countenance. He bled me plentifully and gave
me a doſe of the mercurial medicine. This was
immediately rejected. He gave me a ſecond doſe,
which likewiſe acted as an emetic, and diſcharged
a large quantity of bile from my ſtomach. The
remaining part of the night was paſſed under an
apprehenſion that my labours were near an end.
I could hardly expect to ſurvive ſo violent an attack of the fever, broken down, as I was, by
labour, ſickneſs and grief. My wife and ſeven
children, whom the great and diſtreſſing events
that were paſſing in our city, had joſtled out of
my mind for ſix or ſeven weeks, now reſumed
their former place in my affections. My wife had
ſtipulated, in conſenting to remain in the country,
to come to my aſſiſtance in caſe of my ſickneſs; but
I took meaſures, which, without alarming her,
proved effectual in preventing it. My houſe was
a Lazaretto, and the probability of my death,
made her life doubly neceſſary to my family. In
the morning, the medicine operated kindly, and
my fever abated. In the afternoon it returned,
attended with a great inclination to ſleep. Mr
Fiſher bled me again which removed the ſleepineſs.
The next day the fever left me, but in ſo weak a
ſtate, that I awoke two ſucceſſive nights with a

4 faintneſs

faintnefs which threatened the extinction of my life. It was removed each time by taking a little aliment. My convalefcence was extremely flow. I returned in a very gradual manner to my former habits of diet. The fmell of animal food, the firft time I faw it at my table, forced me to leave the room. During the month of November, and all the winter months I was harraffed with a cough, and a fever fomewhat of the hectic kind. The early warmth of the fpring, removed thofe complaints, and I now enjoy, through divine goodnefs, my ufual ftate of health.

I fhould be deficient in gratitude, were I to conclude this narrative without acknowledging my obligations to my furviving pupils Mr Fifher and Mr Coxe, for the great fupport and fympathy I derived from them in my labours and diftreffes.

I take great pleafure likewife in acknowledging my obligations to my former pupil Dr Woodhoufe, who affifted me in the care of my patients, after I became fo weak as not to be able to attend them with the punctuality their cafes required. The difinterefted exploits of thefe young gentlemen in the caufe of humanity, and their fuccefs in the treatment of the diforder, have endeared their names to hundreds, and at the fame time, afforded

a pre-

a prelude of their future eminence and ufefulnefs
in their profeffion.

But wherewith fhall I come before the great
FATHER and REDEEMER of men, and what
fhall I render unto him for the iffue of my life,
from the grave?

———— Here all language fails ————
" Come then, expreffive filence, mufe his praife."

.

.

F I N I S.